PENGUIN BOOKS

Lost Japan

Alex Kerr was born in Bethesda, Maryland, USA, in 1952. He first came to Japan when his father, a naval officer, was posted to Yokohama from 1964 to 1966. He has lived in Kameoka, near Kyoto, since 1977. Alex holds degrees in Japanese Studies from Yale University and Chinese Studies from Oxford University, and is a passionate and knowledgeable collector of East Asian art.

In the years after purchasing the house Chiiori that appears in *Lost Japan*, Alex went on to restore dozens of old houses in Kyoto and across Japan in an effort to revive beautiful but declining rural regions. The non-profit organization he founded, Chiiori Trust, today manages restored houses in Iya and in several other prefectures.

Alex writes and lectures in Japanese, and is author of many books, including *Dogs and Demons* (2000), outlining the impact of public works on Japan's landscape; *Living in Japan* (2006), introducing old and contemporary houses; and *Bangkok Found* (2010), describing the city as Alex experienced it since first visiting Thailand in the 1970s.

The original edition of *Lost Japan*, written in Japanese, won the 1994 Shincho Gakugei Literature Prize for the best work of non-fiction published in Japan. Alex is the first foreigner to win this prestigious award. After publication in English based on a translation by Bodhi Fishman, the book won the Asia-Pacific Publishers Award, Gold Prize for Best Translation of 1996.

Lost Japan

Last Glimpse of Beautiful Japan

ALEX KERR

Translated by Alex Kerr and Bodhi Fishman

PENGUIN BOOKS

PENGUIN BOOKS

UK | USA | Canada | Ireland | Australia
India | New Zealand | South Africa

Penguin Books is part of the Penguin Random House group of companies
whose addresses can be found at global.penguinrandomhouse.com.

Penguin
Random House
UK

First published by Lonely Planet Publications 1996
Published with a new Preface in Penguin Books 2015

012

Text copyright © Alex Kerr, 1993
Adapted from *Utsukushiki Nippon no Zanzo*
(Shincho-sha, Tokyo, 1993) copyright © Alex Kerr, 1996, 2015
Calligraphies © Alex Kerr, 2015

Calligraphy by Alex Kerr

The moral right of the author has been asserted

Set in 11/13 pt Dante MT Std
Typeset by Jouve (UK), Milton Keynes

Printed and bound in Great Britain by Clays Ltd, Elcograf S.p.A.

A CIP catalogue record for this book is available from the British Library

ISBN: 978-0-141-97974-8

www.greenpenguin.co.uk

Contents

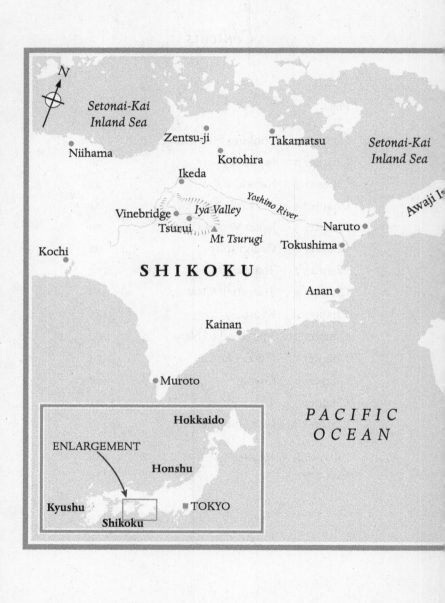

N

Setonai-Kai Inland Sea

Niihama

Zentsu-ji

Takamatsu

Kotohira

Setonai-Kai Inland Sea

Ikeda

Yoshino River

Vinebridge

Iya Valley

Awaji I

Tsurui

Naruto

Mt Tsurugi

Tokushima

Kochi

SHIKOKU

Anan

Kainan

Muroto

PACIFIC OCEAN

Hokkaido

ENLARGEMENT

Honshu

Kyushu

■ TOKYO

Shikoku

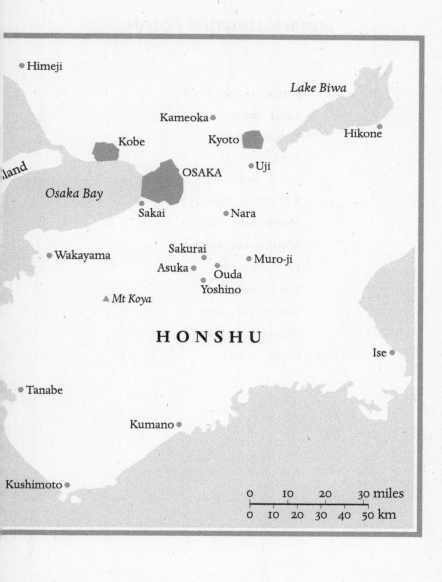

Japanese Historical Periods

Jomon 10,000–300 BC

Yayoi 300 BC–300 AD

Kofun 300–710

Nara 710–794

Heian 794–1185

Kamakura 1185–1333

Muromachi 1333–1576

Momoyama 1576–1600

Edo 1600–1867

Meiji 1868–1912

Taisho 1912–1926

Showa 1926–1989

Heisei 1989–

Chinese Dynasties

Zhou 1100–221 BC

Qin 221–206 BC

Han 206 BC–220 AD

Three Kingdoms 220–280

Jin 265–420

Southern dynasties 420–589

Northern dynasties 386–581

Sui 589–618

Tang 618–907

Later Liang 907–923

Later Tang 923–936

Later Jin 936–946

Later Han 947–950

Later Zhou 951–960

Liao 916–1125

Song 960–1279

Western Xia 1038–1227

Jin 1115–1234

Yuan (Mongol) 1271–1368

Ming 1368–1644

Qing (Manchu) 1644–1911

Preface

It has been twenty-four years since I sat down in January of 1991 to write the first of the articles that were later to become the book *Lost Japan*. I would like to say that since then I've learned and seen much, and now have a new perspective on it all. And yet, looking back, nothing has changed!

Twenty-four years later, I'm still just where I was when, hiking in the hills of Iya Valley in 1973, I pushed open the door of the house Chiiori and saw the dusty black floors and huge old beams sweeping overhead. But I've got the math wrong. That was forty-two years ago.

I found Chiiori just in time. During the ensuing years, I was to witness the gradual disappearance of Japan's delicate natural landscape and old towns of wood, tile, bamboo, and thatch. If anything, the pace of change increased in scale and speed in the 2000s, leaving Iya Valley and Chiiori as remnants of a vanished world. I still own Chiiori, and after all these years, on entering that old room and smelling the smoky *irori* floor hearth, my heart leaps up as it always did. In the intervening years, I've seen dozens, hundreds, of old houses, and never found anything else like Chiiori.

Lost Japan itself has lived on. It's still in publication in the original 1993 Japanese version (titled *Last Glimpse of Beautiful Japan*), and with the exception of this last year as it transited between publishers, the English version never fell out of print. For the translation, I'm indebted to Bodhi Fishman. Starting in 1994 I set out to do an English translation myself, but found that not even one paragraph would go into English acceptably. When I wrote the original articles, I was thinking exclusively of a Japanese audience. For readers outside Japan, the text would have to be radically revised. It was a sobering experience for someone who had spent decades blithely translating other people. Baffled by my inability to translate myself, I let the book sit for almost two years. Finally, in 1996 Bodhi came to my aid with a translation that captured the mood of the original. I revised this, cutting some chapters and expanding others; Bodhi edited the revision; and that's how *Lost Japan* came to be.

The book has brought thousands of visitors to Iya, and many friends into my life. Two decades and several books later, the world described in *Lost Japan* is still my starting point.

If anything has changed, it is that in recent years I've had the chance to put into practice what I had merely dreamed of and spoken about in the 90s. This was made possible by the business experience gained when Trammell Crow dragged me into helping with his real estate investment ventures in the Bubble Era of the late 80s. That bit of time I spent working in the real world allowed me to build, eventually, the 'balance' that Tamasaburo describes in his Afterword.

Starting in 2004 I began restoring old *machiya* town houses in Kyoto, not as historical showpieces, but fitted out with modern amenities – heating, cooling, nice baths and toilets and so forth, so that people today could enjoy them in comfort. We rented these out for visitors to stay in when they visited Kyoto. After that I went on to restore houses in rural areas around Japan, and finally Chiiori itself in 2012.

Chiiori today looks exactly as it did back in 1973. When we did the restoration, we picked up the ancient black floorboards, numbered them, and after shoring up the foundations, and installing plumbing, gas, electric lines, insulation, and underfloor heating, we put the boards right back in their original position. Meanwhile, the corridor behind the house features bathrooms with all the latest in Japanese toilet technology and a lovely cedar bath of the sort we never imagined possible in Iya. Today a freshly thatched – and thoroughly modernized – Chiiori welcomes a new generation of visitors as it enters its fourth century.

In 2004, we established a non-profit organization centered on the house, called Chiiori Trust. It's staffed by young people coming from Tokyo and other big cities who would like to do something for Iya, which continues to age and depopulate. My old neighbour and friend Omo passed away in 2012.

Today our challenge is how to bring a new community into the valley.

The other worlds described in *Lost Japan* – Kabuki, calligraphy, Kyoto, Nara, Tenmangu, art collecting – these continue more or less as before. I still live in the grounds of Tenmangu Shrine in Kameoka, outside Kyoto, and the little emerald-like frogs still hop around in June. I still write calligraphies, some of which appear as chapter headings in the book.

As for art collecting, prices for Japanese art plummeted after 2000. Behind this change in the market was China's rise and the passing of the last generation in Japan who knew what these old things were. Just when I thought I could put an end to my compulsive collecting, a whole new opportunity came my way. How could I refuse a pair of screens by an important eighteenth-century calligrapher that had found no buyer at auction and was now selling for a song? So I'm still buying, because I must.

Kabuki *onnagata* Tamasaburo, now in his sixties, has been designated a Living National Treasure, but in some sort of miracle of nature, remains as meltingly beautiful as he was when I first saw him so many years ago. But slowly he is cutting down the more energetic pieces in his repertoire and no longer dances the *Heron Maiden*.

Tamasaburo and I once promised each other that in our old age we would not turn into our crabby old mentors. For me that was American drama critic and 'saviour of the Kabuki' Faubion Bowers, and for Tamasaburo it was the celebrated older *onnagata* Nakamura Utaemon VI. Faubion and Utaemon spent their later years grumbling bitterly about the new generation.

But I at least couldn't live up to that promise. First with the book *Dogs and Demons* published in 2000, and then with later publications (some only in Japanese) I continue to write and speak about the destruction of precious places and things I see going on around me. For consolation I think back to the words of 'the last of the literati', Shirasu Masako, when I asked her why she had taken her fists to the artist Rosanjin over his bad kimono design. 'If you really love something,' she admonished me, 'then you should get angry about it.'

Lost Japan concludes with a metaphor from Kabuki, in which I keep getting pulled back to Japan in the same way as the protagonist of the play *Kasane* finds himself dragged back onstage by the long bony fingers of dead Kasane's ghost.

These days I have a new metaphor. Again, it's from a play that I once saw Tamasaburo perform in, called *Yashagaike (Demon Pond)*. A young ethnologist travels to a remote village where there's a legend that if the temple bell is not rung every evening at sunset, a dragon princess who lives in the pond will rise up and flood the village. The young scholar moves in with the old bell keeper and stays, eventually marrying the bell keeper's daughter. One day the bell keeper falls dead. It's late afternoon. Soon someone must ring the bell. Although he's a city boy who doesn't believe in old superstitions, the scholar does so. He has become the bell keeper.

There is one big thing that did in fact change since I wrote *Lost Japan*. Time passed, and with it the people who understood and transmitted the lore of old Japan – aesthete David Kidd, Naohi the Mother Goddess of Oomoto, Faubion Bowers, Kabuki *onnagata* Jakuemon, Shirasu Masako, Omo, art collector Hosomi Minoru, screen and scroll mounter Kusaka – they're all gone now. That leaves me – a foreigner, and like the scholar in *Yashagaike*, not really a part of the tradition – stuck with the job of ringing that old bell.

I think the one thing that you want to do when you've really loved something is to pass the memory on to others. That's why *Lost Japan* is still so important to me. I'm delighted that Penguin is reissuing the book, with a new cover and fresh calligraphies at the head of each chapter – but with no other substantive changes.

Preface

It brings me joy to think that a new generation of readers can experience the mists of Iya, the moment of walking into Chiiori, the first view of a young Tamasaburo on stage, the wit of David Kidd, 'the moment before glory'.

Alex Kerr, 2015

Lost Japan

Chapter 1

Looking for a Castle

The Egg in the Dungeon

When I was six, I wanted to live in a castle. I suppose many children dream of living in a castle, but as they grow older the dream is forgotten. However, in my case this desire lingered on until adulthood. My father was a legal officer with the United States Navy, and we lived for a time in Naples, Italy. There was a castle on an island in the harbor called the Castel dell'Ovo (Castle of the Egg). Legend has it that Virgil had presented an egg to the castle, and had prophesied that if the egg ever broke, the castle would be destroyed. But after hundreds of years the egg was still intact in the dungeon, the Castel dell'Ovo still stood, and I wanted to live there.

Practically every day, when my father returned home from work, I would follow him about, repeating, 'I want to live in a castle.' I was extremely persistent, so one day my father grew exasperated and told me, 'A great landlord called Mr Nussbaum owns all the castles in the world, so when you grow up you can

3

rent one from him.' From that time on, I waited expectantly for the day when I could meet Mr Nussbaum.

A typical Navy family, we moved constantly. From Naples, my father was transferred to Hawaii, where we lived by the beach on the windward side of Oahu. Sometimes, large green glass balls encrusted with barnacles floated in on the tide. My father told me that the fishermen in Japan used them to keep their nets afloat. Torn from the nets by storms, the balls floated all the way across the Pacific Ocean to Hawaii. This was my first experience of 'Japan'.

When I was nine, we moved to Washington, DC. I entered a private school there, which taught Latin and Chinese to elementary school students. The school was at once hopelessly behind and ahead of the times. Stern Mrs Wang, our teacher, made sure that we copied our Chinese characters correctly, hundreds to a page. For most of the other students it was drudgery, but I loved the look and feel of the characters. Mrs Wang showed us pictures of Beijing, of temples perched on mountain precipices, and in the process memories of Italy faded and my daydreams began to focus on China.

After three years at the Pentagon, my father was transferred to Japan, and in 1964 we went to live at the US naval base in Yokohama; I was then twelve years old. This was the year Japan hosted the Olympics. In retrospect, 1964 was a great turning point for Japan. The previous twenty years had been spent rebuilding a nation that had been devastated by World War II. The next thirty years were to see an economic boom unprecedented in history, as Japan transformed itself into the richest country in the world.

Although the American Occupation had ended in 1952, signs of the US military presence were everywhere in Yokohama, from the special currency we were issued to foil the black market (printed with the faces of movie stars instead of presidents) to the ubiquitous military police. Outside the military base, the few foreigners living in Yokohama made up a small group of longtime expatriates, many of whom had been living there for decades. The yen was 360 to the US dollar, four times the rate today, and the foreigners lived well. My mother's childhood friend Linda Beech was living in Tokyo and had gained great notoriety as a teacher of English on TV. She would appear underwater in scuba gear and shout, 'I'm drowning! That's d-R-(not L)-o-w-n-i-n-g!' Linda was the first of the 'TV foreigners' who now populate Japan's airwaves in great numbers. Today, foreigners in Tokyo eke out a living in cramped apartments; in contrast, Linda and a group of expat families owned villas at Misaki, on the coast.

I was excited to find that the Chinese characters I had learned in Washington were also used in Japan. Within a few weeks I had taught myself *hiragana* and *katakana* (the two Japanese alphabets), and once I could read train and bus signs, I started exploring Yokohama and Tokyo on my own. When the weekend came, Tsuru-san, our maid, packed a boxed lunch for me, and I traveled the train lines south to Odawara Castle, and north to Nikko. People were always friendly to an American boy asking directions in Japanese. Slowly, my interest in China shifted to an interest in Japan.

Although the country was poised on the verge of a huge economic boom, the old Japan was still visible. All around Yokohama, even in the heart of the city, there were green hills, and many traditional old neighborhood streets remained. I was particularly captivated by the sea of tiled roofs. On the streetcars, most women over forty wore kimono in fall and winter. Western-style shoes were still something of an innovation, and I used to enjoy studying the footwear of streetcar passengers, which consisted of a mixture of sandals, *geta* (wooden clogs) and some truly amazing purple plastic slippers. After dusk fell, you could often hear the clopping sound of *geta* echoing through the streets.

My favorite things were the Japanese houses. At that time there were still many magnificent old Japanese houses in Yokohama and Tokyo. Linda Beech had introduced my mother to a women's group called the Nadeshiko-Kai (Society of Pinks), so-named because Japanese women are supposed to be as lovely as *nadeshiko* flowers (pinks). In those days consorting with foreigners was still something special, and the Nadeshiko-Kai drew its Japanese membership from the elite. Once a month, the ladies would visit each other's homes, so there were many opportunities for me to view great houses, as I was able to go along as well.

Among the houses I visited was a large estate at Hayama, a resort town near Misaki, about an hour south of Yokohama. I recall being told that the house belonged to the Imperial Family, but it seems inconceivable today that the Imperial villa would have been made available to US military personnel, even in those twilight post-Occupation years. The estate must have been merely in the neighborhood of the Imperial villa. At the Hayama villa, I saw neat tatami mats for the first time. From the sunny rooms on the second floor, Mt Fuji could be seen floating in the distance.

Another great house was the mansion of former prime minister Shigeru Yoshida in Tokyo, featuring an enormous living room with dozens of tatami mats under a huge coffered ceiling. My favorite place was the little complex of Japanese-style country houses belonging to Linda Beech and her friends on the Misaki coast. I can still vividly recall the rows of pine trees atop the cliffs at Misaki, blowing in the ocean breeze.

The grand old Japanese houses were not just houses. Each house was a 'program' – designed to unfold and reveal itself in stages, like unrolling a handscroll. I remember my first visit to the house of one of the ladies of the Nadeshiko-Kai. Outside, high walls gave no indication of the interior. We entered through a gate, passed through a garden, and continuing on, met another gate, another garden, and only then the *genkan*, or entranceway (literally, 'hidden barrier').

On arriving at the *genkan*, we were surprised to find that the lady of the house got down on her knees to greet us, her head touching the tatami. It was the sort of greeting royalty might receive; it made me feel that entering this house was a great occasion. Once inside, we passed along a hallway; this was followed by a small room and another hallway. Finally, we reached a spacious living room, absolutely empty except for some flowers in the *tokonoma* (alcove). It was summer, the doors to the hallways and living rooms had been removed, and a breeze from the garden swept through the whole house from one end to the other. However, only the surrounding passageways received light from the garden, so it was dark inside the large tatami room. A secret space removed from the outside world, it conjured up the feeling that I had been transported back to an ancient time, long before I was born. To me, that house had become my 'castle': I knew that Japan was where I wanted to live my life.

In 1966 we moved back to Washington, DC. After graduating from high school in 1969, I entered the Japanese Studies program at Yale University. However, the course was not what I expected. Japanese Studies at the time revolved almost wholly around economic development, post-Meiji government, 'theories of Japaneseness' (known as *Nihonjinron*), and so on, and deep inside I began to wonder if Japan really was the country I wanted to live in. In order to put my doubts to rest, during the summer of 1971 I hitchhiked all around Japan, from the northern island of Hokkaido to the southern tip of Kyushu.

This trip took two months, and during that time I was treated extraordinarily well. It was an easy time for foreigners. The Japanese have always tended to treat foreigners like creatures from another universe. As Japan has become more internationalized, the attitude towards foreigners has grown more, rather than less, complicated. But in those days, outside the big cities, there was only tremendous curiosity: I would be deluged with questions about the American school system, about my parents, my family, my clothing, everything. Old ladies would pinch the hair on my arms to see if it was real; the men of the families I met couldn't wait to get me into a public bath to see if what they had heard about foreigners was true. In two months I only spent three nights in a hotel – the rest of the time, people I met on the road would invite me to stay in their homes.

While I was deeply impressed by the kindness of the Japanese, I reaped another benefit from the trip as well. This was my discovery of Japan's natural environment. In 1971 the onslaught of modernization was already encroaching upon the countryside, but compared to the cities, the rural areas still preserved much of their old appearance. Roads were few, and the mountains were heavily blanketed with old-growth forest. Mist boiled up out of the valleys as if by magic; the slender and delicate tree branches quivered like feathers in the wind, and in the gaps between them the sheer rock surface would show through, only to be hidden again.

Geographically, Japan lies in a temperate zone, but its vegetation seems far more characteristic of a tropical rainforest. As anyone who has hiked through the mountain ranges of Shikoku and Kyushu will know, Japan's mountains are a jungle of sorts. Wherever one looks, the humid, dense slopes are covered with ferns, moss and fallen leaves. Coming along the bend of an unpaved mountain road, I would suddenly have the illusion that I had traveled back hundreds of millions of years. It felt as though at any moment a pterodactyl might come flying out of the mist.

When I think back on the natural beauty of Japan at that time it brings tears to my eyes. With its abundant 'rainforest' vegetation, volcanic mountains and the delicate leafage of its native flora, Japan was perhaps one of the most beautiful countries in the world. During the ensuing twenty-odd years, the country's natural environment has changed completely. The old-growth forests have been logged and replanted with neat rows of cedar trees, and within these cedar groves it is deathly silent. They have become deserts in which the living, breathing presence of plants and animals cannot be sensed. Roads have been carved deep into the mountains, and the hillsides have been covered in erosion-control concrete, obscuring the beauty of the rocky slopes. Even the mist no longer rises from the gorges.

Recently, there has been a worldwide boom in Japanese Studies, and many college students now visit Japan. They see the gardens of Kyoto and come away thinking that these creations of neatly raked sand and pruned hedges are 'nature'. But nature, in Japan, used to be far more mysterious and fantastic, a sacred area that seemed surely inhabited by gods. In Shinto, there is a tradition of *Kami no Yo*, the 'Age of the Gods', when man was pure and the gods dwelled in hills and trees. Today, that tradition is the sort of thing you read about as historical commentary when you study ancient Japanese poetry, or in the brochure when you visit a Shinto shrine. Yet, as recently as 1971, the primeval forest still existed. You could feel the presence of the gods. This environment is now a thing of the past, but if I live to be eighty or a hundred, I doubt that the lost beauty of Japan's mountains and forests will ever fade from my memory.

Shikoku, the smallest of the four main islands of Japan, is the least visited by tourists, and it was not originally on my summer itinerary. When I was a child in Yokohama, Tsuru-san used to sing a song to me about the Shinto shrine of Kompira in Shikoku, and by coincidence the very first person I hitched a ride with in Tokyo gave me a charm from the shrine. This gave me the idea that I was meant to make a pilgrimage to Kompira, so at the end of the summer I traveled to Shikoku. I spent some time with a group of friends at Kompira and the nearby Esoteric Buddhist temple of Zentsu-ji. On the final day of my visit, a friend I had met at the temple offered to take me to a place he said I would surely fall in love with.

We got on his motorcycle and left Zentsu-ji for the heart of Shikoku. We headed towards Ikeda, a small town near the center of the island. From there, the road began to climb the banks of the Yoshino River. The valley walls on either side grew steeper and steeper, and just when I was beginning to wonder where on earth I was being taken, we arrived at the mouth of Iya Valley. I thought this was our destination, but my friend told me, 'This is where we start.' We began to climb up a narrow, winding mountain road.

Situated on the border between the Tokushima and Kochi Prefectures, Iya Valley is the deepest gorge in Japan. The landscape I saw that day was the most fantastic in all of Japan's countryside, bringing to mind the mountains of China that I had fallen in love with as a child. It looked exactly like a mountain scene from a Sung-dynasty ink painting.

Due to the green shale peculiar to the Tokushima area, the rivers were tinged with emerald, and the towering cliff faces looked like carved jade. From a mountain across the valley, white cascades – what the Japanese call *taki no shiraito* (literally, 'the white threads of the waterfall') – fell straight down, as though drawn with a single brush stroke. Against this backdrop, the thatch-roofed houses scattered here and there deep in the mountains looked like the dwellings of sages.

Every country, I believe, has its typical 'pattern of landscape'. In England, the keynote is grass – in town squares, in meadows and in college quadrangles. In Japan, it is the village cluster. Usually, the houses of a Japanese village huddle together in a group on the flatlands, either in a valley or at the foot of a hill, surrounded by an expanse of rice paddies. People do not live up in the mountains, which in ancient times were the domain of gods and considered taboo. Even today, the mountains of Japan are almost completely uninhabited.

Iya is different. Later, back at Yale, I researched Iya Valley for my senior thesis. I discovered that the pattern of its settlement is unique in Japan. In Iya, houses avoid the low-lying land by the river, and instead are built high up on the mountainsides. One reason is that the shaded areas around the riverbanks are inadequate for farming. Also, the many freshwater springs that gush forth on the hillsides make the elevated areas better suited for human habitation. Since Iya's rocky terrain is unfit for rice cultivation, there are very few rice paddies, and therefore there is no need for people to live in a single village compound to tend them. The result is independent households scattered throughout the mountains.

The Yuan-dynasty painter Nizan drew mountains with an inimitable touch. The composition of his works is always the same. There never appears even a single human figure: just a solitary thatch-roofed cottage supported by four pillars, sitting in the midst of a vast mountain range. Deep in the mountains of Iya, I felt something akin to the human loneliness and corresponding grandeur of nature expressed in the paintings of Nizan.

The whole trip that summer had been one large arrow leading me to Iya. My question as to whether Japan was the country I wished to live in had been answered. I spent the next year at Keio University in Tokyo as an exchange student; however, I skipped most of my classes, frequently journeying back to the mountains of Iya. During the course of these trips, I gradually began to learn something about the region and the people living there.

Anyone who travels in China and Japan is bound to come across lists of threes and fives: the Five Famous Mountains, the Three Gardens, the Three Famous Views, etc. So, naturally, Japan has classified its Three Hidden Regions. They are Gokaso in Kyushu, Hida-Takayama in Gifu (famed for its high-ridged thatched houses) and Iya Valley. Since ancient times, Iya has been a hideaway, a place of refuge from the outside world. The oldest written record concerning the valley dates back to the Nara period: a description of how a group of shamans fleeing the capital disappeared into the neighboring mountains. Later, in the twelfth century, during the wars between the Heike and Genji clans, fugitives of the defeated Heike fled into Iya Valley. From that time on, Iya became known as an *ochiudo buraku* (a refugee village). The world was surprised in the 1970s when a Japanese soldier was found to have lived for almost thirty years in a Philippine jungle, still fighting World War II. Thirty years is nothing. The Heike in Iya kept up their struggle from 1190 right up until about 1920. Even now, in a village called Asa in the furthest reaches of Iya, the descendants of the leader of the Heike clan live in a thatch-roofed mansion, still preserving their twelfth-century crimson war banner.

During the period of warfare in the mid-fourteenth century, when Japan was divided between the Northern and Southern courts, Iya became a stronghold of guerrillas fighting to restore the Southern Court. Even during the peaceful centuries of the Edo period, the valley people fought off integration with the rest of Japan. The villagers bitterly resisted incorporation into the Awa fiefdom of Lord Hachisuka of Tokushima, rising in numerous peasant revolts. As a result, prior to the twentieth century, Iya existed virtually as an independent country.

The tunneling of the first public road into Iya began in the Taisho era in the 1920s, but the carving of this road through solid rock by manual labor took over twenty years to complete. Today, there are many roads throughout Iya, but when I first visited the valley there was nothing passable by car except for the original Taisho 'highway', which was for the most part a narrow dirt track. There were no guardrails, and one could look down over hundred-meter precipices to the river running below. One day, I came around a corner to find that the tire of the car in front of me had slipped from the shoulder of the road. I watched as the driver frantically jumped from the vehicle, which proceeded to plummet into the depths.

I began to walk the mountain trails of Iya. Thinking back on it now, I was just in time. The old way of life still remained in Iya in 1972, but it was on the verge of fading out. The people working in the fields still wore the woven straw raincoats seen in samurai movies. Inside the houses, cooking was done over an open hearth sunk into the floor.

New houses had been built alongside the Taisho road, which followed the course of the river. But in order to visit the older houses, it was not unusual to have to hike for an hour or two up from the roadside along narrow mountain paths. Consequently, there was very little contact with the outside world; some old women I met had not descended from their native hamlets for over ten years.

To Iya residents, all outsiders are labeled *shimo no hito* (literally, 'people from below'). Although, as a foreigner, I was an especially strange *shimo no hito*, Japanese from Tokyo or Osaka are lumped together into this group as well. Because of this, the attitude towards foreigners in Iya is relatively relaxed. However, the reality of my being a foreigner was an inescapable fact, much more so as I was quite possibly the first Westerner to have ever ventured into the heart of the region. One day, tired from a strenuous one-hour hike up a steep mountain path to one of Iya's hamlets, I sat down to rest on the stone steps of a small shrine. After about ten minutes, an old lady toiled into view on the path below. As she approached the shrine, I stood up to ask her for directions. She took one look at my face, let out a shriek, and ran off down the path. Later, when I asked the villagers about it, they explained that the old lady had thought I was the god of the shrine, come out for a little air. It was a perfectly logical conclusion, since Shinto gods traditionally have long red hair. I recall this incident even now, when I see the gods in Noh and Kabuki performances come out with their flaming manes.

In the Iya houses of twenty years ago mysterious shadows still abounded. The valley's rocky slopes are completely unsuited to rice paddies, so traditional agriculture consisted of crops such as millet, buckwheat and *mitsumata* (the fibers of which are used to make 10,000-yen notes). But the main crop was tobacco, introduced by the Portuguese into Japan in the early 1600s. Until recently, when a courtesan in a Kabuki play put a long pipe to her lips and inserted a pinch of pipe tobacco, she used Iya tobacco.

Because of the constantly swirling mists in the valley, the tobacco was dried inside, hung from the rafters over the smoking hearths. So Iya houses are ceilingless, and the roofs soar upwards like the vaults of a Gothic church. The first time I entered a traditional Iya dwelling, I was shocked to find that the interior of the house was pitch black. The floor, pillars and walls were all colored a deep ebony from years of smoke rising from the open hearth. The Japanese call this *kurobikari* (literally, 'black glistening'). After a little while, my eyes adjusted and I could gradually make out the thatch on the underside of the roof. The thatch too was a shiny black color, almost as though it had been lacquered.

Iya was always desperately poor, and its houses are small in comparison to those of most rural areas in Japan. The houses of Hida-Takayama are many times larger, rising five stories or more, but since each story has a ceiling, one feels little sense of spaciousness upon entering. Iya's houses, on the other hand, feel extremely roomy inside due to the darkness and the lack of ceilings. Inside, the house is cavelike; outside is a world above the clouds.

Even now, when I travel back to Iya, I feel as though I've left the world behind and entered a magical realm. This feeling is stronger now than ever, because whilst the towns and plains below have been completely modernized, Iya remains little changed. Near the entrance to the valley there stands an Edo-period stone monument inscribed at the command of the Lord of Awa, which reads: 'Iya, Peach Spring of our land of Awa'. The 'Peach Spring' is the subject of an old Chinese poem about an otherworldly paradise. This monument is evidence that even hundreds of years ago, when all of Japan was beautiful, Iya was seen as something unique, as a Shangri-La.

So far, I have only written of Iya's beautiful side, but in truth there was already a snake in this Garden of Eden: *kaso* (depopulation). It began in 1964, when my family arrived in Yoko-hama. In that year, the imbalance between city and rural incomes passed a critical point, and farmers from all over Japan fled the countryside. Much poorer and with a more loosely organized society than the rice-growing communities of the plains, Iya was especially hard hit, as villagers moved down to Tokushima and Osaka. After 1970, the pace of *kaso* increased, and Iya was filled with abandoned houses. It occurred to me that I could own a house there.

These days, all of rural Japan gives the impression of becom-ing one enormous senior citizens' home. Back then, although the tide of depopulation in Iya was advancing, the villages were still alive. Even the abandoned houses were in beautiful condition.

Starting in the fall of 1972, I spent about six months 'house hunting'. I traveled around looking at dozens of houses, not only in Iya but throughout Kagawa, Kochi and Tokushima Prefectures as well. I wound up visiting over a hundred houses in the end. I toured the countryside with friends in search of interesting aban-doned houses, and when we found one, we would brazenly explore inside. It was just a matter of loosening the wooden shut-ters, which were usually not even locked. There were some unbelievably magnificent houses that had been left to rot. One indigo-dying mansion near Tokushima had a two-meter-wide verandah surrounding the entire house, of the sort you would only see today in Nijo Castle in Kyoto. The floorboards were over ten centimeters thick, all cut from precious *keaki* wood.

Breaking into these abandoned houses, I experienced many things that could never have been learned from books. I was able to see with my own eyes the reality of Japan's traditional ways of life. When a family decided to leave their house for the big city, they would take practically nothing away with them. What good were straw raincoats, bamboo baskets and utensils for handling firewood going to be in Osaka? Everything that had been a fea-ture of life in Iya for a thousand years had become irrelevant overnight. On entering one of these houses, it looked as though the residents had simply disappeared. The detritus of their daily life lay undisturbed, like a snapshot frozen in time. Everything was in place: the open newspaper, remains of fried eggs in the pan, discarded clothing and bedding, even the toothbrushes in the sink. The influences of modernization were already visible here and there – ceilings had been tacked up against the rafters to protect against the winter cold, and aluminum door and window frames had been installed – but one could still see much of the original condition of the houses. However, only a few years later, artificial materials were everywhere, covering not only ceilings, but floors, walls and pillars. The interiors disappeared under a layer of plastic and plywood.

Western visitors to Japan, appalled at the disregard for city heritage and the environment, always ask, 'Why can't the Japanese preserve what is valuable at the same time as they modernize?' For Japan as a nation, the old world has become irrelevant; it all seems as useless as the straw raincoats and bamboo baskets abandoned by the Iya villagers. In the West, contemporary clothing, architecture and so on have developed naturally out of European culture, so there are fewer discrepancies between 'modern culture' and 'ancient culture'. The industrial revolution in Europe advanced gradually, taking place during the course of hundreds of years. This is why it was possible for much of the countryside of England and France to be left relatively unspoiled, why numerous medieval towns still remain, and why the residents of these historical areas still treat them with care and respect.

In contrast to Europe, however, change came to China, Japan and Southeast Asia in a truly precipitous fashion. What's more, these changes were introduced from a completely alien culture. Consequently, modern clothing and architecture in China and Japan have nothing to do with traditional Asian culture. Although the Japanese may admire the ancient cities of Kyoto and Nara, and consider them beautiful, deep in their hearts they know that these places have no connection to their own modern lives. To put it bluntly, these places have become cities of illusion, historical theme parks. In East Asia, there are no equivalents of Paris or Rome – Kyoto, Beijing and Bangkok have been turned into concrete jungles. Meanwhile, the countryside has been filled to overflowing with billboards, power lines and aluminum houses. The egg in the dungeon has cracked.

The municipal library where children study in the town of Kameoka, where I now live, is not so different from Oxford's Merton College library, the world's oldest working library. On my first visit to Merton, it struck me that while this library was built nearly seven hundred years ago, the books, shelves, chairs and even the very concept of a 'library' have remained virtually unchanged over the intervening centuries. The children of Kameoka could visit Merton library and feel at home there. But if they visited the *sutra* (Buddhist scripture) storage rooms of a Japanese temple, with shelves filled with folding albums wrapped in silk, or the studios of the literati, lined with hanging scrolls and handscrolls, they would have no idea what they were looking at. These things are so far removed from what the Japanese use today, that they could almost come from a different planet.

The wholesale collapse of the natural environment and cultural tradition in East Asia will one day be seen as one of the major events of this century. Japan, with its vast wealth and thorough way of doing things, has a head start over the other nations of East Asia. But the changes are by no means limited to Japan alone, and viewed from a historical perspective they were probably unavoidable. It was fated for Asia to go this way.

When the native culture of a country has been lost, a 'new traditional culture' is created. This develops as a mix of ancient forms and modern tastes, and ends up a cultural Frankenstein's monster. The most shocking example of this is China. Attempts to repair Chinese temples cheaply have led to buildings and statues drastically different from the originals. The garish colors and grotesque compositions are a wholesale denial of the spirit of Chinese sculpture. Unfortunately, since this is all that tourists get to see, these tacky creations are now regarded as Chinese culture.

While Japan's case is not so extreme, its traditional culture is also being remade. This is especially true of its houses. The 'new' tradition has its myths, one of them being the case of tatami. Most people believe that Japanese interiors cannot exist without tatami, but this is not so. Until the Heian period, palace floors were made of wooden planks, as can be seen in old paintings and handscrolls. A nobleman would sit on a single tatami mat, upon a raised platform set in the middle of the floor. This arrangement can still be seen in certain Zen temples in Kyoto. In commoners' houses, thin reed mats were used when it was necessary to cover the floor with something. In Iya, these mats were laid only around the open hearth, and the rest of the floor was left bare. It was customary to wipe this wooden floor with a wet cloth twice a day, in the morning and evening. As a result, the floors were burnished a shiny black, very much like the surface of a Noh stage.

Noh stages, Shinto shrines, Zen temples and the houses of Iya all date from a pre-tatami age. The psychological difference between the wooden floors and tatami is great. The wooden floors can be traced back to the houses of Southeast Asia, which stood on stilts in forests from the 'Age of the Gods'. Tatami, with their neat black borders, came into vogue in a later era of precise etiquette, tea ceremony and samurai ritual. With tatami, the floor plan becomes quite evident, and the room looks smaller, more manageable. With a floor of black wooden planks, which has no visual interruptions, one feels a sense of limitless space.

So, despite the predominance of tatami today, there are really two types of Japanese interior, dating from different ages. Japan's typical pattern of cultural change can be seen in these two types of flooring. Rather than replace the old with the new, Japan simply lays the new on top of the old.

Back to Iya. The valley is divided into West Iya and East Iya. West Iya is comparatively accessible, and hundreds of thousands of tourists visit its famous Kazura-bashi each year. Kazura-bashi is a suspension bridge made of huge vines. Rehung periodically (these days reinforced with steel cables), the vine bridge dates back to the times when the Heike first fled into Iya, and has become one of Shikoku's premier tourist landmarks. The tourists, however, rarely venture beyond Kazura-bashi to visit the less developed East Iya.

Starting from East Iya's most remote mountain, Kenzan, I hiked from hamlet to hamlet looking for abandoned houses. Such houses were quite numerous, but I could not seem to find one that was just right. Houses that had been inhabited until recently had had ceilings installed, or had been remodeled with concrete or aluminum. On the other hand, houses that had been abandoned for over ten years were run down, with listing floors and cracked pillars, beyond any hope of restoration.

In January 1973 I visited a hamlet called Tsurui in East Iya. I came bearing an introductory letter to Mr Takemoto, a village assemblyman. I asked him if there were any abandoned houses nearby, and he promptly agreed to show me one. We soon arrived at a deserted house, and at that moment, I knew: 'This is it.' There before my eyes was the castle I had been seeking.

Chapter 2

Iya Valley

In Praise of Shadows

The villagers could not tell me the exact age of the house, but the last family to live there had occupied it for over seven generations – dating it back to at least the eighteenth century. It had been abandoned seventeen years earlier, but was basically in good condition. The floors of burnished black planks and the sunken hearths had survived the centuries unchanged. The roof, however, had not been thatched for fifty years, and was near the end of its useful life. Ferns and moss, even a few pine trees, grew rampant in the thatch, and there were numerous leaks when it rained. Nevertheless, I assumed I would be able to deal with it somehow. Little did I suspect the hardships I was to undergo because of that roof!

I made the decision to buy the house the first day, but negotiations ended up taking over four months. This illustrates law number six of my Ten Laws of Japanese Life, namely, the Law of Palaver. Nothing can ever be accomplished without time-consuming discussion. The discussion may apparently have little to do with the matter at hand, but it is absolutely indispensable, and many an impatient foreign businessman has met his doom by disregarding this law.

The reason the negotiations took so long in my case was not because of any particular problem with selling the house – it was mostly a problem of language. Knowing only standard Japanese, I found the dialect spoken in Iya incomprehensible. A neighbor would say, *'Denwa zo narioru'* ('the phone is ringing'): *denwa* (telephone) is twentieth century, *narioru* is Shikoku dialect and *zo* is an archaic particle dating from Heian court language. I had such a difficult time understanding conversations in Iya that in the end I asked a friend from Tokyo to come and help me with the negotiations.

We sat with the villagers until late in the evening, while Mr Takemoto officiated. Village etiquette required that I accept a cup of saké from every man in the room, not once but several times. Heated discussion about the house seemed to go on for an eternity, and my head was spinning. I was barely hanging on to the conversation, but I took comfort from the knowledge that my Tokyo friend would explain the nuances afterwards. At last the evening drew to an end, and we staggered outside and started off down the narrow mountain path in pitch darkness. My friend turned to me and exclaimed, 'What on earth were they talking about?'

In spite of the language difficulties, we finally reached an agreement in the spring of 1973: one hundred and twenty *tsubo* of land (about four hundred square meters) for 380,000 yen, with the house thrown in for free. With the exchange at about 300 yen to the dollar, 380,000 yen amounted to $1300. Still a college student, I did not have that much, but a family friend from the time when we lived in Yokohama in the 1960s agreed to lend me the money. For me it was an enormous sum; it took over five years to pay it back. In the meantime, Iya, remote from the booming urban centers, has seen its population drop by half, and its timber and farming industries collapse. While land everywhere else in Japan has skyrocketed in value, my plot in Iya, cheap though it was, is now worth less than half of what I paid for it.

I welcomed the period of palaver, because it gave me an opportunity to get to know the village. The official introduction was made when Mr Takemoto invited me to attend the spring festival at the local shrine; it happened to be one of the last times this festival was held. Twenty or thirty villagers gathered in the shrine enclosure, under giant cryptomeria pines as large as California redwoods. Boys painted with white make-up beat drums, while young men carried a shrine out of the main building and rested it on a pile of stones. A priest chanted while villagers paraded in bright red, long-nosed masks.

One of the boys in white make-up was Eiji Domai, aged thirteen, who was my first visitor after I bought the house and started to repair it. He was an active boy with a buzz cut who loved chopping things, running and swimming. Another visitor was Omo, my nearest neighbor. Omo – short, stocky and handy with everything – was the classic cheerful woodsman. He lived with his four daughters in a thatched house about a hundred meters away. Just below his house was a smaller thatch-roofed cottage, the 'retirement house' where his father and stepmother lived. Later, Omo became my teacher in the ways of Iya, helping with every aspect of my house, including the roof thatching when the time came.

I moved in that June. I had asked Shokichi, a poet friend of mine, to help. Aside from being a poet, Shokichi was also half Korean, which made him a distinct outsider in Japanese society. Shokichi showed up with a small band of Tokyo artists and hippies, which combined with a foreigner like myself made us a decidedly odd group. But it seemed appropriate somehow for Iya, which had always been a retreat for outsiders.

Mr Takemoto helped me pace the lot to determine exactly where the boundaries were. Then, with the help of Shokichi and his friends, we began cleaning and renovating to make the house livable again. First, we swept the floor. This was not as easy as it might sound, since it was completely covered with five centimeters of powdery black soot. This we gathered into a pile in the garden and burned. But as the smoke began to rise, we suddenly realized that the powder was not soot at all. It was tobacco! During the seventeen years that my house had been abandoned, the tobacco leaves hanging in the rafters had gradually disintegrated and settled on the floor as dust. Unwittingly, that day I burned several pounds of precious tobacco, more than enough to pay off the entire debt for the house.

No antiques of any value came to light in cleaning the house, but the former occupants had left all the objects of their daily life undisturbed, and in these could be read much about the lives of Iya's people. Most remarkable was the diary of a young woman who had lived in the house with her grandparents in the 1950s. In her diary, the poverty of Iya, the gloom and darkness inside the house, and the girl's desperate yearning for city life were frankly and tearfully recorded. About the time she turned eighteen, the diary came to a sudden end. The villagers told me she ran away from home. Her grandparents wrote 'The child does not return' on a piece of paper and pasted it upside down on the door as a charm to bring her back. It failed, but the slip of paper remains on the door to this day.

After finishing the cleaning, we had to install electricity and water and build a toilet. Eiji came by after school and helped to clear the land by hacking down the bamboo. There were no roads to Tsurui at the time, so all necessary materials had to be lugged up on our backs from the road below, about an hour away by foot. Later, we used the village cargo transport, a steel cable strung across the ravine from which hung a rickety wooden box like a ramshackle ski lift. Once or twice, after hauling up a load of lumber, I took a terrifying ride in the box back down to the road below.

One day, Omo dropped by to watch me and my friends from Tokyo – 'people from below' – and out of pity offered to teach us how to use a traditional scythe to clear the grass. His father, a silent man with bold white eyebrows, would also come over to watch. He would sit on the verandah, open his tobacco pouch and puff on a *kiseru*, one of the long silver pipes you see in Kabuki theater. Omo's stepmother, who came from near Kazura-bashi and prided herself on her Heike culture, wrote thirty-one-syllable *waka* poems for us to inscribe on the paper doors.

Other villagers from Tsurui came one by one to look at the foreigner, and then pitched in to help with the renovation. A foreigner was rare enough, but a foreigner who was trying to repair an old thatch-roofed house was doubly bizarre. Old folk took an interest, and would come over with straw to teach me how to weave straw sandals. On awakening in the morning, I would often find that somebody had left a bunch of cucumbers or other produce for me on the porch outside. At times I would discover that someone had cut the grass in front of the house. In spite of, or maybe because of, the charm on the door, the local children came over to play daily. At night, Shokichi and his friends told ghost stories to them in the spooky light of the floor hearth.

Confucius said, 'Kind men love the mountains', and I think it is possible that mountains breed a kinder sort of person than the plains. The fertile plains support a higher population density and require a collective social structure, especially in the case of rice growing, with its intensive irrigation. Much has been written about the complex human relations born from rice cultivation, and Marx even extrapolated from that to posit a uniquely Asian form of society which he called 'Oriental despotism'. In contrast, the hunters and foresters of Iya, whose rocky slopes hardly supported a single rice paddy, were independent, free and easy people.

In Japan, they represented the survival of an earlier stratum of culture related to Japan's Southeast Asian roots. Centuries of feudal government, the militarism of the late nineteenth and early twentieth centuries, and the stifling influence of the modern education system have created a relatively rigid mindset among the modern Japanese. However, when reading literature from early periods, one gets the impression that the ancient Japanese had little in common with the cautious bureaucrats and obedient company employees one so often meets today. Early poetry, such as the eighth-century *Manyoshu* anthology, has all the rough-hewn vigor of the beams in the Iya house. Other remnants from this period are the 'naked festivals', when young men clad only in loincloths take part in frenzied fertility rituals at temples in late winter.

Another custom with roots in the distant past is *yobai*, a folk tradition once prevalent all over Japan, which has died out everywhere except on a few remote islands and in hamlets like Iya. *Yobai*, or 'night crawling', was the way the young men of the village wooed their maidens. The boy would crawl into the girl's room at night, and if she did not reject him, they would sleep together. By dawn he had to leave the house, and if matters went well, he would visit the girl regularly at night until they got married. Some villages also extended the privilege of *yobai* to travelers, which may have been a way of preventing too much inbreeding in remote areas.

Today, many Japanese would hardly know what the word *yobai* means, and it was little short of miraculous that the custom still existed when I arrived in Iya. It was the subject of many a laughing conversation, and villagers slyly asked me now and then when I was going to start on my nocturnal adventures. At the time, *yobai* seemed to me just another local oddity, but later I discovered that there was more to it than I had thought.

In the Heian period, the loves of the aristocrats immortalized in novels such as the *Tale of Genji* were modeled on the *yobai* pattern. Noblemen visited their loves only at night, and had to leave in the morning. A classic poem such as 'Ariake no tsuki' ("The

Moon at Dawn') is essentially the lovers' lament at parting. The aristocrats took the peasant custom of *yobai*, refined it and added elegant trappings like calligraphy, incense and multilayered robes. But at bottom it was still *yobai*, and the emphasis was on darkness. From this, commentators have spun many theories concerning Japanese concepts of eros and romance.

As can be seen in the case of *yobai*, during the Heian period the primal Japanese roughness was tempered by a sensitivity to fine details of art and love. The marriage was made between simplicity and elegance, traces of which can still be seen in many Japanese arts. At the end of this period, in the late 1100s, a major change occurred, a sort of geologic rift cleaving Japanese history. After hundreds of years of rule by effete court nobles, the old system collapsed. The military took over, moving the capital from Kyoto to Kamakura and establishing the Shogunate which ruled Japan for the next six hundred years. One consequence of this military rule is the rigidity we see today. The ancestors of the Iya people fled into the valley just before military rule began.

The achievements of the military period are by no means all negative, since they include Zen, tea ceremony, Noh drama and Kabuki, almost all the arts which today we think of as being high points of Japanese culture. But there was a deeper stratum below this, one of mists and rocks and giant uncarved tree trunks, the 'Age of the Gods' from which was born the religion of Shinto. This is the world which moves me most of all, and I would hardly have known about it had I not met the people of Tsurui.

I started to think about naming my house. I wanted something which would mean 'House of the Flute', since I play the flute. One night, assisted by Shokichi and a group of Iya children, I set out to find a name. The standard words for flute – *sho* and *teki* – were rejected by the children as sounding too stiff. So we searched through an old Chinese dictionary and found the character *chi*, meaning 'bamboo flute'. It was a beautiful character, written with 'bamboo' on the top, a flourish in the middle and 'tiger' at the bottom. No one had ever seen such a character before, but the children were all for it.

The character *an*, meaning a thatch-roofed cottage, was perfect for the 'house' part of the name, but it is used commonly for tea-ceremony houses, and so seemed too heavily 'cultural'. But, thanks to the dictionary, we discovered that the same character also has the less common reading of *iori*. Combined with *chi* for flute, it gave us the name Chiiori, which had a playful ring to it. Shokichi wrote a poem about Chiiori, which was a big hit with the children, and Chiiori became the standard name for my house in the village. Years later, when I started making calligraphies and paintings, I used it as my artist's signature.

When I founded my art business I used the name again, calling my company Chiiori Ltd. It has been the source of endless trouble, since nobody has ever seen the archaic character *chi*, and nobody ever reads the character *an* as *iori*. Special seals had to be carved in order to file tax documents, and a font just for those characters had to be installed in my computer. Even so, I treasure the name. Although my work today keeps me in Tokyo, Kyoto and Osaka, just looking at my company documents triggers memories of Iya.

In the process of restoring Chiiori I picked up certain skills, one of which was how to measure a house. In ancient China, the size of a building was defined by the number of pillars or 'bays' lining the front and side of the structure. Japan inherited this arrangement, and standardized the width of one bay to be the same as the length of a tatami mat. It is from this system of bays and mats that Japan's modular architecture developed. Land is also measured in terms of tatami mats. The standard used even today, when all other measurements have gone metric, is the *tsubo*, defined as one square bay or two tatami mats (3.3 m²). The land my house sits on measures one hundred and twenty *tsubo*. In front, there is a narrow stretch of garden which drops off suddenly over a sheer stone wall. This wall is the boundary line of the property. Standing on the wall is rather like standing on the battlements of a castle; one looks out over a cedar forest to mountain peaks ranging off into the distance. Immediately behind the house is a hillside overgrown with bamboo, through which a path leads to the nearest neighbors.

My house measures four bays by eight bays (approximately seven meters by fourteen meters). There is one large living room, three bays by three bays, fronted by a verandah, with a *tokonoma* and a Buddhist altar lining the back. This room, a stark expanse of black boards, is almost always empty. The middle room, two bays by two bays, centers on a sunken floor hearth. This is where most of the action in the house takes place: making the fire, cooking, eating, talking. Behind it are two small bedrooms, the only rooms in the house with ceilings over them (to protect sleepers from ash falling from the rafters). At the far end of the house is the kitchen and work area, which drops to an earthen-floored entrance.

The lower part of the house is constructed of squared and polished wood, with pillars lined up at regular intervals. But about one meter above head level, the structure suddenly changes. Linear becomes organic. Resting on the squared pillars are brute timbers, so massive as to seem wholly out of proportion to the size of the house. It is a very typical Japanese transition, also found in temple walls, where a sheet of perfectly smooth plaster drops to a base made from a jumble of rocks. Inside the house, all is flat surfaces and ninety-degree angles to a certain point; above are twisted and knotted timbers finished with adz cuts, huge tree trunks laid sideways, arching from one end of the house to the other.

I built shelves, closets and doors, and repaired the wooden verandahs. Carpentry is of course an unavoidable part of renovating a house, but in Japan what is most important is simply how one chooses to use the available space. This is a vital issue because traditional Japanese architecture is almost completely without walls. There are the pillars set at regular intervals that support the roof – all the rest is extra. Sliding doors can be inserted or removed at will, allowing for a sense of openness and visual freedom. Japanese houses can be likened to open-air pavilions through which wind and light pass freely.

Old houses are remarkably spacious, but their inhabitants frequently divide them into small rooms and corridors with *shoji* or *fusuma* sliding paper doors, transforming the houses into cramped living spaces. In earlier times this was necessary to keep out the cold of winter and to protect the privacy of an extended family, but today there is much less need for such partitions. So the first thing to do when renovating a Japanese house is to remove the *shoji* and *fusuma*. The corridors and verandahs merge with the inner rooms, enlarging the space dramatically. When I moved into Chiiori, black wooden doors so heavy you could hardly move them blocked off the rooms. Taking them out banished to a large extent the oppressive darkness the young girl had complained of in her diary.

The use of space has everything to do with lighting. Jun'ichiro Tanizaki's book *In'ei Raisan (In Praise of Shadows)* has become a modern classic. In it, Tanizaki makes the point that Japan's traditional art arose from the darkness in which people lived. For example, gold screens, which look garish in modern interiors, were designed to pick up the last struggling rays of light making their way into the dim interior of a Japanese house.

Tanizaki laments the fact that the beauty of shadows is no longer understood in modern Japan. Anyone who has lived in an old Japanese house will know how one always feels starved of light, as if one were swimming underwater. It was the constant pressure of this darkness that drove the Japanese to create cities of neon and fluorescent lights. Brightness is a fundamental desire in modern Japan, as can be seen in its uniformly lit hotel lobbies and flashing *pachinko* parlors.

In restoring an old house, it goes without saying that fluorescent lighting should be shunned, but this is not yet so obvious to the Japanese. The older generation, who grew up in traditional gloom, wanted only to escape from all those shadows, so they greeted the advent of the fluorescent light with joy. The younger generation knows little else. In the West, people typically reserve fluorescent lights for kitchens, workspaces and offices, while the use of incandescent lamps, ceiling lights and spotlights for living and dining rooms is so standard as to be taken for granted. So visitors to Japan are unprepared for the complete and utter victory of fluorescent lighting, whose flat bluish glare has penetrated homes, museums, hotels, everywhere. Recently I spoke to a group of students of interior design and asked them how many had thought about illumination and done something to decrease the fluorescent lighting in their homes. Of forty students, there was only one.

Bando Tamasaburo, the Kabuki actor – who also performs in and directs movies – once said to me: 'In Western movies there is a warmth and depth to the color. Not only are shadows abundant, but the shadows themselves have color. In Japanese films, there are few shadows, and the colors are flat and insipid. Living their lives under fluorescent lighting, the Japanese are losing their sense of color.'

The depopulation of Iya had made it a treasure trove of castaway objects of folk handicraft. I filled my house with a collection of old saws, baskets, buckets, *tansu* chests, carved bamboo implements, and so on, turning Chiiori into a handicraft museum. But no matter how magnificent these objects were, I found that the fewer I placed in the house, the more beautiful it became. I removed more and more, eventually leaving the thirty-six square meters of polished floorboards in the main room completely bare. With nothing except the 'black glistening' of the open floor, the house took on the majesty of a Noh stage.

This openness reveals the Southeast Asian and Polynesian origins of the traditional Japanese lifestyle. The way the entire house rests on high supports (essentially poised on stilts) and the

A-frame construction of the roof beams are also from Southeast Asia. But most characteristic of all is the ethos of the 'empty room'. Once I went on a sailing voyage with my father through the islands near Tahiti, and I noticed that the people sat in simple open rooms, with nothing but a TV. In my travels to Southeast Asia I have noticed that in old Thai and Burmese houses there is little other than a Buddhist altar.

Chinese, Korean and Tibetan houses are a completely different story. Even the house of a poor person in these countries is filled with stools and tables, and in the case of China, the placement of furniture developed into an art form in its own right. Japanese houses, however, were built for the lifestyle of the empty room. Tatami mats and polished wooden floors reject things. They want to be empty. One eventually has no choice but to give up all decoration and surrender to the serenity of the empty room.

With the interior of the house cleaned and restored, it was now time to attend to the leaky roof. Thus began my long 'thatching saga'. Japanese roofing thatch is made of a high-growing grass with long, blade-like leaves and delicate seed fronds. Known as *susuki*, it appears in countless screens and scrolls as the 'autumn grass' so beloved of poets and painters. Cut and bound to a farmhouse roof, it is called *kaya*. It is more durable than rice straw: roofs thatched with *kaya* can last for sixty or seventy years.

The way to thatch a roof is as follows: strip away the old *kaya*, revealing the timber construction of the roof; then mount a frame of split bamboo over the timbers, and on top of that lay fifty centimeters or more of thatch, lashed to the timbers with straw rope. It sounds straightforward enough, but I was wholly unprepared for the huge amount of thatch required. One day, as I was blithely planning the reroofing, Omo took me aside and calculated the volume of thatch Chiiori would need. Including the area under the eaves, the floor area of the house is about one hundred and twenty square meters. The area of the roof would be three times that figure. For each square meter of roof, about four bundles of thatch would be needed, bringing the total required to fourteen hundred and forty bundles of thatch. A single bundle cost 2000 yen, bringing the cost of the thatch alone to 2,880,000 yen; in today's dollars, that comes to about $36,000!

For me, who took five years to repay a loan of 380,000 yen, repairing the entire roof with new thatch was out of the question. Instead, Omo helped me buy another abandoned house, about half an hour's walk away. I bought the building for 50,000 yen and, assisted by the villagers, Shokichi and a friend from Colorado, I dismantled it. Stripping the thatch from the roof, we strapped it to our backs, four bundles at a time, and carried it over the mountain paths to my house. As it was old thatch, the accumulated soot of decades of hearth fires puffed out with every step, and by the end of each day we all looked like coal miners.

In the summer of 1977 we used the thatch to repair the roof at the back of the house. Facing north, this section of roof was constantly in shade and so suffered from damp, and was in considerably worse shape than the thatch at the front. The local thatcher was busy rethatching the roof of the Asa mansion deeper in the valley, the enormous farmhouse where the descendants of the Heike leader lived. In festive spirit, the villagers, my friends and I rethatched the back of the roof ourselves. Omo warned me that the old thatch was already weak and would not last long, but for the time being Chiiori was saved.

The next few years in Iya were happy, dreamlike ones. Sometimes I would hike with friends and the village children to a swimming hole deep in the mountains, known as Kunze, which means 'Smoky World'. Omo's mother wrote a poem about it, in which she used the name to suggest the smoky atmosphere inside Chiiori. There was no trail leading to this pool; only Eiji knew the way. For three hours we would scramble over boulders while Eiji hacked his way through brambles until we reached a waterfall that cascaded into the pool. It was blue, cold and so deep that none of us were ever able to dive all the way to the bottom. The villagers believed it to be the abode of a dragon. We would take off our clothes, dive in and swim about, even though the villagers warned us that swimming in the nude at Kunze would not be taken well by the dragon. After spending an afternoon happily splashing around in the pool, we would start home, and then, invariably, it would begin to pour. The dragon, god of rain, was showing his wrath.

In the evenings we would go out into the garden to watch the shooting stars, so common that we often saw as many as seven or eight in an hour. Later we would go inside and tell ghost stories, and then crawl into a cave of green mosquito netting and sleep huddled together in the middle of the floor.

It is said that owning an old Japanese house is like bringing up a child. You have to constantly buy new clothing for it. You must replace the tatami mats, repaper the sliding doors, restore rotten timbers on the verandahs – you can never leave the house unattended. Chiiori was of course no exception, and the problem with the roof in particular eluded any quick and easy solution. By the early 1980s the second-hand thatch on the rear part of the roof was leaking again, and it became clear that I had no choice but to get the local thatcher to undertake a full-scale rethatching.

So I set out on my second quest for thatch. However, with the 1980s had come an even more serious wave of emigration from the valley, and the people left in Iya had cast away most elements of their traditional lifestyle. After a long search, I finally tracked down the valley's last surviving field of cultivated *susuki* grass. Over the next five years, I gathered fifteen hundred bundles of thatch. In the process, I saw how even in the peasant culture of Iya, the complex use of natural materials was far advanced. For example, there are several different varieties of thatch, one of which is called *shino*. This thatch is cut in early spring, when all the leaves have fallen from the dry stalks. Denser than ordinary thatch, *shino* is used only on the corners of the roof.

In addition to thatch, we needed several truckloads of rice straw. The thatcher inserts a layer of straw under the edges of the roof, thereby creating a slight upward curve at the eaves. We also needed six types of bamboo, each of which had different dimensions, came from a different part of Shikoku, and had to be cut at a certain time in order to prevent insect damage. Add to this three types of rope (rice straw in two weights, and palm fiber), a hundred cryptomeria pine logs to replace rotten roof timbers, and cedar planks for the eaves. Finally, there are arcane implements, like the meter-long iron needle used during the roofing process. The thatcher runs rope through the eye of the needle and jabs it through the thatch. Someone below ties the rope around a beam, runs the end of the rope through the eye again and the needle is yanked back out. The thatcher then ties the ends of the rope, thereby securing the thatch to the roof beams.

The cost of thatching Chiiori the second time proved a truly tremendous burden. Including travel and labor costs, it ran to twelve million yen. No bank was about to loan money to the owner of the only piece of real estate in Japan to have dropped in value. I had to pay it all in cash, relying on loans from friends and family.

The thatching was completed in 1988, and was a six-month project involving Omo, the rest of Tsurui village, and friends from America, Kobe, Kyoto and Tokyo. When it was over, the *susuki* field we had used was replanted with chestnut trees. The village's aging thatcher had no successor, and in any case there was no further need for his services: apart from two houses designated by the government as national treasures, there were no plans to have a roof thatched in Iya. Some decades in the future the government will have to rethatch the houses in its care, but by then all the materials and workers will need to be brought in from outside. Chiiori was the last house ever to be roofed by the Iya thatcher using *kaya* grown in Iya.

From the cottages of rural England to the palm-frond-roofed dwellings of the South Pacific, houses covered with leaves instead of stone, metal or tiles have a unique appeal. I suppose it might be because the other materials are more or less artificial, while leaves are closer to nature. A thatch-roofed cottage does not seem to have been manufactured, but rather to have sprung from the earth like moss or mushrooms.

In Japan, the era of thatched roofs is at an end. The last examples may be seen in temples, teahouses, cultural landmarks protected by the government, and a few surviving farmhouses. By and large, roofs have been covered over with tin or aluminum. Driving through the countryside, you can easily spot houses that were originally thatched because of their distinctive high-pitched roofs; under the tin, the old roof beams and often even the thatch itself remains.

It is often argued that thatched roofs are difficult to maintain and expensive, which I can hardly deny, having personally suffered the dire financial consequences of thatching a roof. But there is an interesting lesson to be learned here with regard to the preservation of traditional industries. Thatch is not inherently expensive. Traditionally, every village had a thatch field, and the villagers harvested thatch in winter as a regular part of the agricultural cycle. They stored it along with the various types of bamboo, straw and lumber, and used these supplies communally whenever a house needed reroofing. The materials were plentiful and did not have to be specially ordered; the thatcher had work year-round, so he did not need to charge high rates. When demand for thatching dropped, however, a vicious circle set in: the price of humble materials like thatch and bamboo skyrocketed, and as it did so, fewer people wanted or were able to go to the expense. The irony is that thatching did not die out because it is expensive – it is expensive because thatching died out.

In Europe the same forces were at work, and as thatching declined, prices rose, so that today, thatching is something of a luxury. However, in England and Denmark, thousands of thatched houses still exist, including entire thatched hamlets. Thatchers continue to have work, thatch continues to be cut, and the expense, while high, is not astronomical. As a result, thatched roofs have retained an important place in the rural landscape.

Japan's rejection of thatch was tragic because it had been a critically important part of the country's cultural tradition. Many other countries used thatch, but it had remained the property of peasants. From China to Ireland, churches, palaces and the villas of the rich were universally roofed with tiles, stone or metal. But in Japan, since the Heian period, thatch was the preferred material of the elite. The Imperial Palace in Kyoto is thatched with cedar chips; the most important Shinto shrine, the Grand Shrine of Ise, is thatched with *kaya*; the most famous tea-ceremony houses are thatched with *kaya* or wood bark. In painting, poetry, religion and the arts, thatch was considered the very keynote of elegance. This ability to make sophisticated use of humble natural materials was one of the defining characteristics of Japan's tradition. In that light, the loss of thatching is not just a quirk of modern rural development: it is a blow to the heart.

This brings me to the dark side of the fairy tale of Iya Valley. When I first entered Iya twenty-five years ago, Japan's systematic environmental destruction was already becoming visible, but there was virtually no popular resistance or dialogue regarding the matter. This destruction has continued at an ever-increasing rate, and now Japan has achieved a position as one of the world's ugliest countries. My friends from abroad who come to visit are almost universally disappointed. Apart from showpieces such as Hakone Park, Japan's countryside has been utterly defiled. When my friends ask me, 'Where can you go to escape the billboards, electric wires and concrete?', I am at a loss for an answer.

It is said that of Japan's thirty thousand rivers and streams, only three remain undammed, and even these have had their streambeds and banks encased in concrete. Concrete blocks now account for over 30 per cent of the several thousand kilometers of the country's coastline. The government manages the national forests with complete disregard for ecological balance (there are no forest rangers in Japan). The thrust of hundreds of millions of dollars of government subsidies is devoted to establishing a forestry industry in these reserves, with owners of mountain land being encouraged to log virgin forest and replace it with uniform ranks of cryptomeria cedar. Thanks to this policy, when one goes to view autumn foliage, it is very difficult to find and widely scattered.

And then the electric wires! Japan is the only advanced nation in the world that does not bury electric lines in its towns and cities, and this is a prime factor in the squalid visual impression of its urban areas. Out in the suburbs, the use of electric lines is even worse. I was once taken to see the new Yokohama residential district Kohoku New Town, and was amazed at the multitudes of enormous steel pylons and smaller utility poles clustered everywhere – a hellish web of power lines darkening the sky above one's head. This in a site which is considered a model of urban development. Further out into the countryside, power companies have been free to erect steel utility pylons without the slightest restraint. The effect of these towers marching across hills and valleys is so overwhelming that one feels they were raised with the express intention of destroying the beauty of the landscape.

The movie director Akira Kurosawa said in an interview a few years ago, 'Because Japan's wilderness has been despoiled in recent years, it is becoming increasingly difficult to make movies here.' It has reached the point where a simple litmus test applies unfailingly to the landscape: whenever you see a sweeping wilderness scene on TV or on a poster, look for concrete or electric wires; if you can't find any, the odds are overwhelming that the scene is a set, or it was filmed outside Japan.

A poem by the Tang poet Tu Fu includes the famous line,

'Though the nation is lost, the mountains and rivers remain'. In Japan, the opposite is true: the nation prospers, but the mountains and rivers are lost. The architect Sei Takeyama has pointed out that one reason for this state of affairs is the ability of the Japanese to narrow their focus. This is what led to the creation of a haiku in which the poet shuts out the entire universe to concentrate on just one frog jumping into a pond. Unfortunately, in the case of landscape, the same ability allows the Japanese to concentrate on a pretty green rice paddy without noticing the industrial estate surrounding it. I recently gave a talk to the Junior Chamber of Commerce in the town of Kameoka, where I live. When I remarked that looking out from the highway one could easily count over sixty giant utility pylons towering over the surrounding mountains, my audience was shocked. Not one of them had ever noticed these pylons.

However, I do not believe that the Japanese have completely lost the delicate sensibility of the Heian era. Somewhere, deep in their hearts, they know that Japan is becoming an ugly country. Since I began speaking and writing about this issue, my mailbox has been filled with correspondence from Japanese who feel just as heartbroken as I do about the situation. I am convinced that this is one of the most important issues Japan will face in the coming century. For a long time, the destruction was dismissed, even by foreigners, with excuses like, 'it's more important to have electricity' and 'it was necessary to develop economically'. But surely such comments are condescending to a country which is one of the world's most thriving economies. The Japanese are no longer poor peasants excited about their first experience of electricity. Other countries have developed ways of managing electric pylons. For example, Switzerland mandates the bundling together of electric lines to reduce the number of pylons as much as possible, painting pylons green and building them lower than ridge lines so as not to interfere with the line of sight. Germany has developed a technology of shoring riverbanks with stones and rough concrete in such a way as to nurture grasses and insects, thereby protecting the ecosystem. But Japan has completely overlooked such technologies.

The effects on the domestic tourist industry are already beginning to show. Internal travel is declining, while foreign travel is at an all-time high, reflecting the millions of people who are traveling abroad to escape the domestic ugliness. Nevertheless, in spite of an increase in grass-roots awareness, Japan's environmental destruction has accelerated. Sometimes when driving through the countryside I come across another mountain being bulldozed or a river being concreted over, and I can't help but feel a sense of fear. Japan has become a huge and terrifying machine, a Moloch tearing apart its own land with teeth of steel, and there is absolutely nothing anyone can do to stop it. It is enough to send a chill down one's spine.

Today, I rarely visit Chiiori. Luckily the mountains around the house still retain their beauty; however, the road to Iya, the Inland Sea, and Kagawa and Tokushima Prefectures have been drastically transformed, so the trip to Chiiori is becoming depressing. Inside Iya, the construction of a forest road recently filled even the remote Kunze pool with sludge and debris. Looking out from the stone wall at the edge of the garden, the mountainsides opposite are now dotted with concrete retaining walls, and steel pylons line the banks of the Iya River. It is only a matter of time before the mountain-eating machine comes to Tsurui, so it is impossible to view the scenery without a sense of unease.

When I found my house in Iya, I fancied that I would live like a sage deep in the mountains, in a solitary thatch-roofed cottage perched atop a soaring emerald crag high above the clouds – just like a mysterious Nizan painting. However, it became increasingly evident that the mountain life I loved would be a short one. So I turned my eyes away from Iya, beginning the search for the world of dreams elsewhere. In 1978, I met the Kabuki actor

Tamasaburo, and was invited into the world of the traditional arts. My dream of living in a castle shifted away from Iya: from a mountaintop castle to one of the stage.

That year, I decided to come down from the mountains and headed for the Kabuki theaters of Tokyo. Of course, I did not wholly give up on Iya. Over the ensuing years my friends and I have continued to have a variety of experiences there, including the saga of Chiiori's rethatching. The Noh stage of the living room has seen numerous performances, including one where Eiji and Omo's youngest daughter dressed up in old puppet costumes and performed a samurai story for the villagers. Another time, Shokichi's wife, Setsuko, who is now one of Japan's leading *buto* dance artists, performed an ecstatic dance which began on the black floorboards inside the house and ended outside in the snow. A photographer lived in Chiiori for six months and later produced a book of photographs capturing Tsurui life. A pair of British anthropologists spent a summer there. In this way, Iya has continued to be a refuge.

And there are some bright signs for the region. Until recently, one problem has been that Iya men have had trouble finding wives in wealthy modern Japan; women from elsewhere do not want to move to a poverty-stricken mountain area like Iya. So, in the 1980s, Iya pioneered a novel scheme to bring in brides from the Philippines, which generated nationwide controversy. It was a success and has since been copied by other remote villages. Although depopulation is still severe, the scheme is bringing fresh blood to Iya, and restoring its ancient Southeast Asian roots. While many young men have left, Eiji, for instance, returned to the valley with his earnings from a decade spent working outside as a designer of tunnels; he lives with his Filipina wife and their young son in a house further up the hillside. Also, with Chiiori thatched and another house nearby designated an important cultural property, there is even talk of making Tsurui a 'special cultural zone'. Perhaps some day it will happen.

Iya Valley

The winter of 1978 was bitterly cold. On the day of my descent from Tsurui, Omo's mother composed a haiku for me:

> *Powdered in snow*
> *The morning mountains*
> *Tug at my back.*

Chapter 3

Kabuki

Only the Salt Remains

In the summer of 1977 my long college years ended, and I returned to Japan to work at a Shinto foundation called Oomoto, based in the small town of Kameoka, west of Kyoto. The founder of Oomoto had said, 'Art is the mother of religion', and in keeping with his philosophy, Oomoto sponsors a summer seminar in traditional Japanese arts (tea ceremony, Noh drama, etc.), which I had attended in 1976. My job at Oomoto was to help with arts-related international activities.

However, my first months in Kameoka were extremely lonely. Although Oomoto provided the opportunity to study tea ceremony and Noh drama, their world of ritual failed to interest me. For a person of serious temperament, the quiet of the tearoom and the formality of Noh should be an inspiration. But with some feelings of guilt, I had to admit to myself that I did not have a serious temperament. I tried to distract myself by making the rounds of Kyoto's temples, but soon reached my limit of raked sand. It was very frustrating. There had to be more than this zestless, ritualized Kyoto, with every tree pruned, every gesture a formula.

That summer, the old Mother Goddess of Oomoto had a visit from an important guest – the Tibetan lama Domo Geshe Rinpoche, abbot of a monastery in Sikkim. He was famed for his psychic powers. At the end of the summer, we met one day in a beer garden in Kameoka. Knowing Domo Geshe's reputation as a psychic, I came straight to the point and blurted out, 'What should I do?' He looked me over and said, 'You must seek out another world. If not on this earth, then the moon. If not the moon, then somewhere else. Without fail you will find that world by the end of the year.'

Domo Geshe went on to America, leaving his secretary, Gail, to take care of odds and ends in Kyoto. One day in December, Gail invited me to go and see a Kabuki play. I had been dragged to Kabuki as a child, but my only memory was of ugly old women with harsh croaking voices – the *onnagata* (male actors who play women's roles). I was not very enthusiastic about the invitation, but having nothing better to do I accompanied Gail into Kyoto to see the play at the Minamiza Theater.

It was Kyoto's *kaomise* (literally, 'face showing'), when leading Kabuki actors come down from Tokyo to act in the gala performance of the year. Geisha dressed in their finery sit in the boxes that line the theater, and the refined matrons of Kyoto throng the lobby exchanging cruel politenesses with each other. But we were too poor to be a part of all that. We bought the cheapest tickets available and climbed to our seats high in the rafters.

As the dance 'Fuji Musume' ('Wisteria Maiden') began, I saw that the *onnagata* playing the maiden was not one of the ugly old women of my childhood memory, but was truly picture lovely. The flute and drums were fast-flowing; the sliding feet and impossible turns of the neck and wrists of the dancer were playful and sensuous – everything I had been missing. I was stagestruck.

After the dance, Gail informed me to my surprise that the *onnagata*, whom I had thought to be about twenty-five years old, was the veteran actor Nakamura Jakuemon, aged sixty at the time. On leaving the theater, Gail took me to a nearby teahouse called Kaika. The master of the teahouse asked me what I had thought of *kaomise*, and I replied, 'Jakuemon was amazing. His sixty-year-old body managed to be totally sensuous.' The master gestured to the woman sitting next to me, and said, 'She has an appointment with Jakuemon right now. Why don't you go along?' So before I knew it, I was backstage at the Minamiza Theater. One minute, Jakuemon was a vision dancing on a stage miles below me, someone I could only view from afar with no hope of ever meeting; the next, I was backstage talking to him.

Jakuemon, still in make-up, looked fortyish, like a refined Kyoto matron. But he had a sly grin, and a coquettish sideways glance flashed from eyes lined with red and black. This sideways glance, called *nagashime* (literally, 'flowing eyes'), was a hallmark of beautiful women in old Japan, and is found in countless woodblock prints of courtesans and *onnagata*. I was seeing it at close range. An attendant dressed in black brought out a small saucer, in which Jakuemon blended white face powder and crimson lipstick with a gentle hand. Dipping a brush in the resulting 'onnagata pink', he wrote the character *hana* (flower) for me on a square *shikishi* (calligraphic plaque). Then, with the removal of wig, robes and make-up, there emerged a tanned, short-haired man, who looked like a tough Osaka businessman. With a brusque 'See ya', spoken in a gravelly voice, he strolled out of the room in white suit and shades.

In my case, the secret door to the world of Kabuki was the Kaika teahouse. *Kaika*, which means 'transformation', refers to the Bunmei Kaika (Transformation of Civilization) that took place in Japan after the Meiji Restoration in 1868. The master of Kaika was a former Kabuki *onnagata*, and the interior of the teashop was covered with Meiji- and Taisho-period theater decorations. As it was close to the Minamiza Theater, Kaika was a meeting place for actors and teachers of traditional Japanese music and dance.

After my audience with Jakuemon, I was taken to see various other actors, among them Kawarazaki Kunitaro, a childhood friend of the Kaika master. Kunitaro, who was in his sixties, was a true child of the Meiji 'transformation', his father having founded Tokyo's first coffee house on the Ginza at the turn of the century. As a young man, Kunitaro joined a group of leftist intellectuals who broke away from traditional Kabuki and cofounded a theater troupe called Zenshinza (Progressive Theater). Kunitaro was especially adept at *akuba* roles – sharp-tongued townswomen. Other actors would come to him to study his distinctive technique of *sute-serifu* – catty quips 'tossed' at the audience.

I found it curious that the Progressive Theater featured something so retrograde as *onnagata*. Kabuki was founded by a troupe of women in the early 1600s, but during the Edo period, women were banned from the Kabuki stage because they were considered conducive to immoral behavior. The *onnagata* took their place. There was a brief attempt in early Meiji to replace *onnagata* with real women but the audience rejected them. By that point, Kabuki was so thoroughly imbued with the art of *onnagata* that real women did not play the roles properly. After Meiji, women found their place in modern theater. However, in certain unexpected pockets, such as Zenshinza and in Japanese dance, *onnagata* continue to exist even outside of Kabuki.

I soon heard of a particular *onnagata* called Tamasaburo. Unlike the others, he had achieved fame outside of Kabuki as his face was everywhere – on TV, on posters, in advertisements. In 1967, at the age of seventeen, Tamasaburo had caught the eye of the public with his appearance in the play *Sakurahime Azuma Bunsho (The Scarlet Princess of Edo)*. Yukio Mishima wrote a play for him; teenage girls besieged the theaters. For the first time in a century, a Kabuki *onnagata* had become a popular star.

The February after the Minamiza *kaomise*, I saw Tamasaburo perform for the first time, at the Shinbashi Enbujo Theater in Tokyo, in the dance 'Sagi Musume' ('Heron Maiden') – Kabuki's *Swan Lake*. In it, a young maiden dances as a white heron in the snow. Through successive costume changes, from white, to purple, to red, she passes through the stages of girlhood, young adulthood and first love. Then comes heartbreak: her wing (or sleeve) is wounded. She becomes deranged and whirls madly through the snow. At the end, mounting a red felt-covered platform, her face distorted with suffering and rage, she strikes a final pose.

The beginning of the dance was quiet. Sagi Musume, dressed in a pure white kimono, a white hood over her head, turned slowly at the center of the stage, her movement so smooth and perfectly controlled that she seemed like a marble statue. Though Tamasaburo had yet to show his face, he had already conjured up a quiet, twilit, snow-covered world. The hood fell, revealing the pure face of an angel, radiantly white. The audience gasped; this was not the usual *onnagata*. Impossible to describe, the beauty of Tamasaburo is almost a natural phenomenon, like a rainbow or a waterfall. At the end, when, her long black hair disheveled, Sagi Musume mounted the red platform brandishing a magic staff, she was like a shaman of ancient times, evoking the wrath of heaven. The audience around me wept.

Afterwards, a friend of the Kaika master took me to Tamasaburo's dressing room backstage. Out of make-up, Tamasaburo was a tall, thin young man, who looked not much different from somebody one might sit next to on the subway. In contrast with his sadness-tinged femininity of the stage, he was no-nonsense, cheerful, funny. He was then aged twenty-seven, two years older than me.

Kabuki, an almost perfectly preserved remnant of Japan's feudal past, is dominated by a handful of old families. Actors are ranked according to the importance of their hereditary names, like barons and dukes in the peerage. Actors not born into a Kabuki family are doomed to spend their whole lives as *kuroko* – the black-clad attendants, supposedly invisible to the audience, who appear onstage to supply a prop and remove or adjust a piece of costume. At best, they might appear in a row of maids or retainers. But occasionally someone manages to gain entrance to the hierarchy from outside, and Tamasaburo was one of these.

Although not born into the Kabuki world, Tamasaburo began dancing when he was four. At the age of six he was adopted by the Kabuki actor Morita Kanya XIV, and appeared as a child actor under the name of Bando Kinoji. From then on, his entire life was devoted to the stage; he never went beyond high school. When I met him, he had just returned from his first trip to Europe and was dying to talk to someone about world culture. Fresh from Oxford, I seemed to him to be the ideal candidate. For my part, having just watched Sagi Musume, I was still marveling at his genius, and had a host of questions to ask about Japanese theater. We hit it off at once, and soon became fast friends.

From then on, I neglected Oomoto and stole every opportunity to take the train to Tokyo to see Kabuki. Jakuemon and Tamasaburo gave me free run of the backstage, and Tamasaburo's adoptive mother, Kanshie, was a master of Nihon Buyo (Japanese dance), so I would often watch her classes. For five years I more or less lived inside the Kabuki theater.

Kabuki seems to me to have the perfect balance between the sensuality and ritual which are the two poles of Japanese culture. On one hand, there is Japan's freewheeling sexuality, out of which was born the riotous *ukiyo* (floating world) of Edo: courtesans, colorful woodblock prints, men dressed as women, women dressed as men, 'naked festivals', brilliantly decorated kimono, etc. This is a remnant of ancient Southeast Asian influence on Japan, and is more akin to Bangkok than to Beijing or Seoul. In fact, early Jesuits traveling from Beijing to Nagasaki at the end of the sixteenth century wrote letters in which they contrasted the colorful costumes of the Japanese with the drab gowns of the common people of Beijing.

At the same time, there is a tendency in Japan towards over-decoration, towards cheap sensuality too overt to be art. Recognizing this, the Japanese turn against the sensual. They polish, refine, slow down, trying to reduce art and life to its pure essentials. From this reaction were born the rituals of tea ceremony, Noh drama and Zen. In the history of Japanese art you can see these two tendencies warring against each other. In the late Muromachi period, gorgeous gold screens were in the ascendant; along came the tea masters, and suddenly the aesthetic was misshapen brown tea bowls. By late Edo the emphasis had swung back to courtesans and the pleasure quarters.

Today, this war goes on. There are garish *pachinko* parlors and late-night pornographic TV, and there is a reaction against all that, which I call the 'process of sterilization': the tendency to fill every garden with raked sand and every modern structure with flat concrete and granite. Kabuki, however, has the right balance. It began as a popular art, and is rich in humor, raw emotion and sexual appeal. At the same time, after hundreds of years, it has been slowed and refined to the point where, within the sensuality, there is that timeless 'stop' – the meditational calm which is Japan's special achievement.

Kabuki, like all theater, is a world of illusion. With its extreme elaboration of costumes, make-up and the *kata* (prescribed 'forms' of movement), it may be the most illusionistic of all: when the elegant court lady removes her make-up, one is left facing an Osaka businessman. Once, I was translating for Tamasaburo when an Englishman asked him, 'Why did you want to become an actor?' Tamasaburo answered, 'Because I longed for a world of beauty beyond my reach.' I, too, was bewitched by this elusive world of illusion.

In the play *Iriya*, there is a scene where the woman Michitose is about to meet her lover after a long separation. Her samurai is being hunted by the police but has crept through the snow to see her. He waits in front of some *fusuma* sliding doors. Hearing of his arrival, she bursts into the room and the lovers are reunited. When Tamasaburo was once playing the part of Michitose, we were sitting together backstage, next to the *fusuma* doors and more or less on the stage itself, just prior to Michitose's dramatic entrance. Tamasaburo was chatting casually and was not the least bit feminine – very much an average man, although he was in full costume. When the time came for his entrance, he stood up, laughed, said, 'OK, here I go!', and walked over to the *fusuma*. He adjusted his robe, flung open the *fusuma*, and in that instant was transformed into a beauty straight out of an Ukiyoe print. In a silvery voice fit to melt the audience's heart, he cried out, '*Aitakatta, aitakatta, aitakatta wai na!*' – 'I've missed you, I've missed you, I've missed you so much!' A world of illusion had sprung up from one side of a *fusuma* to the other.

The illusion is achieved by Kabuki stagecraft, probably the most highly developed in the world. The *hanamichi* ('flower path') through the audience is a particularly famous example. Actors enter and leave the stage via this walkway; separated from the action on the main stage, the actor on the *hanamichi* enters a solitary realm where he is free to reveal the inner depths of his role. For instance, the play *Kumagai Jinya* (*Kumagai's Battle Camp*) is a traditional tale of *giri-ninjo* (the conflict between love and duty): Kumagai must kill his own son and substitute the boy's severed head for the son of his lord. His ruse is successful, but in remorse Kumagai shaves off his hair to enter a life of asceticism, and exits down the *hanamichi*. When the late Kanzaburo XVIII played Kumagai, he imparted such a sense of personal desolation as he exited down the *hanamichi* that *Kumagai Jinya* seemed not a tale of *giri-ninjo*, but an antiwar play.

Kabuki stagecraft sometimes seems symbolic of life itself. An example of this is *danmari*, or pantomime scenes, in which all the lead characters come silently out onto the stage at the same time.

As though walking in pitch darkness, they move about in slow motion, oblivious to each other's existence; they run into each other or drop things which are retrieved by others. There is an eerie quality about *danmari* which has nothing to do with any specific play. Watching scenes of *danmari*, where a man picks up a letter his lover has dropped, or two people looking for each other pass by unawares, one senses the blindness of human existence. What begins as just another bit of eccentric Kabuki stagecraft ends up symbolizing a deeper truth.

Why did stagecraft develop to such a level in Japan? At the risk of oversimplification, I would say it was because Japan is a country where the exterior is more often valued over the interior. One may see the negative effects of this in many aspects of modern Japanese life. For instance, the fruits and vegetables in a Japanese supermarket are all flawless in color and shape as if made from wax, but they are flavorless. The importance of the exterior may be seen in the conflict between *tatemae* (officially stated position) and *honne* (real intent), which is a staple of books written about Japan. Listening to the debates in Japan's Diet, it is abundantly clear that *tatemae* is given precedence over *honne*. Nevertheless, this emphasis on the surface is not without its positive side, for Kabuki's unparalleled stagecraft is a direct result of such prizing of the outward.

Though I learned many things from Kabuki stagecraft, the aspect I found most fascinating was the artistry used to capture and accentuate the emotion of a single fleeting moment. The *mie*, when actors pose dramatically with eyes crossed and arms flung out, is an obvious example of this. But it may be said of many other Kabuki *kata* as well. For example, there might be a scene where two people are casually talking; then, from some detail of the conversation, the characters suddenly comprehend each other's true feelings. In that instant, action stops, actors freeze, and from stage left wooden clappers go '*battari!*'. The two characters resume speaking as though nothing has happened;

however, in the instant of that '*battari!*', everything has changed. While most forms of theater try to preserve a narrative continuity, Kabuki focuses around such crucial instants of stop and start, start and stop.

This can also be said of Kabuki audiences' expressions of appreciation. At a Western play or concert, the audience waits politely until the very end before applauding; nothing could be more ill-mannered than to clap between movements of a symphony. In contrast, during highlights of a Kabuki play, audience members will show their appreciation by shouting out the *yago* (house names) of the actors. When the play is over, they just get up and leave.

The shouting of *yago* is an art in itself. One doesn't shout at any time, but only at certain moments of dramatic tension. You can recognise the amateurs in the audience by their poorly timed shouts. There is a group of knowledgeable old men, called the *omuko* (literally, 'men in the back'), who are the masters of this art form; they frequent the upper rafters, where I sat at my first *kaomise*. From there, they shout *yago* such as '*Yamatoya!*' for Tamasaburo or '*Nakamuraya!*' for Kanzaburo. Or they will vary their repertoire with '*Godaime!*' ('Fifth generation!'), '*Goryonin!*' ('The pair of you!') or '*Mattemashita!*' ('I've been waiting for this!'). I remember watching the legendary *onnagata* Utaemon, then aged seventy, appearing as the grand courtesan Yatsuhashi. At the climactic moment, when Yatsuhashi turns to the peasant following her and bestows upon him the smile which is going to destroy his life, there was a shout from the *omuko*: '*Hyakuman doru!*' – 'A million dollars!'

I have only shouted once in my life; it was in the early days, for Kunitaro. His yago was *Yamazakiya*. I practiced and practiced, and then at the right moment I shouted '*Yamazakiya!*' from the rafters as best as I could. It wasn't easy. The timing is so important that the actors depend on the shouts to sustain the rhythm of the performance. I once saw Tamasaburo in rehearsal pause at a critical moment, whisper '*Yamatoya!*', and then glide into the next movement of the dance.

Focus on the 'instant' is characteristic of Japanese culture as a whole. In Chinese poetry, the poet's imagination might begin with flowers and rivers, and then suddenly leap up into the Nine Heavens to ride a dragon to Mt K'un-lun and frolic with the immortals. Japanese haiku focus on the mundane moment, as in Basho's well-known poem: 'The old pond; a frog leaps in – the sound of water'. The frog leaps into the pond, not up to heaven. There are no immortals, just 'the sound of water'. In the concision of haiku and *waka*, Japan created unparalleled literary forms. On the other hand, long poems of narrative or ideas are almost completely absent from the history of Japanese literature. Long verse was created by stringing pearls together into longer chains, as in *renga* (linked *waka* poems).

This 'instantaneous culture' is something I also noticed in the real-estate world, where I was later to work in Tokyo. There are innumerable detailed building codes, but the overall design of a building and its aesthetic relation to street and skyline are ignored; the result is careless, disjointed, ugly. The sorry state of the highway system is also the result of *renga* thinking: there is no master plan, just a stringing together of annual budgets to build highways piecemeal.

Kabuki is no exception. The arrangement of a play's elements are ambiguous, and sudden narrative leaps are often made. For anyone expecting dramatic unity, Kabuki seems weak. My friends who value logic invariably dislike Kabuki. However, with its emphasis on the depth of a single instant, Kabuki creates an atmosphere of intense excitement which is rare in other theater. Tamasaburo once told me, 'In ordinary drama, the story proceeds step by step. What a bore! Kabuki's fascination lies in its outrageous leaps of logic.'

Kabuki, like everything else in Japan, is torn between the poles of refinement and hedonism – hedonism being represented by *keren* (acrobatic tricks), refinement by the actors' measured grace. These days, plays featuring multiple costume changes, actors attached to cables flying through the air, and waterfalls onstage are all the rage. The popularity of *keren* is a sign of the sickness currently plaguing the traditional Japanese arts in general. When one looks at Japan's wilderness breathing its dying gasps, the traditional arts seem comparatively healthy. Kabuki has actually experienced a box-office resurgence over the last twenty years, and the theaters are often sold out. But trouble is brewing because of Kabuki's irrelevance to any life a modern audience can now experience. There is hardly a single object on the Kabuki stage recognizable to young people today. When stage chanters sing of fireflies or autumn maples, such things are now almost mythical subjects in this land of vast cedar plantations.

Actors such as Jakuemon or Tamasaburo spend hours with the kimono dyers discussing the precise shade of purple a certain kimono should be, what color the actor Kikugoro VI ('the Great Sixth') used, what is chic or not chic by standards of the Edo period. Certain older attendants, who came in from outside and therefore can never achieve major roles, have amassed incredible knowledge about such Kabuki arcana. In many cases, these men, not the actors you see onstage, are the true standard-bearers of the tradition; they know by heart not only what Kikugoro VI used, but what was used before him.

An example is Tamasaburo's old retainer Yagoro, now in his eighties, whom Tamasaburo inherited from his adoptive father Kanya. Yagoro performed major roles in his youth as a member of the small troupes that used to travel the countryside. As the tide of Westernization swept Japan after World War II, these smaller troupes disappeared or were gradually absorbed into one large troupe. The 'Grand Kabuki' we see today consists of several hundred actors (and their assistants), all based in Tokyo. 'Grand' though it is called, it is actually the shrunken remnant of a larger Kabuki world which once numbered thousands of performers spread throughout the provinces. Yagoro belongs to the last generation who knew that larger Kabuki world.

Yagoro will come into the room backstage after a show and sit there with a smile on his face. Then Tamasaburo will say, 'What do you think, Father?' (actors address each other as 'elder brother', 'uncle', 'father'). Yagoro will say, 'The Great Sixth used a silver fan, but that was because he was short and it accentuated his height. For you it would be inappropriate. Use gold, like the former Baiko did.' This is how their knowledge is passed down.

But what use are all these refinements when you are performing to an audience whose familiarity with the kimono is about on a par with that of Americans? Fine details tend to be lost, and the audience goes for the obvious crowd-pleasers, like *keren*.

Another problem is the generation gap. The training of actors, including those of Tamasaburo's generation, used to be fierce. Intense dedication was required. Jakuemon told me how he used to memorize *nagauta* (long narrative lyrics) by chanting them on the train on his way to the theater; one day, the train suddenly stopped and he found all the other passengers staring at him as he chanted loudly in the ensuing silence. In those days, Kabuki was more of a popular form, and less of a formalized 'traditional art', so audiences were more knowledgeable and demanding. A bad actor would find the *omuko* shouting, '*Daikon!*' ('big radish!'), to his everlasting humiliation. Now there are no calls of *Daikon!*, and audiences sit reverently with their hands in their laps, no matter how good or bad the actor might be. The younger actors, born into privilege because of their family names, have it easy. Tamasaburo once said, 'Communism in Russia was a terrible thing, but it produced great ballet dancers. In order to be great you need a Moscow in your background.'

After I began watching Kabuki, I discovered Nihon Buyo (Japanese dance) and Shinpa (Meiji-style drama) as well. I realized that 'Grand Kabuki' is just the tip of the iceberg – the arts connected to Kabuki are vigorously active in their own right. There is a constant round of recitals, called *kai* (gatherings), of Nihon Buyo, flute, *nagauta* (long lyrics), *kouta* (short lyrics), *samisen*, and more.

While one invariably sees foreigners at Kabuki theater, I have found it extremely rare to see another foreigner at any of these recitals. But given the diversity of Nihon Buyo, which includes dozens of styles, tens of thousands of teachers and millions of students, it is a broader world than Kabuki. Many of the finest dancers are women, which is a return to Kabuki's pre-*onnagata* roots. Some of them are legends such as Takehara Han, who began as a geisha in Osaka and ended up as the premier master of Zashiki-mai (sitting-room dance), a subtle form of dance which originated in the intimate quarters of the geisha house. If you included classical Kabuki dance styles such as Fujima-ryu, as well as the numerous varieties of Zashiki-mai, Kyo-mai (Kyoto dance) and even *enka* (modern pop dancing), you could spend your life watching Nihon Buyo.

When the Fates were planning my introduction into the world of Kabuki, they arranged not only the Kaika teahouse and my meeting with Tamasaburo, but also that I should become friends with a man named Faubion Bowers. Faubion traveled to Japan as a student before World War II, and had become enamored of Kabuki, sitting up in the rafters night after night learning from the *omuko*. He was especially a fan of the prewar actor Uzaemon.

During the war he was a translator and ended up as General Douglas MacArthur's aide-de-camp, and at war's end MacArthur dispatched Faubion a few days in advance of his arrival to make arrangements. So, when Faubion and his group arrived at Atsugi air base, they were the first enemy soldiers to set foot in Japan. A contingent of Japanese officials and press nervously awaited them, fearful of what the Americans' first move would be. But Faubion approached the press and asked, 'Is Uzaemon still alive?' The tension instantly relaxed.

Following the war, all 'feudalistic' customs were banned by the US Occupation, and Kabuki, with its subject matter of samurai loyalty, was banned as well. However, Faubion managed to get himself appointed as censor of the theater, and so was able to revive Kabuki. He later received an award from the Emperor in recognition of his historic role. Having seen Kabuki's prewar greats, and having been close to postwar leaders Baiko, Shoroku and Utaemon when they were still young, Faubion has an unparalleled knowledge of Kabuki.

During our lifetimes, Kabuki has undergone a critical transformation. The art form will of course continue, but we will never see the likes of actors such as Utaemon and Tamasaburo again. As foreigners, Faubion and I both had access to Kabuki in a way that is unlikely to be repeated. We hope to put our knowledge together in a book some day for future generations.

However, Faubion and I disagree about everything. For instance, I am not partial to Kabuki's historical plays such as *Chushingura* (*The Forty-Seven Samurai*); most of them involve tales of *giri-ninjo*, and for me there are more interesting themes. For an earlier audience, trained fanatically to obey their superiors, these plays about sacrificing oneself for one's lord were truly heart-rending; it was what all Japanese did every day of their lives, at the office or in the army. There is a moment in *Chushingura* when the lord has committed hara-kiri and is dying, but his favorite retainer, Yuranosuke, is late. Finally, Yuranosuke arrives, only to see his master expire with the words, 'You were late, Yuranosuke.' Yuranosuke looks into his master's eyes and silently understands that he is to wreak vengeance for his lord's martyrdom. I have seen older audiences weeping uncontrollably at this scene. But for people who have grown up in soft, affluent, modern Japan – including myself – resonances of personal sacrifice are growing faint. Faubion, however, insists that these historical plays embody the essence of Kabuki. He also contends that the ugly old ladies I remember from my youth epitomize the true *onnagata* art, and that the beauty of Tamasaburo and Jakuemon is far too striking, even 'heretical'.

On no point do Faubion and I disagree so much as on the subject of *onnagata*, which brings me to the difficult question of what *onnagata* really are. Obviously, they have something in common with a drag show. From English pantomime to traveling performers in India, the desire to see male actors dressed up as women seems to be universal. In China and Japan the primeval drag show developed into art. The *dan* (Chinese *onnagata*) have largely disappeared (although they may be making something of a comeback), not because the public gradually lost interest, but because the Cultural Revolution dealt such a blow to traditional theater; once a tradition like *dan* is weakened, it is difficult to reconstruct. Japan, however, escaped the turmoil of the Cultural Revolution, and so it is only here that the tradition survives in healthy form.

Development into high art meant that *onnagata* concentrated on the romantic rather than the comic, the essential feminine rather than the physical body. This is why Faubion values older *onnagata*: the fact that they are old and unattractive allows their art to shine unadulterated by common sensual appeal. According to him, 'The art of old Kabuki actors is like sea water which has been sitting in the sun. As actors get older, more and more water evaporates, and it gets more and more salty. In the end, only essential salt remains.'

Due to their exact preservation of details of the old lifestyle, Kabuki plays may be seen as a 'living museum'. How to light an *andon* (paper floor lantern), open a *fubako* (lacquered letter case), arrange hair with *kanzashi* (hairpins), handle a scroll – these and countless other techniques live on in Kabuki's use of stage properties. Kimono fashions, shops and houses, prescribed movements of hands and feet, the ways to bow, the ways to laugh, samurai etiquette and many other aspects of Japan that existed prior to the arrival of Western culture are all reflected in Kabuki's mirror. Kabuki is one giant nostalgia for the past; I cannot think of any other theatrical art form that preserves ancient daily life so thoroughly.

Especially in the light of the modernization that has swept over Japan in recent years, the world of Kabuki seems particularly poignant. There are, of course, no longer any *fubako* or *kanzashi* (except as souvenirs in tourist shops in Kyoto), but the disappearance of these things is no more significant than the disappearance in the West of the bustle and fringed parasol. In the West, modernization, while drastic, did not wipe away every single reminder of what life once was. But in Japan, cities and countryside alike have been bulldozed. Even the trees and rice paddies painted on backdrops are fast vanishing from day-to-day surroundings. Only in Kabuki does the dream world of the past live on.

Over eighteen years have passed since I first went to meet Jakuemon, and since then I have entered the backstage door countless times. Yet even now I get butterflies in my stomach every time I approach it. I live in fear of the doorman, I wonder if I am neglecting some bit of backstage punctilio. Kabuki's window into Japan's traditional lifestyle does not end on the stage.

Lesser actors make the rounds of greater actors' rooms, entering on their knees to make official greetings and to ask for good wishes before they go onstage. Actors are addressed by titles that sound strange to modern ears, such as 'Wakadanna' ('Young Master') for an *onnagata* like Tamasaburo. ('Danna', or 'Master', is the title for an important male-role player, but an *onnagata*, no matter how old he gets, remains 'Young Master'.) Each backstage room is decorated with banners carrying the distinctive emblems of the actors, just like aristocratic heraldry. There is a constant exchange of gifts: fans, hand towels or rolls of fabric, all of which carry symbolic significance. It is a truly feudalistic world, far removed from that of ordinary mortals. Once, when I told Tamasaburo about my trepidation on going backstage, I was surprised when he answered, 'I feel exactly the same way!'

I sometimes think that what bewitched me about Kabuki was

not the plays themselves, but the life behind them. What is so remarkable is the tenuous line between illusion and reality which exists backstage. At the opera, the performance does not continue backstage; the actors don't sing arias at you, and on removing their costumes they become just ordinary people, no matter how famous they are as artists. Backstage at Kabuki, however, the illusion continues. Most people wear kimono, which is rare enough in Japan today, and the kimono – all black for *kuroko* attendants, printed *yukata* (a cotton kimono) for other attendants and gowns for major actors – clearly indicate social status; the backstage kimono are sometimes as striking as anything you might see onstage.

Occasionally, an actual play may even continue behind the scenes. For instance, during a performance of *Chushingura*, which is considered Kabuki's supreme play, the actors and attendants maintain a particularly serious demeanor backstage. Another example is *Kagamiyama*. In this play, the court lady Onoe is humiliated by Iwafuji, who is trying to bring ruin to Onoe's house. Onoe exits slowly down the *hanamichi* deep in thought. When Jakuemon played this part, he remained seated alone, in silence, in the small room behind the curtain at the end of the *hanamichi*, until it came time for Onoe's next entrance; although not onstage, he was still in character. Later, when I asked Jakuemon about this, he replied that it was a *Kagamiyama* tradition, which allows the depths of Onoe's emotional concentration to remain unbroken until she reappears the second time.

Faubion once pointed out that Kabuki actors spend a greater percentage of their life onstage than almost any other actors. First put on the stage at age five or six, they appear in two performances a day, twenty-five days a month, month after month, year after year. In essence, the Kabuki actor spends his entire life onstage. As a result, says Faubion, older actors sometimes find it difficult to differentiate between their stage personas and their real selves.

The actor Utaemon's normal movements, the distinctive turn of hands or neck, bear striking resemblances to his body language onstage. After performing as the character Onoe, Jakuemon remarked to me that he felt very tired; when I asked why, he replied, 'Onoe bears a great responsibility. I was very worried about Ohatsu.' Ohatsu is Onoe's protégé in the drama, and Ohatsu also happened to be played by Tamasaburo in that performance. In Jakuemon's concern for Ohatsu/Tamasaburo (it was not clear which), the onstage and offstage worlds were so intertwined as to be inseparable.

Kabuki's themes provide much insight into Japanese society. For instance, many plays are about the relationship between a lord and his retainers, or that between lovers, but there are none about friends. Friendship has been a key theme of Chinese culture since ancient times. The second sentence of Confucius's *Analects* – 'When a friend comes from afar, is this not a joy?' – demonstrates the Chinese attitude towards the subject. But in Japan such examples are rare. True friendship is not easy here. Long-term foreign residents complain that after ten or twenty years in the country they are lucky to know one Japanese they consider to be a true friend. Yet the problem goes deeper than the culture gap between foreigners and Japanese. The Japanese often tell me that they can't make friends with each other; they say, 'There are the people you knew in high school who remain bosom buddies for life. Everyone you meet after that cannot be trusted.'

One reason for this could be that the educational system traditionally discourages the Japanese from speaking their mind. They never quite trust each other, making friendship difficult. Another reason might be that hierarchical structures of society get in the way. In the old society the master–retainer relationship was a familiar one; relationships between equals were not. This is a question for sociologists to ponder, but in any case, the culture of friendship is strikingly absent from Kabuki.

And yet it was through Kabuki that I eventually made my best friends. Over the years, I became close to a number of Kabuki actors; I am still mystified how this came to pass. The world of Kabuki, with its nebulous border between illusion and reality, is at once very Japanese, and not of Japan at all. As Domo Geshe had predicted, it's a world which is not of this earth, nor of the moon – a 'world beyond reach'. That's why when I pass through the scary barrier to the backstage, though it is a world of illusion, I feel at home. My good friends are here.

Chapter 4

Art Collecting

The Moment before Glory

I spent the fall of 1972 commuting between Iya Valley and Tokyo, where I was supposedly attending Keio University as an exchange student. Actually, I spent most of my time sitting beside a Chinese table in Linda Beech's house drinking gin and listening to her talk hilariously about the old times, when she arrived in Japan just after the Occupation. One night, conversation turned to the Chinese table. 'It's Ming,' she remarked casually. 'I bought it from a man in Ashiya, near Kobe, whom I think you should meet. His name is David Kidd, and he lives in a palace. Next time you go to Iya, you should drop by.'

So, in January 1973, less than a week after finding Chiiori, I visited David Kidd's house on the way home from Iya. Linda had told me a bit about him in advance. David lived in Beijing before the war and married into a wealthy Chinese family. He resided in the family mansion, one of the great houses of old Beijing, but when the Communists took over in 1949 the family lost everything, and David and his wife fled to America. After a short period in New York they went their separate ways, and soon afterwards David came to Japan. He started all over again from nothing, became an art dealer and built up a collection by buying Chinese treasures discarded by the Japanese after the war.

David's house really was a palace. Standing in the entrance, I could see a Chinese statue of Ida-ten, guardian of Buddhist temples, to my right; to the left was a flower arrangement set on a Ming table like Linda's; and before me were wide sliding doors papered with silver leaf. The doors flew open and David appeared. He led me into a huge living room, easily sixty tatami mats in size, with blue-and-yellow Chinese-dragon rugs covering the floor. Tables, couches and stands glowing softly with the tan, brown, orange and purple-black hues of various rare woods were aligned with several grand *tokonoma*. Inside the alcoves, gilt Tibetan statues stood in front of mandala paintings three meters high. In every nook there were mysterious objects, such as a table bearing a collection of what looked like pieces of driftwood, each piece labeled with calligraphy on gold paper. I had no idea what most of these objects were, but I could see instantly that everything was beautiful, everything was precious and everything was there for a reason. The day I walked into that room was the day I realized that the impossible was possible. I meant to stop by for afternoon tea; I left the house three days later. Those three days were filled with long and intense conversations with David. It was the beginning of my artistic apprenticeship.

The foundations for my love of Asian art were laid in early childhood. My grandfather and father were both naval officers, and they brought back many souvenirs from their travels to Japan and China. The result was that I grew up with Asian art as part of my daily life: scrolls hung from our walls, and the dining table would be set with Imari porcelain for the occasional dinner party.

One day, not long after we arrived in Yokohama, my mother took me to Motomachi, a popular shopping district. Unlike the

Motomachi of brand-name boutiques today, the street at that time was more homely and practical, with small shops selling cakes, office supplies and crockery. We entered a china shop and my mother asked the shopkeeper in her rudimentary Japanese, 'Do you have any Imari ware?' Naturally, she thought every china shop in Japan would stock Imari, but she had just done the equivalent of walking into Woolworths and asking for Limoges porcelain. The shopkeeper looked completely baffled, but suddenly he remembered something and rushed into the back of the shop. He came back with a wooden box, and explained, 'This has been around since before the war, but because no one would buy it, it's just been sitting here . . .'

He opened the box for us. Inside were ten Imari plates, wrapped in the straw rope in which they had come from the kiln. I still have one of those plates, and judging by its age, it is possible that the box had sat in storage since the nineteenth century. Aged only twelve at the time, I untied the rope, touched the plates and was overcome with awe. I felt just like the people who opened up King Tutankhamen's tomb for the first time in three thousand years. So strong was the impression that even now the image of those plates and straw rope remains fresh in my memory.

My mother began to frequent the antique stores of Yokohama and Tokyo, and we returned to America two years later laden with folding screens, lacquerware, ceramics and *tansu* chests.

My first purchase of an antique came years later when I was an exchange student at Keio. I like old books, and used to frequent the Kanda booksellers' district of Tokyo. On one occasion I noticed a pile of antique Japanese books set out on the sidewalk. They were being sold for 100 yen apiece. Although I was majoring in Japanese Studies, until that day I had never laid eyes on a genuine old block-printed Japanese book; I picked one up out of curiosity and opened its navy blue cover. It happened to be *The Great Learning*, one of the Confucian classics, dated about 1750. I was surprised that this 100-yen throwaway was an eighteenth-century edition. The hand-engraved block-printed characters were strikingly beautiful, and so large that a single line of text filled a whole page. Although I was ignorant of Chinese, my familiarity with Japanese made it possible for me to roughly grasp the meaning. On the page I had happened to open was written: 'If you wish to rule the state, first pacify your family. If you wish to pacify your family, first discipline yourself. If you wish to discipline yourself, first make right your heart'. This single line struck me forcibly, and for the first time I sensed the appeal of Chinese philosophy. That 100-yen volume of *The Great Learning* became my introduction to classical Chinese literature.

After that, I set about looking for old Japanese books in earnest. It was simply incredible what you could find. These books were so little valued that they were being sold as scrap for mounters, who used them as backing for screens and sliding doors. I started with Chinese classics such as the *Analects*, the *I Ching*, the *Chuang-tzu*, and so on, but I gradually formed an interest in Japanese-style books. Unlike the Chinese classics, printed in blockish standard type, the Japanese texts featured pages of flowing cursive script. As I leafed through them I realized that Japan's traditional calligraphy is fundamentally different from China's, and my interest in Japanese calligraphy steadily grew.

Meanwhile, I was traveling to Iya and slowly accumulating folk craft and old kimono. I once passed through the city of Tokushima on my way, and in an antique shop there I found four large baskets filled with puppet costumes. They were the entire wardrobe of Otome-za, one of the lost puppet theaters of Awaji Island. The boxes had been set aside during the war, and then apparently forgotten. I brought the costumes back to Tokyo, carried them with me to Yale and then to Oxford, and I have them still today.

Then I met David Kidd. He is one of the world's great conversationalists, and like me he is a creature of the night. Following that first encounter, I visited David's house constantly. We would sit out on the moon-viewing platform while David read aloud Ouyang Xiu's 'Ode to Autumn', only going to bed at dawn and waking in early evening. During the first three days I spent at David's house, I never actually saw sunlight. Sometimes we would sit on the *kang* (Chinese sofa) in the living room, discussing the finer points of landscape painting, while David amused his guests with his great wit. 'Humor is one of the four pillars of the universe,' he once said, adding, 'I forget what the other three are.' At other times, we lounged on the rugs and drank endless cups of tea while David divulged the secrets of a Tibetan mandala.

That is when I learned that artworks have secrets. In the case of a Tibetan mandala, there is a universe of esoteric symbolism: colors, directions, the names of Buddhas and their attributes. But even the most simple painting of trees or grasses might also conceal secrets. One night, David opened a pair of six-paneled gold screens in the living room. They made up a willow-bridge painting, a conventional theme in which weeping willows stand beside a curving wooden bridge. These screens, however, were particularly old, and seemed to have an expressive power lacking in later versions. We began to discuss what made them so different. As we talked, we noticed that the willow branches to the left hung straight, while those on the right swayed, as if a breeze were blowing though them. To the left was the moon; on the right, no moon. We realized that the screens were depicting the transition from night to day, the breeze being the first breath of dawn. Then someone pointed out that the branches on the trees to the left were bare; the branches on the right were sprouting young leaves. So the screen was also depicting the moment when winter passes into spring. In the river under the bridge, waterwheels were turning, and the bridge itself, which in Japan symbolizes the arrival of messengers from the other world, was a great arc curving towards the viewer. Everything in these screens was turning and transforming from old to new and from dark to light. 'And so,' concluded David, 'these screens are a painting of the moment before glory.'

Unlocking the secrets of things has much to do with observation. One night, David sat me down in front of a set of Chinese snuff bottles, and said, 'Tell me what you see.' I saw ceramics, lapis lazuli, iron, gold, silver, ivory, glass, lacquer, copper, jade and amber. It was a lesson in looking at materials. The main thing I learned from David, however, was the interrelation of all his pieces, the way in which they were all links in a single worldview. I have since met other collectors of Chinese art whose pieces are more important from an art-history point of view. But not a single one of them understood and manifested the relationship between things as David did. This came from having lived in an old mansion in Beijing's declining days. While Japan has lost much in the twentieth century, China lost infinitely more during the turmoil of the Maoist years. There are only a handful of people alive who have any idea of the lifestyle of the Chinese literati in the old days. In that sense, David's knowledge is a unique resource, as fragile and mysterious as Iya Valley.

For example, Chinese furniture is not something you arrange by setting here and there to taste. Those *kangs* and tables demand to be arranged along symmetrical axes, which David aligned with the center of the living room and the *tokonoma* alcoves. Each ceramic vessel or statue needs to rest on a stand, and that ensemble in turn relates to the painting behind it. The books, jade scepters, brushes and whisks displayed on tables symbolize the pleasures and amusements of a gentleman. For example, what I had taken to be driftwood were pieces of rare aloes incense wood, and nearby could be found the silver cutting knife, the bronze chopsticks and the celadon burner that were needed for burning incense.

David taught me an important lesson that I would never have heard from art historians and curators: beauty comes first. 'It should be old, it should be valuable,' he said. 'But first ask yourself, "Is it beautiful?"'

'How can I know if a new thing I have bought is beautiful, or if I have simply become carried away?' I asked.

He answered, 'There are two ways. One is to have a beautiful house. The other is to surround the new thing with beautiful things. If it's not right, they will reject it.'

After that, whenever I bought an antique, I would put it in David's living room to see how it looked. Most of the time my purchase would be revealed as an eyesore. But one time I bought an old Chinese table in Kyoto, brought it back to David's and set it in a *tokonoma* without telling anyone. We got through the whole evening without David noticing it, and so I knew that the table was good.

Fascinated as I was by David's collection, I was in no position to start collecting jades and Chinese ceramics. Instead, I continued with old books and calligraphy. By 1977 I had moved to Kameoka, so I had ample time to explore the antique shops of Kyoto. One day, the master of an old bookstore showed me a set of ten *shikishi* (square plaques) and *tanzaku* (rectangular plaques) – small pieces of paper with calligraphy in an archaic and refined style. They were decorated very delicately with gold, silver and mica, on papers dyed red and blue. He was offering them to me for 5000 yen each, roughly $20 at the time. I turned them over and was shocked to read 'Prince Konoe', 'Regent Nijo', 'Minister of the Left Karasumaru', and so on. These were genuine pieces of calligraphy by court nobles of the seventeenth century! I could not believe that they could be bought so cheaply, but at the time there was simply no interest in Japan in such things. So I began collecting *shikishi* and *tanzaku*. After I had acquired several dozen of them and the general style became clear, my curiosity was aroused. The hair-thin lines of elegant calligraphy on these plaques were different from anything I had ever seen in Japan. I began to inquire into the history of these princes and ministers, and was thus introduced to the world of the *kuge*, the court nobles.

The *kuge* were descended from the Fujiwara family, who ruled every aspect of court life during the Heian period. They controlled almost all the important court posts, reducing the Emperor to puppet status. It was the Fujiwara nobles and related families who built fantasy pavilions like Byodoin near Nara, and penned the poems and novels for which the Heian period is famous. After several hundred years of Fujiwara dominance, the extended family grew so large that it became necessary to distinguish between the various branches. So people started calling the branch lineages by their street addresses in Kyoto: for example, the Nijo family, the Karasumaru family, the Imadegawa family, etc. Over time, there grew to be about one hundred families, called the *kuge*. They were seen as having semi-Imperial status, and were carefully distinguished from the *buke*, or samurai families.

When the samurai class overthrew the system of noble rule at the end of the twelfth century, the *kuge* lost all their lands and revenue. They had no choice but to find work, but after four hundred years of writing poetry by moonlight, the only work they were able to do was in the field of the arts. So they became teachers of poetry, calligraphy, court dance and ritual. Over time, they developed a system of hereditary franchises, in which each family purported to be the holder of 'secrets' passed down to the head of the house. Outsiders could only acquire these secrets by paying for them.

The next step, naturally, was the proliferation of secrets. The *kuge* organized their secrets into hierarchies, with lesser secrets for beginners and more profound secrets for advanced students, on an ascending pay scale. This was to become the prototype for the 'schools' of tea ceremony, flower arrangement and martial arts predominant today. Typically, these schools have a hereditary grand master, a system of expensive titles and licenses granted to students, and ranks (such as the different colored belts in karate and judo).

With the coming of peace and prosperity at the beginning of the Edo era in the early 1600s, a renaissance of *kuge* culture occurred in Kyoto. Each family taught its specialty, the Reizei concentrating on poetry, the Jimyoin on Imperial calligraphy, the Washio family on Shinto music, and so on. The one art they all had in common was their delicate calligraphy, which they wrote on *shikishi* and *tanzaku* at tea parties and poem festivals.

The *kuge* lived in cramped quarters in a village surrounding the Imperial Palace. They never had money. The story goes that right up until World War II, they would pay a visit to their neighbors just before the New Year, when all debts must be settled. 'I am very sorry,' the *kuge* would say in polite accents, 'but our family will not have enough money to pay our debts by the end of the year, so we will have to set fire to the house and flee in the night. I hope that will be no trouble to you.' This was a disguised threat, since setting fire to one house in the crowded inner city of Kyoto might destroy an entire district. So the neighbors would take up a collection and bring the money over to the *kuge* on the last day of the year.

All the impoverished *kuge* possessed was their memory of the Heian era's refinement, so they developed ways of living elegantly in poverty. Examples of this can be seen in every *kuge* art, and it exercised an incalculable influence on the city of Kyoto. For example, the construction of teahouses such as the famous Katsura Detached Palace, the utensils of tea ceremony, even the dainty displays one sees today in store windows can be traced back to the *kuge*.

People who come to Kyoto hear much about Zen and tea ceremony. But Kyoto is not just Zen and tea; it was also the center of the culture that grew from the fine-grained sensibility of the *kuge*. When the capital was moved to Tokyo in 1868, many of the *kuge* moved north with the Emperor. Their village around the Imperial Palace was razed, leaving the large open spaces you see today surrounding the palace. As a result, almost nothing tangible remains of *kuge* history, and their culture never became a tourist attraction; there is very little written about their world, so most people are hardly aware that it ever existed. Nevertheless, their romantically delicate sensibility survives in *waka* poetry, incense ceremony, geisha dance and Shinto ritual. But if I had not purchased a few 5000-yen *shikishi* on a whim, I would never have discovered it.

As the years I spent in Kyoto went by, the scope of my collection grew. The next step from *shikishi* and *tanzaku* was hanging scrolls, and then folding screens, ceramics, furniture, Buddhist sculpture, and more. My collection expanded to include not only Japanese art but pieces from China, Tibet and Southeast Asia as well. However, no matter how underpriced the folding screens or Buddhist statues were, they never cost Mere hundreds or thousands of yen, so collecting began to involve real money. In order to pay for it, I began to sell or trade pieces to friends, and before I knew it, I had become an art dealer.

As the business grew, I eventually found my way into Kyoto's art auctions; in Kyoto, these auctions are called *kai*, or 'gatherings'. These gatherings are a closed world known only to dealers. They are completely unlike Christie's or Sotheby's, where the auction houses research the pieces and publish a catalogue in advance, and buyers can examine objects at their leisure before bidding. In a Kyoto *kai*, no information is made available, and there is no time to even get a close look at the work. With a flourish, the auctioneer unrolls a handscroll across a long table, and with no mention of the work's author or date, the bidding commences. Buyers have only an instant in which to look over the seals and signature on the work and to examine the quality of the paper and ink before placing their bids. So participation in these auctions requires a highly trained eye, to say the least. At first I found myself utterly at a loss.

Rescue came in the form of my scroll mounter, Kusaka. At eighty, Kusaka had close to sixty years' experience of the Kyoto auctions, and over that time had seen tens of thousands of screens and hanging scrolls. I had sent him some of my screens for repair, and through this connection, he allowed me to accompany him to the *kai*. As a mounter, Kusaka could judge paper and ink with the eyes of an expert, and he had an encyclopedic memory of signatures and seals. Muttering, 'No signature, but that's the seal of Kaiho Yusho – looks like the real thing . . .' or 'The characters have vigor, but the paper is dubious. Maybe you ought to pass this one by . . .', Kusaka became my teacher at the *kai*. In this fashion, I was able to acquire knowledge that decades of university study could never bring.

There are two types of antiques. One consists of objects already circulating in the art world, in good condition and with artist, period and provenance well documented. The other type is made up of objects which in Kyoto are called *ubu* (literally, infant). *Ubu* objects are those surfacing in the art world for the first time; very often they have sat for years in old storehouses. These storehouses, called *kura*, have defined the special character of the Japanese art market.

Traditionally, most houses in Japan of any size or wealth had a *kura* built alongside. These storehouses were necessary because of the 'empty room' ethos. Furniture, paintings, screens, trays and tables appeared in a Japanese house only when needed, and varied by season and by occasion. I was once shown into a *kura* belonging to a prominent family in the mountains of Okayama. The mistress of the house explained that she kept three full sets of lacquer trays and bowls there – one for the household, one for guests, and one for VIPs. Well-to-do families needed a place, separated from the house itself, where they could store such things. You can spot *kura* by their unique architecture: tall, squarish structures with peaked roofs, a few tiny windows and walls of thick white plaster. The plaster walls protected the building against damage from the fires and earthquakes that were the scourge of Japan.

There was a strong taboo against entering the *kura* unless you were the head of the house. In Kyoto, a maid would boast about her status by saying, 'I'm the number-one maid. I'm allowed to enter the *kura.*' Even in the prewar years, when Japan's culture was still more or less intact, *kura* were rarely entered, and obscure objects inside tended to get forgotten. And after the cultural shock of World War II, there was suddenly no need at all for the trays, plates and screens kept inside them, so their huge wooden doors were shut for good. Their present-day owners, caught up in the rush for modernization, deem the *kura* and their contents almost completely worthless: when it comes time to tear down an old compound, the owner calls in an antique handler, or 'runner', who buys the entire contents of the *kura* in one lot, more or less as scrap. The runner carts it all away in a truck and delivers it to the auctions, where dealers such as myself see it for the first time. These things are *ubu.* When an artwork which has been sleeping for years in a *kura* arrives at auction, it is as if it has popped out of history. Sometimes I open a screen – stiff from mildew, damp and insect damage – and realize that I am likely to be the first person to see it in a century. At such times, memories come welling up of a child unwrapping straw rope from Imari plates in Motomachi long ago.

Ubu objects are the ultimate risky venture for an art collector. There are no guarantees, and huge problems of repair and restoration. But this is where the excitement lies. David Kidd once said to me, 'Having a lot of money and using it to buy great pieces of art on the world market – anyone can do that. Not having money, but still being able to buy great pieces – that's fun.'

Which brings me to the secret of how 'the impossible was possible' for David and me. Neither of us had much money at first, but we were able to build art collections wildly out of proportion to our means. And we didn't achieve this in some poverty-stricken third-world country, but in an advanced economic superpower. It was possible because of the lack of interest of the Japanese in their own cultural heritage. Chinese art maintains its value on the world market because as the Chinese get rich, the first thing they do is invest in traditional cultural objects; there is a large community of Chinese art collectors. In prewar Japan there existed such a community, in which Japanese collectors vied with each other for fine paintings, calligraphies and ceramics. They were the ones who stocked the *kura*.

After the war, this community evaporated, so today there are almost no significant private collectors of Japanese art. The only exception is tea masters. The tea-ceremony world is still very active, so utensils such as tea bowls, scoops and scrolls for the tearoom are highly valued; in fact, they are very often overvalued, and command ridiculous prices. But step outside the world of tea, and Japanese artworks sell for a song. For example, I made quite a collection of handscrolls, some of them with calligraphy by artists greatly prized by tea masters. Handscrolls roll sideways and can be ten or even twenty meters long. Unlike hanging scrolls, they are difficult to use in the tearoom. So they sell for a fraction of the cost of hanging scrolls, although they have equivalent, or even greater, artistic and historical value.

I once acquired a handscroll of the Kabuki play *Chushingura* (*The Forty-Seven Samurai*), an enormous piece just over one meter high and ten meters long. It was originally a banner illustrating each of the eleven acts of the play, and was probably used by a traveling Kabuki troupe in the mid-nineteenth century. On doing some research, I found there was nothing comparable in any of Japan's museums, and that possibly I had chanced into ownership of the finest *Chushingura* scroll in all Japan. But being young and very poor I had no choice but to sell the work.

I first approached my friends in the Kabuki world. But these actors spend their daily life immersed in Kabuki trappings, and they told me that the scroll was hardly what they would want to relax with at home. I could see their point, so I then tried selling the piece to Shochiku Inc, the entertainment giant that produces movies and manages Kabuki. They weren't interested. Foreign companies in Japan often display gold screens or folk art in their lobbies, so I thought Japanese firms might do the same. I took every opportunity to look around the premises when I happened to be visiting an office building. But everywhere I turned, Western Impressionists hung from the walls, and I could only conclude that Japanese companies had zero interest in the traditional art of their country.

Next, I decided to try my luck with Japan's art museums. However, on hearing of this, my veteran art-dealer friends in Kyoto were quick to dissuade me. Without proper introductions, there was virtually no chance that these museums would give a young foreigner like me a hearing. I tried other avenues, such as approaching the Sengaku-ji Temple in Tokyo, which is dedicated to the memory of the forty-seven samurai, but received only a brusque rebuff on the telephone. In the end, an American friend bought the scroll for the absurdly low price of $4000, and it went to Fargo, North Dakota.

Most people assume that Japan's cultural properties left the country during the nineteenth century, when people such as Ernest Fenollosa, who helped to create the collection of the Boston Museum, saved Nara-period statues from destruction in the wake of the *haibutsu* anti-Buddhist movement. There is also a belief that foreigners capitalized on Japan's disastrous situation after World War II, which is true to some extent. But what few people realize is that the flow of cultural assets out of Japan continues today.

In my early days at the Kyoto *kai*, it seemed strange to me that old artworks sold far more cheaply than new ones. Garish late-nineteenth- and early-twentieth-century paintings easily outsold classic Muromachi ink paintings. This phenomenon exists everywhere in the modern art world, where, for example, Monet and Van Gogh sell for stratospheric prices many times higher than most Old Masters. But in Japan the situation is extreme.

Muromachi ink paintings and Edo literati calligraphy were being auctioned off at ridiculously low prices. Thanks to this, over the course of about fifteen years, I was able to acquire paintings, ceramics, furniture and hundreds of pieces of calligraphy.

In the process of collecting and dealing, I found that collectors belong to several distinct breeds. Perhaps the most common is the 'stamp collector' type. These people seek out large numbers of small objects that resemble one another – a sort of magpie mentality. Collectors of old coins, sword guards, woodblock prints and Chinese snuff bottles tend to fall into the stamp-collector category.

Then we have the 'Sunflower' type: people or corporations who buy artworks only to impress others. Hence the worldwide popularity of easily recognizable big-name artists such as Picasso and Van Gogh. I call this type 'Sunflower' after the museum in the Yasuda Fire & Marine Insurance building in Tokyo, which essentially exists to house only one painting: Van Gogh's *Sunflowers*, which was purchased at vast expense in the 1980s. Yasuda Fire & Marine is not, properly speaking, a collector at all; its only reason for owning *Sunflowers* is to impress the Japanese public.

I cannot deny having inclinations towards both these types. For instance, my *shikishi* and *tanzaku*, a collection of hundreds of little bits of paper, clearly fit the stamp-collection mode. When I was buying *shikishi*, I tried to assemble complete sets of certain categories, such as calligraphy by every head of the Reizei family from 1500 until 1900. I suppose this is not far from compiling a full set of baseball cards. As for big names, I must admit that it brings me satisfaction to own works by well-known artists, and I am not above displaying these just to impress my friends.

But for me the highest pleasure of art collecting lies elsewhere. I use my collection to create a world. For example, in the *tokonoma* I will hang a scroll of rubbings from Mt Tai in China, with three strong characters reading, 'The virtuous man is not alone'.

Below this I will set a Ming-dynasty table on which rests a copy of the *Analects*, opened to the passage reading, 'The Master said, "The virtuous man is not alone, he will always have neighbors".' Next to the book is a Ruyi scepter, thought to enshrine magical powers – evoking the world of the sage. A flower from the garden floats in a celadon bowl; in other parts of the room stand unusually shaped 'spirit stones' (in whose ins and outs the Chinese saw workings of the Tao). Before the stones are fans inscribed by Edo literati. Everything fits together into a single, interrelated theme. This is a world which one cannot find in a museum. Spirit stones standing by themselves in a case are nothing special; a scroll saying 'The virtuous man is not alone', by itself, is of little interest to anyone but a calligraphy master. Yet by gathering together a number of such objects and arranging them with their essential meaning and artistry in mind, the world of the literati or Kyoto court nobles comes to life.

Today's young Japanese are unaware of their country's cultural history. There are many who yearn after a lost world of art and beauty, but wherever they go, concrete and fluorescent lighting confronts them; the problem is even more severe in other Asian countries, such as China or Tibet, where ancient cultures have sustained near-mortal damage. In Japan there are only a handful of houses where a breath of this ancient beauty lives on, and ironically, many of them belong to foreigners like myself or David. When young students visit my house and come away deeply moved, it leaves me feeling elated. I feel that my mission as an art collector has been fulfilled.

As the twentieth century draws to a close, the art-collecting world stands at a major turning point. There is a shift from private ownership to public institutions, a trend which can be seen throughout the world. The objects in my collection were passed down from individual to individual, or treasured in families, for centuries. I imagine that their former owners studied and enjoyed them just as I do; as they lived with these artworks, they slowly unraveled the secrets hidden within them, and in the process honed their own understanding of art and life. However, the age when individuals can own such things is drawing to a close. One way or another, I expect that most of my pieces will eventually end up in museums. A private collector from the next generation would need to be very wealthy to create a similar collection. It is likely that my current lifestyle may not survive this century.

In recent years, antiques have become scarce in Japan. For fifty years after World War II, artworks from the *kura* kept flowing into the market like a bubbling spring. But after fifty years of destruction, there are few *kura* left to demolish, and *ubu* objects are gradually disappearing from the Kyoto auctions. Folding screens, in particular, have declined drastically in quantity and quality, and ink paintings have only a few more years before they vanish as well. The spring is running dry. My ability to keep collecting depends on just one thing: the lack of interest in Asian art displayed by the Japanese. As long as this continues, I will be able to keep adding to my collection. So, although it's a self-centered wish, I pray they will stay asleep a little while longer.

Chapter 5

Japan Versus China

Hapax Legomenon

A. F. Wright, my professor of Chinese history at Yale, used to begin his lectures like this: 'When gazing over the vast historical sweep of China, I hardly know where to begin. Shall I begin with the efflorescence of the Tang dynasty in the eighth century? Or a thousand years before that with the First Emperor and his burial of the scholars? Or a thousand years before that with the Duke of Zhou, sage and statesman? No!' Here he would rap on the podium and there would be a pregnant pause. 'I shall begin with the rise of the Himalayas!'

On the other hand, Roy Miller, my professor of Japanese, began his term by inviting the students over to his house for sushi and Japanese dance. Here lies the difference between Japanese and Chinese studies: superficially similar, they are actually worlds apart. As someone who is drawn to both, I have found the differences intriguing, and nowhere are they so pronounced as in the field of academic study.

Although I started with Chinese language classes in elementary school, the two years I spent in Yokohama in the mid-1960s set me firmly on the path of Japanese Studies. When we returned to the US, I listened avidly to the folk songs and Kabuki music which I had taped from the radio. We had brought back several cases of instant noodles, and what with the noodles, the music and the artworks my mother had collected, my love of Japan remained fresh. By the time I entered high school I already knew that I wanted to major in Japanese Studies at college. Universities offering Japanese Studies were scarce back then, and Yale happened to be one of them. So I set my sights on Yale, and in the fall of 1969 matriculated there.

The first step in Japanese Studies is of course to learn the language. Now there are dozens of Japanese textbooks on the market, but until the mid-70s most American universities used a textbook called *Jordan*. The book was originally written for diplomats, and it taught Japanese with a step-by-step approach grounded in linguistic analysis, which at the time was revolutionary. *Jordan* has since become known as the 'Mother of Japanese language textbooks'. Its teaching method consisted of repeating speech patterns again and again and again; compared to the average language textbook, *Jordan's* use of repetition is almost unbelievable. Having lived in Japan, I expected the textbook to be pure tedium. Mrs Hamako Chaplin, who had coauthored the book, happened to be teaching at Yale, so I went to see her to explain that I already spoke Japanese. But she would have none of that, saying, 'Certainly you can speak Japanese, but it is the typical foreigner's Japanese picked up in the international schools – a kind of child's speech. Unless you correct this, you'll never be able to speak in a way widely acceptable to Japanese society. You will have to start over again from zero.'

Attending the beginners' class not only meant using *Jordan*, but also arriving every day for class at eight o'clock. This was the cruelest blow of all for a night person like myself, and the class was boring to the point of paralysis, as I had foreseen. But thanks to *Jordan*, I mastered fundamental grammar and the system of honorifics, which is critically important, as I discovered in my very first oral exam. Mrs Chaplin began by asking me, 'What is your name?', and I responded, 'My name is Alex-san.' There was a pained silence. She said, 'This interview is over.' I remembered, as I slunk out of the room, that the particle *san* is not a neutral 'Mr': it always implies honor, and therefore must never be used for oneself.

Although Yale offered an excellent Japanese Studies program, almost all the classes were available only to postgraduates. This was well before the Japan boom hit American education, and there were still very few undergraduate students majoring in this field. When I graduated in 1974, only one other student received a bachelor's degree in Japanese Studies; today, Yale alone has numerous students in this field, and the number of colleges offering Japanese Studies has mushroomed to well over a hundred (compared to about twenty when I was a student).

Japanese Studies encompasses literature, art, social studies, economics and more, but overwhelming weight is given to the study of social and economic structures. It would seem obvious that there is a need to study Japan's economy, but perhaps more has been written and taught about its social structures than any other aspect of the country. Experts in Japan and abroad have developed numerous theories to explain social behavior here. Lafcadio Hearn, the American journalist who became a naturalized citizen of Japan in the early 1900s, had a theory that Japanese society was fundamentally similar to that of the Ancient Greeks. Ruth Benedict, in her groundbreaking book *The Chrysanthemum and the Sword*, put forth the idea that while Westerners internalize their 'guilt', the Japanese regret an action only when it results in externally imposed 'shame'. In addition to these theories, we hear about 'the vertical society', *amae* (reliance on others or the system for support), *tatemae* and *honne* (an officially expressed view versus an actually held opinion), and so on. Such theories have mounted up into a vast bibliography which the student must read.

My own theory (to add one more to the pile) is that the regimentation of society that began with the Kamakura Shogunate at the end of the twelfth century did indeed succeed in repressing individualism. As Japan is an island country, rules could be imposed with a thoroughness impossible in a large continental nation like China. As a result, Japan's pyramidal structures, which you can find everywhere from companies to tea ceremony, really do determine patterns of behavior. In my experience, a Japanese is much less likely to say or do the unexpected than a Chinese; whatever he may think, he is more likely to do what the rules tell him to do. The muffled scream of the individual being strangled by society is psychologically what the tragic Kabuki loyalty plays are all about. Since social rules do play such a pivotal role, it is very important to study them.

Another reason for the emphasis on social theories is the profusion of books on *Nihonjinron* (theories of Japaneseness), written by Japanese authors for domestic consumption. For students of Japanese Studies who expect to spend their lives interacting with the Japanese, failure to read this literature can lead to major problems. The books on Japaneseness cover a wide spectrum, including titles such as *The Japanese and the Jews*, *The Japanese and the Koreans*, *The Japanese Brain*, and so forth. In general, the tenor of the argument is somewhat aggressive, the majority of these theories being designed to prove that the Japanese are better than everybody else in some way. We hear, for example, that the Japanese process language with the right side of the brain, which therefore means that their brains are unique and superior. Surely no other country in the world has such an extensive literature in praise of itself.

Foreign scholars in the field of Japanese Studies must be very careful where they step. Ezra Vogel of Harvard was lionized when he wrote *Japan as Number One*. But when Roy Miller wrote a book entitled *Japan's Modern Myth*, confronting the linguists who are trying to prove that the Japanese language is unique and superior to all others, he was ostracized as a 'Japan basher'. When I was a student in the early 1970s, this debate was already raging. Despite my fondness for Japan, the rhetoric of the 'theories of Japaneseness' made me feel a distinct foreboding for the country's global future.

From the fall of 1972 I spent a year studying at the International Center of Keio University in Tokyo as an exchange student. Keio is Japan's oldest university, founded in 1867 by Fukuzawa Yukichi, who was one of the first Japanese to travel abroad in the nineteenth century. I lived in Shirogane-dai, not far from the old Keio campus in Mita, where I attended classes in Japanese language and audited courses on architecture.

However, I can remember almost nothing of interest regarding the time I spent at Keio. That was partly a result of Japan's university system. High-school students must study relentlessly to pass college entrance examinations, giving up all extracurricular activities and commuting to cram schools, in what is called 'examination hell'. But once they get into college, the pressure suddenly relaxes and the next four years are spent almost completely at play. Companies place little stress on what new employees know before they are hired; the real education begins on the job. The result is that college classes do not matter much, and academic rigor lags far behind Europe or the States. The lectures I attended on architecture were deathly boring and almost inevitably put me to sleep. After about two months I simply gave up and stopped going.

Classes at Japanese universities tend to be very large, and because students do not live in dorms, there were few opportunities to meet people. Perhaps also due to the set-up of the International Center at the time, foreign exchange students at Keio were relatively isolated. In any case, I did not make a single friend at the university – though I ate daily in the student dining hall, not once did any Japanese student strike up a conversation with me.

Meanwhile, outside of Keio, I was having a great year. I became close friends with people I met in the public bath in the Shirogane-dai area. After the bath I would go to a coffee shop, and there I met more people. I traveled constantly to Iya Valley, and on the way I would spend days or even a week at a stretch at David Kidd's house in Ashiya. The year was a very rich one, but this was thanks to what I learned in Tokyo, Ashiya and Iya, and had very little to do with Keio.

When the exchange program came to an end, I returned to Yale. For my senior thesis I chose to write about Iya Valley, but meanwhile, my childhood interest in China had been rekindled by David Kidd. I realized that I could never understand Japan if I did not know something about China, so I made plans to travel to China or Taiwan after graduation. However, around this time I was urged to apply for a Rhodes Scholarship. Not taking it very seriously, I applied to study Chinese at Oxford, and before several months were out, the unexpected had happened: I was designated a Rhodes Scholar. I realized with horror that I would have to study at Oxford, in England, the opposite direction from where I wanted to be! But I could hardly refuse, so in the fall of 1974, I boarded a plane for England.

One night, soon after my arrival in Oxford, a friend took me to the Merton College dining hall. I happened to glance at the beer mug in my hand and noticed a number: 1572. This, my friend explained, was the year the mug had been donated to the college – I was drinking from a mug which had been in continual use at Merton for the last four hundred years. It struck me then that the scale by which Oxford measures history is graduated by centuries, not years.

This 'scale of historical memory' is a fascinating thing. In Japan, the events of the pre-World War II decades have been all but erased from the nation's textbooks, and there have been drastic changes in the written language as well. The language suffered two major revolutions: one in 1868, the other in 1945. Hundreds of *kanji* characters that were common before the war have fallen out of use, and the spelling of *kana* alphabetical endings has also changed. It is difficult for most younger people to read prewar prose, and almost impossible, even for older, educated Japanese, to read anything written before 1868. As a result, Japan's 'scale of memory' is about fifty years for historical events, and one hundred and thirty years at most for literature.

The years at Oxford gave me a different perspective on Japan. On hearing that a tea-ceremony bowl dates from the Muromachi period, people in Japan are always deeply awed and impressed. In Oxford, however, old objects surround you, living on as a normal part of everyday life. I am no longer impressed by the mere fact that a tea bowl is Muromachi: even the beer mugs at Merton College were Muromachi. What is important is that old things continue to be used.

The thrust of Chinese Studies at Oxford, as could have been expected, was on the classics; China was regarded as a dead culture. In the Oriental Studies Department, to which Chinese Studies belonged, Ancient Egyptian, Chaldean and Coptic were being taught in the neighboring classrooms. As a result of the Oxford attitude, I was given very little opportunity to learn conversational Chinese, and I can hardly speak it today. On the other hand, I read Mencius, Confucius and Zhuangzi to my heart's content. One of my tutors was a Dutchman named Van der Loon, and his explications of how sounds and meanings of characters changed over the centuries color my appreciation of Chinese writing to this day.

There are some characters, like the *chi* of Chiiori, which occur only once in ancient literature and never again; such a character is called a *hapax legomenon*. In the case of *chi*, a bamboo *chi* flute was actually found a few years ago in a Zhou-dynasty tomb, so now we know what the character represents. But usually we are confronted with a sentence which reads something like, 'The vessel shone with the color X', and although we can guess at X from its sound or structure, or what later commentators had to say, we cannot be sure since X is a *hapax* and never appears elsewhere. 'Hah!' Van der Loon would pounce, when one turned up in our readings of Zhuangzi. 'A *hapax legomenon*. Watson translates it as such-and-such, but actually we will never know what it means.'

Although Chinese Studies at Oxford concentrated overwhelmingly on the classics, the course did not wholly ignore modern China, and we also read passages from Mao Zedong and studied the contemporary Chinese political scene. I noticed then that writings on China contrasted with writings on Japan in that the emphasis, far from being on social theories, was on politics: which faction was in, which faction was out, and so forth. This is not just a modern phenomenon – because of its sheer size, China has been plagued throughout its history by political turmoil. In order to govern such an enormous country, drastic measures are called for; as a result, politics attracts a great deal of discussion and debate, and the country has always been riven by political issues.

For example, during the Sung dynasty, a group of ministers conceived an ideal system which they called the well-field system. It was based on the character for 'well', which is written with two vertical and two horizontal lines, like a tic-tac-toe game. This character represented a plot of land divided into nine portions: the outlying eight fields were for peasants to cultivate by themselves; the innermost field was to be cultivated communally, and the proceeds given as tax to the government. In order to institute the well-field system, millions of peasants were displaced, wreaking havoc with agriculture. There was loud opposition, and soon the anti-well-field faction came into power. They banished the pro-well-field ministers and, at tremendous human cost, dismantled the whole system. Some time later, the pro-well-field group came back into power, and the sequence of events was repeated. This went on for a century, and can be credited with weakening the Song dynasty and leading to its final collapse.

An overconcern with politics likewise afflicts Chinese poetry. A large number of ancient poems are protests over some injustice or government policy, and as a result, many of them remain mired in the circumstances of their time and fail to interest us today. Wherever you turn, politics is everything: during the Oing dynasty, debate raged over whether to allow Western civilization into China; then, with the twentieth century, came the warlords, the Japanese and, finally, the Communists, who proceeded to practically destroy the country in the name of their own modern version of the well-field system.

When I was at Oxford, the effects of the Cultural Revolution were still strong, and the Beijing-published Chinese language textbooks we used in class were almost comically politicized. Lesson One taught the numbers from one to ten; Lesson Two taught 'thank you', 'you're welcome', etc.; and then in Lesson Three, the vocabulary list introduced 'dissident elements' and 'Japanese devils'. In 1977, the year I graduated from Oxford, all this abruptly changed. The leaders of the Maoist era were reviled as the Gang of Four, and 'Japanese devils' became 'Japanese friends'. In contemporary Chinese art, the same forces can be seen at work: while modern art in Japan is almost totally devoid of political intent, Chinese contemporary art is inseparable from the history of dissident movements.

The Chinese have published very few books endorsing the Chinese equivalent of 'theories of Japaneseness', and so I found the atmosphere of Chinese Studies relatively free and relaxed. I came across no attempts to impose theories about the wonderfulness of China upon the people of other countries. However, as is evident from China's very name – Chung Kuo (the Middle Kingdom) – the Chinese are firmly convinced that their country lies at the center of the earth. Until very recently, China bestowed its culture on neighbors such as Vietnam, Korea and Japan, but received relatively little in return; practically the only thing which ever went from Japan to China was the folding fan. Consequently, the Chinese take their superiority for granted. It is the air they breathe, so there is no need to prove it to themselves or others.

Japan, in contrast, was always on the receiving end of cultural imports from other countries, and deep in their hearts, the Japanese are haunted by a sense of insecurity about their cultural identity. What can you call truly 'Japanese', when almost everything worthwhile, from Zen to the writing system, came from China or Korea? People are constantly made aware of the relations of superiority and inferiority; for example, through the honorifics which Mrs Chaplin thought it so important for me to learn. This thought pattern has become a reflex, and the Japanese cannot be at peace without setting up hierarchical ranks for countries as well. Naturally, Japan must stand at the top of the pyramid, and this is what has given birth to the aggressive 'theories of Japaneseness'.

I will surely be criticized for making broad generalizations about the nature of Japanologists and Sinologists – but I can't resist. Lovers of China are thinkers; lovers of Japan, sensuous. People drawn to China are restless, adventurous types, with critical minds. They have to be, because Chinese society is capricious, changing from one instant to the next, and Chinese conversation is fast moving and pointed. You can hardly relax for an instant: no matter how fascinating it is, China will never allow you to sit back and think, 'All is perfect.' Japan, on the other hand, with its social patterns designed to cocoon everyone and everything from harsh reality, is a much more comfortable country to live in. Well-established rhythms and politenesses shield you from most unpleasantness. Japan can be a kind of 'lotus land', where one floats blissfully away on the placid surface of things.

When I compare the paths taken by my friends in Japanese

Studies, Chinese Studies and Southeast Asian Studies, the differences are striking. For example, two of the most memorable people I met at Oxford were my Tibetan teacher, Michael Aris, and his wife, Aung San Suu Kyi. Michael, a modest, soft-spoken man, was a remarkable and dedicated scholar. I remember being impressed when, in the middle of one of our classes, the phone rang and Michael began speaking in rapid Tibetan – it was the Dalai Lama on the line. Suu Kyi is Burmese, the daughter of General Aung San who fought the British and established the modern state of Burma (now called Myanmar). In 1988 she returned to Burma to lead the democratic movement against the military dictatorship that had ruled Burma since the 1960s: it earned her six years of house arrest and the Nobel Peace Prize.

Another friend I met at Oxford was Nicholas Jose, a Rhodes Scholar from Australia. At the time, Nick was studying English literature, but he later took up Chinese and eventually became very fluent. After several years in China, he was posted to the Australian Embassy, where he served as cultural attaché. He became a central figure in the community of artists, poets and musicians in Beijing prior to the Tiananmen Square massacre, and personally rescued some of the dissidents from the police.

In contrast, when I ask my foreign friends in Japanese Studies to describe the most exciting moment of their lives, they respond along the lines of, 'I was meditating in a Zen temple, and I heard the swish of the silk robes of the monks as they walked by.' Since World War II, Japan has had fifty years of uninterrupted peace, during which time the concrete of its social systems has set hard and fast. It has become the land of social stasis, and the foreigners drawn to Japan tend to be those who find comfort in this.

Japan's peaceful and secure society is one of its major achievements. Hygiene and literacy are higher than in many Western countries, and the benefits of its booming economy are distributed more equitably among the population than anywhere else in Asia. There is relatively little violent crime or drug abuse, and life expectancy is high. At the same time, the serious social problems that do exist, such as discrimination against the *burakumin* (descendants of the old untouchable caste) and Koreans, are carefully hidden. Speaking out against the system is discouraged, with the result that advocacy groups for women, the ecology, legal issues or consumers are pitifully weak.

The curious sense of isolation from the rest of the world which you get when living in Japan has its roots in the harmonious social systems which make Japan seem even more peaceful than it really is. These systems reject sudden change and exclude foreign influence, with the result that global issues such as AIDS, ecology or human rights fail to penetrate into the national consciousness. From here, these things look like other people's problems, and foreigners living in this lotus land can easily get caught up in the minutiae of office life, or the aesthetics of tea ceremony, and forget that there are larger issues.

There is also the fact that more traditional culture survives in Japan in a form accessible to foreigners than is the case in most other Asian countries. Its elegant forms exert an almost irresistible sway over those who come into contact with them, and Japanologists tend to abandon their critical faculties and 'convert' to Japan. This is partly because of the country's insecurity about itself, which results in everyone being seen as either a 'Japan basher' or a 'Japan lover'. People think they need to approach Japan with a worshipful attitude in order to gain access to its society and culture. The conversion mentality is something I often run across in Kyoto: foreigners studying the arts there tend to mouth tea-ceremony slogans such as 'Harmony, Respect, Purity, Solitude' with the same zeal that born-again Christians talk about Faith. Sometimes I think 'Japanese Studies' would be more accurately described as 'Japan Worship'.

However, one must not overlook the positive side of this 'Japan Worship'. Although concepts like 'Harmony, Respect, Purity, Solitude' have been overused and debased, the aesthetic they express still survives in Japan. Consequently, those who study traditional culture here do not merely bring the cold eye of scholarship to bear, but take their subjects to heart in a very personal way. The foreigners who have converted and become 'followers' of tea ceremony or Noh drama in Kyoto exist as an extreme example of this, but they represent a side of Japanese Studies that we must be grateful for: it is through them that important aesthetic and philosophical insights, unknown in the West, will be passed on from Japan to the rest of the world.

China, on the other hand, is still suffering from the effects of forty years of cultural repression under the Communist government. The Cultural Revolution, in particular, had a devastating impact on traditional culture. One casualty was its Buddhist and Taoist temples: tens of thousands of temples were destroyed, and a Chinese art expert once described to me the sight of truckloads of ancient bronze Buddhist statues being carted away to the smelting furnaces. I have visited many of Beijing's famous temples, and only very rarely did I catch sight of an original Buddha figure. Most of them were confiscated or destroyed by the government, and all there is to see today are cheap copies.

Nor was it only the cultural products that were destroyed. Artists and artisans were sent to labor camps, theater groups were disbanded and the few who remained of the literati were mercilessly persecuted. Religion was almost eradicated, and even the daily routines of life changed down to their very roots. For example, according to the stories of those who lived in Beijing in the 1920s and 30s, the old city had developed a courtly code of manners derived from centuries of being the center of Imperial rule; even the exchange of daily greetings was something of an art form. But the old residents of the city were moved, and their houses and livelihoods wiped out; today, travelers often express surprise at the rudeness and surliness of Beijing's taxi drivers and hotel waiters.

The efforts to revive Chinese Opera, Buddhism, Taoism and

Confucianism in recent years are nothing less than heroic, providing some hope for a genuine revival as the Chinese rediscover pride in their heritage. But at present, China's traditional culture is still weak, just staggering to its feet after receiving a massive blow to the head. As a result, scholars from abroad tend to look on traditional Chinese culture not as a living force, but as a dead relic. I once had an argument with one of my tutors at Oxford over this point. I wrote an essay on the *I Ching* for a tutorial, and after covering the historical background and various philological issues, I ended by saying, 'What needs to be studied in the future with regard to the *I Ching* is not its historical background. The *I Ching* is a book of divination, intended to advise people as to what the future will bring. The interesting thing about the *I Ching* is that it works.' At the end of term, the Master of Balliol read aloud to me from a letter he had received from my tutor: 'Mister Kerr's way of thinking is typically American, soft and woolly-headed, full of spiritual truths, but with no regard for academic rigor.'

My tutor's attitude was not just symptomatic of Oxford. In general, Chinese Studies tends to be a little dry, keeping a discreet distance from the subject; Japanese Studies, in contrast, takes almost too reverent an attitude towards traditional culture. I cannot imagine any student in Japanese Studies being criticized by his teacher because he expressed an interest in Zen enlightenment.

In the summer of 1976, my last year at Oxford, a letter arrived from David Kidd containing a brochure about the Oomoto Foundation, a Shinto organization in the city of Kameoka near Kyoto. Oomoto was holding a seminar for foreigners in traditional Japanese arts, and David wanted me to attend as both student and interpreter. I sent off a reply: 'I'm very sorry, but having lived in Japan since I was a little boy, I've already seen Noh, tea, and the rest. I'd rather spend my summer in the US with my family, so I won't be attending the traditional arts seminar.'

About a week later I was called to the porter's lodge to receive an international phone call. It was David. 'I have bought you a round-trip ticket to Japan,' he said. 'If you don't come to the seminar, never speak to me again!' And he hung up. I was mystified by this zeal on the part of David, who had always had a far greater interest in China than Japan. But it had been made clear that this was an offer I couldn't refuse, so I went to Japan and took lessons in tea ceremony, Noh dance, martial arts and calligraphy for one month at the Oomoto seminar.

The seminar was my third gate into Asian Studies, after Japanese at Yale and Chinese at Oxford. The policy of the seminar is to keep academic lectures to a minimum, and to concentrate on the actual physical practice of the arts. Students learn how to fold the *fukusa* (a silk cloth used by the tea master to wipe utensils), and how to whisk the tea and serve it; and they learn as guests how to hold and turn the bowl, how to sit, where to put their hands and what to say to the other guests. In Noh drama, the students study *shimai* (short Noh dances), which they perform on a Noh stage for an audience on the last day. Though I had written to David that I had already seen tea, Noh, and the rest, every single thing I encountered during the seminar was new to me.

The folding of the *fukusa*, the sliding movement of the feet in Noh, the grip of the wooden sword in martial arts – everything was difficult. Moreover, as the seminar progressed, it became clear that these movements were not merely ornamental, but expressed a philosophy. For instance, I encountered the rhythm *jo, ha, kyu, zanshin*; basically this is quite simple, amounting to 'slow, faster, fast, stop'. When wiping the tea scoop with the *fukusa* in the tearoom, we were taught to start slowly (*jo*), speed up a bit at the center of the scoop (*ha*) and finish off at the end quickly (*kyu*). At the instant one draws the *fukusa* off the tip of the scoop, there is the closing *zanshin*, which means 'leaving behind the heart'. Then one returns to zero, in preparation for the next rhythm of *jo, ha, kyu*.

At first I thought this rhythm was a peculiarity of tea, but I soon found that it applies in exactly the same way to the foot movements and raising of the fan in Noh drama. In martial arts and calligraphy as well, this rhythm governs all movements. Over the course of the seminar I realized that *jo, ha, kyu* underlies every single one of Japan's traditional arts. The teachers went on to explain that *jo, ha, kyu, zanshin* is the fundamental rhythm of nature – it defines the destinies of men, the course of eras, even the growth of galaxies and the very ebb and flow of the universe.

Before long, I became infected with the same enthusiasm that I had been so surprised to see in David Kidd. Of course, in a single month we could hardly master tea or any other art, but by experiencing with my own body *jo, ha, kyu*, and other principles such as the *kamae* (fundamental pose) of Noh, my way of looking at traditional arts changed radically.

In a sense, these arts are Japan's most important heritage. Religious monuments, sculpture, ceramics and literature can be found in any country. But the sophisticated traditional arts in Japan, which have been refined and elaborated over centuries, are unparalleled throughout the world. *Matcha* (Japanese-style tea ceremony), *sencha* (Chinese-style tea ceremony), Noh theater and dance, martial arts (judo, karate, kendo, aikido, and many others), incense ceremony, calligraphy, Japanese dance (dozens of varieties, including Kabuki dance, geisha dance and folk dance), flower arrangement (ikebana, tea flowers, modern table arrangement, tray landscapes), music (flute, *koto*, drum), poetry (seventeen-syllable haiku, thirty-one-syllable *waka*, linked verse, Chinese poem recitation) . . . the list is endless. When you realize that each of these fields is also divided into countless schools, it's enough to make your head spin.

The philosophies of China and Japan are to be found in different places. Beginning with Confucius and Mencius, the first of a long stream of eminent philosophers and theorists, the Chinese skillfully put their thoughts in writing, thus leaving them behind for later generations. One can scour the history of Japan, however, without finding much in the way of articulated philosophy; to put it strongly, Japan is not a country of thinkers. As a result, before coming to Oomoto, both David and I had felt far greater respect for China than for Japan. But at the seminar I discovered that Japan does have its own philosophy, every bit as complex and profound as China's. Rather than being expressed in words, it flows within the traditional arts – although Japan had no Confucius, Mencius or Zhu Xi, it did have the poet Teika, Zeami, the creator of Noh drama, and the founder of tea, Sen no Rikyu. They were Japan's philosophers.

The year after that first seminar, I graduated from Oxford and came to work for Oomoto's International Department. Since then, I've helped out as a member of the seminar staff every summer, and the process of watching how the arts are taught to foreigners has been very educational. For example, as part of the tea-ceremony course, the students take a brief class in pottery. The idea is for them to fashion a tea bowl or sweet tray with their own hands, and every year, this ceramics class is truly amusing to see.

A tea bowl is a very plain object. Its form is bound by function, so its height, thickness and shape are all largely predetermined. A tea bowl is simply a tea bowl – I believe that people who get caught up in the wonderful artistry and design of a particular tea bowl are largely missing the point. The simple approach dates back to the sixteenth century, when Rikyu established tea ceremony in the form we now know it. Tea had originally come from China, and for generations tea ceremony in Japan existed as a way to show off expensive utensils, including bowls made of gold or jade. But originating in the Zen temple of Daitoku-ji in Kyoto, there grew up a new approach to tea, called *wabi*. *Wabi* refers to rustic simplicity. The *wabi* tea masters modeled their tearooms after thatched cottages, and included a hearth cut into the floor. In utensils, as well, their preference was for the simple and unadorned; this is why

Rikyu chose to have his tea bowls made by a tile maker. The rough, black surface of tile was perfectly *wabi*.

Another word for simple and unadorned might be 'boring'. The genius of Rikyu and the other early tea masters was to reject bright colors and interesting shapes, because these seize the attention and distract us. They brought boring objects into the tearoom and used them to create a peaceful and meditative atmosphere. But the seminar students have great difficulty in making something boring. At all costs, they must inject some originality into their work, and they are not satisfied until they have made their bowls 'interesting'. They mold their bowls into a square shape, drape the sides with dragons and curling snakes, attach jagged teeth to the rim or paint the entire surface with inspirational slogans like 'Peace, Respect, Purity, Solitude'. The results are anything but meditative. David used to say, 'The pottery class exists so the clay can draw the poison out of the students' fingers.' Among our students, however, there are occasionally some Japanese, and they obediently make their tea bowls as they are told to. Boring is fine by them, and their bowls turn out to be quite beautiful.

It has often been pointed out that the Japanese educational system aims to produce a high average level of achievement for all, rather than excellence for a few. Students in school are not encouraged to stand out or ask questions, with the result that the Japanese become conditioned to a life of the average. Being average and boring here is the very essence of society, the factor which keeps the wheels of all those social systems turning so smoothly. It need hardly be said that this is one of the major drawbacks of Japanese life. However, in watching the pottery class at Oomoto, the weak points of the American educational system became evident as well. Americans are taught from childhood to show creativity. If you do not 'become a unique person', then you are led to believe you have something wrong with you. Such thinking becomes a stumbling block: for people brought up in that atmosphere, creating a simple tea bowl is a great hardship. This is the 'poison' to which David was referring. I sometimes think that the requirement to 'be interesting' inculcated by American education might be a very cruel thing. Since most of us lead commonplace lives, it is a foregone conclusion that we will be disappointed. But in Japan, people are conditioned to be satisfied with the average, so they can't fail but be happy with their lots.

If so many revelations can boil up out of one day in the pottery studio, one can imagine how much there is to be learned from the study of the traditional arts. I don't believe that Japanese philosophy, such as the essence of *jo, ha, kyu, zanshin*, can be conveyed by words. When one tries to explain these things verbally, there is a sense of 'slow, faster, fast, stop – is that all there is to it?' Only by experiencing the arts with one's own body does one understand their true meaning. In that sense, the traditional arts are the true gateway to the country's culture.

In recent years I have also come to see that Japan's roots lie as much in Southeast Asia as in China or Korea. As a result, I spend much time traveling in Thailand and Burma – this is my fourth gate to Asian Studies. But the more I travel, the more I must reluctantly grant that the authors of 'theories of Japaneseness' have something of a point: every country in the world is unique, but Japan is a treasure house of uniqueness. As an island off the Asian mainland, it was able to absorb cultural influences from China and Southeast Asia while at the same time preserving near-total isolation as a society. It became a sort of cultural pressure cooker into which many ingredients went, but from which none came out.

Japan is a *hapax*. You can try to approach it by comparing it to China and Southeast Asia, or you can read the voluminous literature on the subject of Japaneseness. But as Van der Loon used to warn his students, in the end you cannot understand a *hapax* – you will never really know what it means.

Chapter 6

Calligraphy
The Signs of Ginza

When I began writing the articles that make up this book, I asked a friend for advice. 'Roof thatching in Iya and Kabuki seem interesting enough subjects to write about, but I'm not so sure about calligraphy,' he replied. 'Interest in the art of calligraphy is limited to a very small group, isn't it?'

This may be so, but I would say that calligraphy is the one traditional art which is seen everywhere in Japan. From letters, shop signs, newspaper and book advertisements, down to the labels on the little white envelopes containing chopsticks, the Japanese are surrounded by the art of Chinese *kanji* characters in myriad forms. From this point of view, calligraphy is one of the defining traits of life in Japan, and you can hardly get through a single day without encountering it. Which is reason enough to write about the subject, but actually I have another motive: I loved calligraphy as a little boy.

My first meeting with *kanji* characters was at the age of nine at school in Washington, DC. Our teacher, Mrs Wang, explained that each character was made up of pieces called 'radicals', using the character *kuo* (country) as an example. First, she wrote a large square on the blackboard, representing the borders of the country: this square is the 'containment radical'. Inside the large square, she put a small square – the 'mouth radical'; that is, many mouths to feed. Under the mouth, she added a straight line to represent the expanse of land. And next to the mouth she wrote the four-stroke combination of dots and slashes that makes up the 'spear radical', symbolizing the defense of the country.

She then wrote three more characters – *wo, ni, ta* (I, you, he) – on the blackboard. We were to copy them one hundred times each, putting emphasis on the stroke order. She insisted that unless we wrote each character in the right order, they would never look beautiful. But when we were shown the stroke order for the character *wo* it struck me as a very strange way of writing, especially the order for the right-hand part of the character, which happened to be the spear radical again.

The correct way to write 'spear' is to first draw a horizontal line, followed by a diagonal line down through it. However, the latter is not just a straight line: it curves slightly, and has a hook at the bottom turning back up to the right, producing a pleasant springing sensation as you write it. After this, you write another diagonal near the bottom, and finally return to the top to add a dot. Left to right, swoop down and spring up, right to left, and then jump back to the top again – the movement of the hand seemed like a dance to me. Writing *wo* a hundred times was great fun. Even today, when I write this character, or others that include the spear radical, all my childhood pleasure at practicing the strokes comes flooding back.

When I was twelve and my family moved to Japan, we crossed America from shore to shore by car. We stopped at Las Vegas on the way, and I was stunned by the city's neon splendor. But my father only said, 'This is nothing compared to Tokyo's Ginza district.' He was right. Not only the Ginza but Yokohama as well were brimming with gorgeous neon signs, and everywhere I looked there were *kanji* characters and the *hiragana* and *katakana* alphabets, leaving an impression of chaotic and feverish brilliance. People often ask me, 'What made the biggest impression on you in Japan?', and I always reply, 'The street signs of Ginza.'

From that time on, I began to study *kanji* in earnest. Our housemaid was a sixty-year-old woman named Tsuru-san. As we watched the sumo bouts on TV together, Tsuru-san would explain the characters of the wrestlers' names to me. They included everyday characters such as 'mountain' or 'high', but there were also some extremely unusual ones – such as 'phoenix', used in the name of the great Taiho, the sumo hero of the 1960s, whose record has never been beaten. As a result, my *kanji* vocabulary became rather unbalanced, but nevertheless, with time, I gradually became able to read shop signs around the city.

I learned 'phoenix' partly because I worshipped Taiho and partly because it had so many strokes. Years later I was to discover that this love of many strokes appears to be something built into children. In 1993, my two young cousins from Olympia, Washington, came to stay with me for a year; Trevor was aged sixteen, Edan was nine. Although they didn't know a single word of Japanese, they attended the local schools in Kameoka and had to tackle *kanji* and the two alphabets. Edan hated studying in any way, and was quite hopeless at mastering the alphabets, so I was surprised when he came home from school one day, very excited, with a *kanji* to show me. It was the *kanji* for 'nose', which is extremely complicated. He was proud of his achievement, and I could see that part of the appeal lay in the complicated nature of the character. The way all of its pieces fitted together had the appeal of a model made with a toy construction set. Trevor, for his part, was fond of *kirin* (unicorn), which consists of two detailed characters with a combined forty-two strokes. *Kirin* also happens to be a brand of beer.

Back to my own childhood. I attended St Joseph International School in Yokohama. At that time, about a third of the students at St Joseph were Japanese, a third were Chinese from Chinatown and the rest were children of the city's foreign consular staff and long-time business residents. My best friend was a Chinese boy named Pakin Fong. Though only thirteen, Pakin was amazingly skilled at both calligraphy and ink painting, and I still have a painting of bamboo that he made for me when we were students together. The bamboo leaves are painted delicately in thin, greenish ink, and look almost like feathers; the piece is rendered as expertly as the work of any professional Japanese painter. Pakin became my teacher and instructed me in the use of the brush.

I was not improving much under Pakin's guidance alone, so I went out and bought a beginner's calligraphy lesson book. Tsuru-san was delighted, and presented me with a calligraphy set. Inside the set's red lacquer box were an inkstone, a brush, an ink stick and a small ceramic water-dripper for wetting the inkstone. When I returned to America, Tsuru-san gave me another water-dripper, this one made of bronze. Tsuru-san had been the daughter of a well-to-do family before the war, but she had lost everything during the air raids. The only thing she had been able to salvage from the flames was this tiny water-dripper. Even today, it is among the most treasured of all my possessions, and only used on special occasions.

Pakin Fong turned out to be my first and last calligraphy teacher. Since the age of fourteen, I have studied entirely by copying, using textbooks and practice pieces like *Senjimon* (*The Thousand Character Classic*), which distills Chinese wisdom into 254-character lines, never repeating a character. Later, when I built my art collection, I copied from the handscrolls and *shikishi* and *tanzaku* plaques in my collection.

So began my interest in calligraphy, but it was not until my second year at Oxford in 1975 that I went 'professional'. During the spring break, I visited my friend Roberto in Milan. Roberto was only twenty-two, but he had found friends and patrons in the jet set and was already doing a brisk business as an international art dealer. At his apartment he showed me a notebook in which Man Ray, Jasper Johns and Andy Warhol had sketched drawings for him. I looked at them and thought, 'I can do that!' Above Roberto's bed was a large Andy Warhol portrait – a few splashes of bright color over a blown-up photograph. It was all the encouragement I needed. I asked Roberto to bring me some paper and colored Magic Markers, and seated under the Andy Warhol I penned several dozen calligraphies. On returning to Oxford, I went to an art-supply store and stocked up on a variety of different colors of *washi* (Japanese rice paper), brushes and ink, and began pouring out calligraphies. Not all of them were calligraphies per se; some were ink paintings, which are just one step away from calligraphy.

One day, a friend of mine from Hong Kong named Kingsley Liu bought one of these pieces for five pounds. It was an ink painting of three peaches, one of which bore a remarkable resemblance to a person's derrière. Kingsley found it quite humorous and promptly put it up in his bathroom. I think all artists remember the day they sell their first work. I was quite excited, in spite of the fact that my first commercial work hung on a bathroom wall.

My first teacher was Chinese, and my first buyer was Chinese. On reflection, most of my calligraphic inspiration comes from China. This is hardly surprising, however, since *kanji* characters originated in China. *Kanji* are perhaps China's single greatest cultural contribution to the world. In antiquity there were other hieroglyphic scripts, such as Ancient Egyptian and Mayan. These scripts showed signs of the same development which *kanji* underwent: first there were pictographs – drawings of things like a spear or a mouth; the next generation of glyphs combined these 'radicals' into more complicated forms; they were then abstracted and simplified, and in the final stage a kind of shorthand developed. But the other hieroglyphic scripts failed to survive to the present day. Only *kanji* did.

The fascination of *kanji* is such that many of China's neighbors, including Korea, Vietnam and Japan, fell under their sway. However, in the twentieth century, Vietnam has discarded *kanji* completely, and Korea is slowly phasing them out. *Kanji* are simply too difficult to learn. Linda Beech used to say that she felt all her *kanji* were lined up on a long bridge inside her head: as soon as she added a new character to one end, an old one fell off the other end. Today, other than in China and Chinese communities, it is only in Japan that *kanji* continue to thrive, supported by the two alphabets, *katakana* and *hiragana*. This is a sign of Japan's essential conservatism, for which the Japanese pay a high price, spending years in school memorizing the eighteen hundred *kanji* in common use and their thousands of variant pronunciations and combinations. I shudder to think what a large expanse of gray matter in my own brain must be devoted to *kanji*, at the expense of other, more worthwhile, knowledge.

However, once you have learned *kanji*, unique mental pleasures become possible. What distinguishes *kanji* from an alphabet is that each single character contains a concept. It is my theory that the mental process which occurs in the brain when you see *kanji* is different from that which occurs when you read characters in an alphabet. When you read a word made up of alphabetical letters, you must first line these up in the brain before you can understand what is being said. But when you look at a *kanji* character, its meaning penetrates the brain directly. As a result, one cannot ignore *kanji* signs, even if one wants to. I almost never read signs when I'm in America, but whenever I ride the Japanese subway I find myself unconsciously reading the advertisements hanging in the carriages. Nor is this just a weakness of mine – my fellow passengers are doing the same, some of them even reading out loud.

Each character has many layers of meaning, giving *kanji*

especially rich connotative powers. For example, the character *t'ai* means 'peace' or 'perfect balance'. It is the name of a hexagram of the *I Ching*, and the character used for China's sacred Mt T'ai; it can also mean 'Thailand'. In the language of every country, vocabulary takes on added meanings over time, but I can think of no example like Chinese, in which the same words have been in continual use for three thousand years. A *kanji* is surrounded by a cloud of meanings, like the colors radiating from the halo of a Buddha.

The gaudy street signs which struck me in childhood are not just confined to Japan. In Hong Kong, China or most large cities of Southeast Asia where ethnic Chinese live, a pandemonium of signs can be seen. This is partly due to these countries lagging behind Europe and America in sign restriction and city planning. There is also the practical matter that *kanji* can be read from top to bottom as well as right to left or left to right, allowing for those long vertical signs along the sides of tall buildings. But the main reason for all these signs is that the shapes and meanings of the characters are appealing. They are one of the pleasures of daily life.

It was the use of the brush that allowed the Chinese to develop *kanji* into forms of such expressive power. There is a saying, 'A line is a force', and calligraphy is essentially nothing more than a flowing line; the brush allows the line to be thick or thin, wet or dry, tightly or loosely outlined. In this way, the 'force' is turned inwards or outwards, quietly repressed or explosively released. Force combines with meaning.

With regard to meaning, hanging scrolls commonly display phrases of three, five or seven words. Nowadays, they are as often as not slogans such as 'Harmony, Respect, Purity, Solitude'. Traditionally, calligraphy scrolls were more subtle: poems, suggestions of the season, or Zen *koans* (illogical thoughts designed to force you to enlightenment). As I sit here writing, there is a calligraphy hanging beside me by a Zen abbot of Manpuku-ji Temple in

Kyoto. It reads, 'The voice of the clouds enters the night and sings'. It is the perfect description of rainy nights here in Kameoka, when the rain patters on the roof and I can hear the rush of the stream at the foot of the garden. I have another Manpuku-ji scroll, which I like to set out when old friends come to visit, which reads, 'I turn the flowers and wait for the butterfly to arrive'. Another scroll which comes to memory is one I first saw at the headquarters of one of the tea schools in Kyoto: 'Sitting alone on a great noble peak'. What could better conjure up the solitariness of a quiet tearoom? An example of a Zen *koan* is, 'I gaze at my loved one in a corner of the sky'. The 'loved one' means the moon, and this is the gateway to the *koan*.

For myself, I prefer to write single characters. Favorites are 'the Creative' and 'the Receptive' from the *I Ching*, or nuance-laden 'dragon', 'night' and 'dawn'. Actually, when you look at old pieces, calligraphies of just one character are quite scarce. People of ancient times were more cultivated than we are today and had greater leisure time. Perhaps they also had more to say. The writing of only a single character could be seen as a sort of 'instant' calligraphy, a degenerate form of the art. But I like writing one *kanji* at a time because it allows me to close in on the meaning of that one character. Take the word for 'heart'. One day, I drew this character in black ink and then superimposed the same shape in red. Looking at these overlapping black and red hearts, a friend who was visiting from America said, 'It's like a man and a woman.' He bought the piece and hung it in his home. Some time later his house burned down and the calligraphy was damaged. I received a phone call from him saying the piece had become a talisman for him and his wife, and could I please make another. It was a great pleasure to see this piece of calligraphy fulfilling its true purpose.

When I began my art collection, I started with calligraphy. Of course I loved it, but this was not the only reason: more than anything, calligraphy was cheap! For example, an ink painting by

Edo literati Ike no Taiga or Buson ran to tens of thousands of dollars, while calligraphy by the same artists could be bought for a tenth of this. Even calligraphy by an internationally known figure like Sen no Rikyu, founder of tea ceremony, was available until recently for about $20,000. This compares with the price of some of the more famous prints by Hokusai. But only a few dozen genuine works by Rikyu survive, whereas Hokusai prints were produced by the thousands. The low cost of calligraphy reflects its lack of popularity today among the Japanese.

This was not always so. Traditionally, calligraphy was the highest of the arts. The T'ang-dynasty Emperor Taizong loved the calligraphy of Wang Xizhi so much he ordered that his copy of Wang Hsi-chih's 'Orchid Terrace Preface' be buried with him in his tomb. From that time on, calligraphy formed the heart of the Imperial collection, and the court and wealthy families vied for scrolls and rubbings by famous calligraphers. In Japan, the most valued possessions of Zen temples are the calligraphies of the temple abbots. Among the *kuge* nobles, *shikishi* and *tanzaku* plaques were treasured above all other works of art; it would not be too much to say that the calligraphy of the *kuge* was their very identity.

Calligraphy held the highest rank because it was believed to capture the soul of the writer. There is an ancient Chinese saying, 'Calligraphy is a portrait of the heart'. Even ordinary handwriting can be a 'portrait of the heart'. In the stateroom of my former employer Trammell Crow's yacht there hung a pair of love letters written by Napoleon and Josephine. No painting could have captured their presence with more intimacy than these autographs. But more than any pen, the brush subtly reflects every slight variation in pressure and direction, thus expressing vividly the artist's state of mind. Calligraphy provides a direct link between one mind and another.

I have never met a court noble of old, and no amount of reading can convey a clear idea of what the life of the *kuge* was really like. But the hair-thin lines of almost impossibly elegant script that they wrote at their poem festivals cause the *kuge* world to spring clearly into view. On reading the poems and essays of the legendary fifteenth-century Zen master Ikkyu, you find nothing but opaque Zen theorizing; only a scholar could possibly figure out what he is getting at. But visit Shinju-an Temple in Kyoto, where a pair of Ikkyu's scrolls hangs in the Founder's Hall, and in an instant the wit of this crabby old abbot jumps out at you. The calligraphy reads, 'Don't do evil, do only good!' This refers to an old Chinese story in which someone asked a master to define the essence of Buddhism. The reply was, 'Don't do evil, do only good', to which the questioner asked, 'What is so special about that? Even a child knows that.' 'Well then,' said the master, 'if even a child knows that, why can't you do it?' Ikkyu wrote these lines in a rough hand, at what seems to have been a lightning pace. On first sight, the characters give you quite a jolt – Ikkyu is mocking us, scratching at us, shocking us.

Even when the author is unknown, calligraphy remains a portrait of the heart. Among my favorite scrolls is a rubbing of three characters carved on Mt Tai in China in the sixth century. The carver is unknown, but the characters have a heavy, rough-hewn power for which they have been prized by collectors. The scroll reads, 'Virtue is not alone', referring to the statement by Confucius that 'The virtuous man is not alone; he will always have neighbors.' As I live alone in the rural town of Kameoka, this scroll has always been a comfort to me.

One reason why calligraphy serves as a bridge from mind to mind is that it is a thing of the instant – there is no going back to touch up what you have written. As my tutors at Oxford noticed, rigor is not my strong point. I like the way in which you throw a calligraphy off and then you are done with it. There is none of the gradual development of an oil painting or a musical performance. Calligraphy is perfect for impatient types, and spending an evening drinking wine with a friend while writing calligraphies is for me the highest form of relaxation. From that first evening as a student writing calligraphy at Roberto's house in Milan, this approach has never changed.

When I am planning to do some calligraphy, I invite a friend to come over and spend the night at my house. We select various weights of *washi* paper and then I make the ink. For me, ink is by no means always black. Perhaps as a lingering bit of Warhol influence, I tend to use a range of colorful inks: from gold and silver powders to ground rocks such as cinnabar and azurite, and artist's materials such as poster paints and acrylics. Grinding the powders, boiling the water, adding the glue and, finally, mixing the colors can take several hours. If I do decide to use black ink, I bring out Tsuru-san's water-dripper, and slowly grind the ink on an inkstone.

When at last I pick up the brush to begin writing, the evening is wearing on, and my friend and I have drunk a fair amount of wine. As we talk, I try writing characters on various subjects. The style may be standard script, semi-cursive or cursive – it changes at the whim of the moment. As each piece appears, I ask my guest what he feels about it. Curiously, the ability to judge calligraphy does not seem to depend on any familiarity with *kanji*. Even people who have never seen a *kanji* in their whole lives can sense balance and quality of line. My sixteen-year-old cousin Trevor was one of my best critics.

I write until dawn. On awakening in the late afternoon I find the room littered with dozens of creations from the night before. Most are failures, but from amongst them I select those that best convey the flavor of the previous evening. One summer night, when the frogs in the neighboring rice paddies were in full voice, clouds of moths and mosquitoes came flying into the house, attracted by the brightness inside. On rising the next day, I found only one piece worth saving. This was the *kanji* for 'night', written large in black ink. Scattered all over the page, in some places merging with the 'night' character, were myriad small *kanji* in gold and silver. They said 'frog', 'moth', 'cicada', 'mosquito' and 'gnat'.

The great calligraphers of the past also drank as they worked. The tradition goes all the way back to Wang Xizhi in the fourth century, who would gather his friends at the Orchid Terrace, where they floated wine cups down the river while writing poems. Wine is the perfect companion to calligraphy. I once owned a folding screen by the Edo literati Kameda Bosai, written with an unbelievably wild brush. His usual 'earthworm' *kanji* had become eels, swimming madly across the paper. Looking over the twelve panels of the screen, you could see the characters squirming more agitatedly as Bosai moved from right to left, until on the last panel his *kanji* looked more like Arabic than Chinese. At the end, he had signed, 'Written by old man Bosai, totally drunk'.

I learned much from pieces like the Bosai screen in my collection that I might not have discovered if I had depended on modern teachers. For instance, in the process of collecting calligraphy by *kuge* nobles I found that there had once been a style called *wayo*. Meaning 'Japanese style', *wayo* designates the soft, flowing form which grew up in the late Heian period and became the base of *kuge* and samurai scripts, and later design styles such as those in Kabuki and sumo writing. In contrast to *karayo*, the 'Chinese style' used by monks and literati, *wayo* was delicate and feminine, definitely not the sort of thing which Ikkyu used to put his Zen message across. The *kata* (forms) had been rigidly fixed over centuries, and *wayo* did not allow for much variation or personality; it was not a portrait of the heart as much as a portrait of an elegant ideal. In this aspect, *wayo* has much in common with Noh drama, where the aim is not to express the individual, but *yugen* (dark, mysterious beauty), beyond the individual.

With the coming of the Meiji period, schools removed *wayo* from the curriculum. It was too attached to the samurai classes which had been overthrown, and it was too rigid. Some of the design styles survived, but *wayo* as an artistic style died out, and most calligraphy we now see is *karayo*. Today, 'non-individual' has negative connotations, but the 'supra-individual' world of calm and elegance created by the *wayo* calligraphers was one of Japan's great achievements. The Chinese, ceaselessly trying to express their individuality, never produced anything like it.

When, as an adult, I first saw Kabuki *onnagata* perform, I remembered the dancing sensation I had felt when writing the spear radical as a child. Kabuki dance is a play between yin and yang. The fan goes up before it can go down, the neck turns left as the feet turn right. When the courtesan points, she first draws her finger back, describes a circle and then brings her finger outwards. But at that very moment, her shoulders are turning in the opposite direction. It is the harmony of these opposites that makes Kabuki dance so satisfying. Exactly the same thing occurs in the writing of calligraphy.

Today, Japanese are often taught to write in *seiza*, the formal seated position with legs tucked underneath. Not only is *seiza* very uncomfortable, it allows for very little range of movement. I write standing at a long table, and when I do calligraphy with friends I tend to move around a great deal. Standing up, crouching down, walking back and forth – calligraphy is born from these movements. I can well understand why the T'ang-dynasty artist Chang Xu dipped his hair into a pail of ink and used his own head as a brush! Chang Xu also painted lotus leaves by wetting his buttocks with ink and then sitting on the paper, but that was perhaps going too far.

Which brings me to why calligraphy is not prized in Japan today. It has to do with the way it is taught. Alone of all the traditional arts, calligraphy is instantaneous and free, ideal for busy modern people. But at some point it became a very serious affair. Students must sit still in *seiza*; they must slave for years to acquire technical ability in ancient styles that are completely obscure to the average person. In addition, calligraphy is afflicted by a 'society disease'. Most professional calligraphers are members of societies that have a pyramidal structure, with grand masters at the head, vice-chairman, board members and judges below that, and lower strata of members and students at the bottom. Art yearbooks list the calligraphers in the same way that sumo posters list the wrestlers: the people at the top of the pyramid get more space. A chairman gets a photograph and a fourth of a page; a vice-chairman gets a photograph, but only an eighth of a page; and so on, on down to mere 'provisional members' who get only their name in small print. A glance at the name cards of typical modern calligraphers confirms their commitment to the society system. You will find one or more titles – 'Board Member of X Society', 'Associate Member of Y Society', 'Judge of Z Society' – all indicating that modern calligraphers are as busy establishing their place in committees as they are producing works of art.

As a result of *seiza*, the emphasis on arcane technique and the pyramidal societies, calligraphy these days has slipped from the mainstream. One gets the impression that most young people think of calligraphy as something that old people do in their retirement. Millions still practice it, but the elite of the art world tend to look down on calligraphy as a sort of hobby. Today, far from being ranked first among the arts, calligraphy is something of a lost child. It has for the most part failed to meet the challenge of modern art imported from the West, and its influence on contemporary art is therefore negligible.

Perhaps the prime factor for the decline of calligraphy is the fact that few people can read cursive script anymore. The Japanese language has changed drastically since 1945, and few people use the brush for daily correspondence. Since the advent of the computer, which automatically transfers words into *kanji*, people find it harder and harder to remember the characters. I myself suffer from this trouble: I recognize *kanji* when I read them, but having become dependent on my computer for writing, I often forget surprisingly simple words.

This loss of literacy was inevitable, but in my view it really does not make much difference. Kameda Bosai's earthworm squiggles were unintelligible, even to his friends at the time; there is a comic poem which says that the only writing of Bosai's which anyone could read was a letter asking for a loan. In the old days, being able to read the characters was of secondary importance to the quality of line and the 'heart' of the author. Today, ironically, it is foreign collectors who have the least trouble with the fact that they can't read the characters. They look at calligraphy as abstract art, which, in the end, is what it is. But for the Japanese, not being able to read calligraphy is unsettling. I once had a Japanese assistant who told me that he hated calligraphy; Bosai's earthworm *kanji* especially bothered him. 'Foreigners can appreciate it as abstract art, and that's fine for them, but for us calligraphy must have a meaning,' he said. His inability to understand the meaning was a source of great unease: it would seem that modern Japanese have a complex about being unable to read things.

Calligraphy as fine art – *shikishi, tanzaku* and hanging scrolls for tea ceremony – is slowly losing its place in the culture. But calligraphy as design is very active. Japan has always been a design country, perhaps because of its love for the surface of things. Even such simple things as *geta* (wooden clogs) exist in a huge variety of designs: standard double clogged, single clogged, tall for sushi chefs, extremely tall for courtesans, square toed, round toed, made of white wood, dark wood or lacquered. In the field of calligraphy, dozens of design styles grew up during the Edo period, far more than ever existed in China. There were separate styles for Kabuki, Noh drama and puppet theater; for sumo; for samurai documents; for men's letters and women's letters; for tea masters' signatures; for the writing of receipts; for coins and bills; for seals, and many other things.

With such a wealth of traditional styles to draw upon, graphic design using *kanji* is one of Japan's most vibrant modern fields. From matchboxes to animated TV commercials, *kanji* are still alive and squirming as madly as anything Bosai ever wrote. This is why the signs of Ginza are so remarkable. There is nothing anywhere in the world, not even in China, to compare with them.

Chapter 7

Tenmangu
Ghost Concert

When I was caught up in Kabuki in the late 1970s and early 80s, I would go to Tokyo and stay at a friend's house for months on end, visiting the theater every day. Ten years later, while working for the Trammell Crow Company, I had an office and an apartment in Tokyo. I would spend Monday to Friday minding Trammell Crow's business, then commute to Kameoka on weekends. These days, although my work consists mostly of writing and public speaking, I still need to spend a considerable amount of time in Tokyo. It is the center of almost every form of dynamic cultural activity, and most of the artists I know live there.

When Friday evening rolls around after a busy week in Tokyo, I hail a cab for the Yaesu exit of Tokyo Station and take the bullet train back to Kyoto. When I first get on board, my mind is still abuzz with business matters, but as the train draws away from the city, these thoughts subside. I start thinking about my house in Kameoka. Are the water lilies in the pots in front of the house

blooming yet? I wonder how the repair work on the dragon painting I sent to the mounter is coming along . . . By the time the
train pulls into Kyoto a few hours later, all work concerns are
totally forgotten.

The first thing I notice in Kyoto is the difference in the air. As
soon as I get off the train, it always strikes me that there's not
enough oxygen in Tokyo! Drinking in the clean air after a week's
absence, I get in the car and head for the mountains to the west.
Finally, at about eleven o'clock at night, I arrive at my destination
of Kameoka, a town about twenty-five kilometers outside Kyoto.
My base for the last eighteen years has been here. My home is a
traditional Japanese house in the grounds of a small Shinto shrine
called Tenmangu, dedicated to the god of calligraphy. Like Chiiori, the house measures four bays by eight bays, but it is tiled
rather than thatched. While the house is not large, it has considerable garden space because of its location in the grounds of a
shrine. One side of the property fronts a small road, while the
other side overlooks a mountain stream; the grounds sandwiched
within cover about a thousand *tsubo* of land. The mountain rising
up on the other side of the stream is also shrine property, so the
'borrowed scenery' of the garden actually extends over several
thousand *tsubo*.

A long white wall with a tiled roof borders the grounds of the
shrine on the side towards the road, and in the center of the wall
there is a high gate. Entering, you see directly before you a stone
torii (the entrance gate to the shrine itself), and a small Tenmangu Shrine with an old plum tree standing beside it. To the
right is the 'shrine forest', a stand of giant old cryptomeria cedars.
To the left of the stone path is my domain. Water lilies float in
large pots, and an assortment of vessels scattered here and there
hold peonies, ferns, lotuses, Chinese lanterns and heron grass.
After crossing six or seven stepping stones, you reach the entrance
to my house.

When you enter the living room, the back garden comes into

view – although 'jungle' might be a more appropriate description. Just a few square meters have been cleared near the house, a stretch of grass and moss with some stepping stones in it. The edges of this plot are planted with azaleas and *hagi* (bush clover), which have been long unattended and are beginning to spread unruly twigs outwards and upwards, hiding a mossy stone lantern and some ceramic statues of badgers. Towards the back are a variety of trees: an ancient cherry tree (propped up with wooden supports), a maple, camellias and a gingko tree. Behind these trees, the garden drops away to a waterfall in the stream, and a heavily wooded mountain soars up from the far bank. When I arrive home on Friday night, I throw open the glass doors of the verandah, and the sound of the waterfall swells up into the house. In that instant, all thoughts of the week in Tokyo blow clean away, and I feel like I have returned to my true self.

Finding this house was a piece of great good luck. At the end of the Oomoto seminar in 1976, the foundation suggested that I come to work there after going down from Oxford, and without thinking much about it, I agreed. Over the next year, when people asked me for whom I would be working, I had pleasure of telling them, 'For the Mother Goddess of Oomoto.' But I had neglected to discuss my salary. When I arrived in 1977 to take up my position in Oomoto's International Department, I discovered that all those who worked at the foundation were considered to be 'contributors of service'; in other words, the pay was nominal. I found to my horror that my monthly salary was to be 100,000 yen (about $400 a month). Art activities were all very fine, but how was I going to pay the rent?

For the first two or three weeks I stayed in the Oomoto dormitory, but one day near the end of summer I had an inspiration. A friend from Thailand, Ping Amranand, was taking the seminar. I said to him, 'Ping, let's go look for a house!' So we set out, walking away from the Oomoto grounds. Kameoka is a flat-bottomed bowl of rice paddies, and you cannot walk for long without running up against mountains. As we walked towards them, I noticed an unusual building. Through a gate in a white wall was a large garden, rank with weeds, and by it an empty house. Drawing on my wealth of experience in breaking into abandoned houses in Iya, we were inside the house in a matter of moments. It was dark and dusty inside, and spiderwebs clung to our hands and faces. Walking gingerly across the floor of the dim living room, which winced and threatened to collapse at every step, we came out onto the back verandah, which was sealed shut with a row of heavy wooden doors. I gave one of the doors a shove, and the entire rotten row collapsed and fell into the garden in a heap. In that instant, warm green light from the back garden flooded the living room. Ping and I looked at each other: in a single summer day, we had found my house.

The old woman who lived next door told me that the caretaker of the house was the head priest of the nearby Kuwayama Shrine, so I paid him a visit. The priest explained the history of the house to me. It was very old, having been built around four hundred years before. It had originally been a Buddhist nunnery, but around the end of the Edo period it was dismantled and moved to its current site in the grounds of the Tenmangu Shrine. The gate, from another temple further into the mountains, was moved here at about the same time. The house then took on a second life as the shrine-keeper's home, and also doubled as the village school. But after the 1930s there was no more shrine-keeper, so the house was rented out to local residents. In recent years, nobody had wanted to live in such an old and dirty house, so it lay vacant. Though at a loss to imagine why a foreigner would want to live in such a place, the priest decided then and there that I could rent it.

Although the Tenmangu Shrine, which is tended by the villagers, is separate from the house, my friends and I have taken to calling the house 'Tenmangu' as well. Today, it looks considerably better than it did in 1977. Guests arrive and think, 'Ah, a quaint country residence,' but they can have no idea of the long years of toil it took to bring the house to its present state. At first there was not even running water; there was only a well, which dried up in the winter months. Although I don't mind 'run-down', I do mind 'dirty'. So I invited a group of friends from Oomoto over for a house-cleaning party. Carrying buckets of water from the well, we wiped the ceilings, pillars and tatami mats until they gleamed. Happily, the roof did not leak, so the tatami had not rotted and I did not face the horrific roofing problems which had colored my experience in Iya. Gradually, I brought in running water, repaired the doors and walls, and weeded the garden. The back garden which Ping and I had discovered that first day was an impenetrable mass of weeds and vines. A few months after moving in, I took sickle and machete to it, and saw for the first time the stepping stones, lanterns and azaleas that are typical of a Japanese garden.

However, on a salary of only 100,000 yen a month, the repair of the house could not be done all at once. As a result, for the first three or four years, life in Tenmangu was very much like dwelling in a haunted house. Not long after I moved in, an eighteen-year-old friend named Diane Barraclough came to live with me. Diane was a blonde British-French girl who had been raised in Kobe and spoke a colorful form of Kobe dialect. Although her Japanese lacked delicacy, she was certainly fluent. She had also inherited French from her mother and an upper-class British accent from her father, doctor to the expatriates in Kobe. Diane was the sort of long-haired beauty who inhabits the comic books which are popular among young girls in Japan. She was pure Edgar Allan Poe, and completely happy in the dark and dilapidated atmosphere of Tenmangu.

I was initially unable to replace the rotten verandah doors, so the entire eight-meter expanse of the verandah was left open facing the garden. On summer evenings, hordes of moths and mosquitoes would come flying in, so I went to one of the second-hand shops in Kyoto and bought a couple of old mosquito nets. These nets were among the most hauntingly beautiful objects in old Japanese life. They were like enormous square tents, each one the size of a whole room, and they hung from hooks high up on the ceiling. The body of the net was pale green linen, and the borders were of brilliant red silk. We laid our bedding inside the green tents and set out floor lamps. Dressed in a kimono, Diane would sit inside her tent to read, a silver *kiseru* pipe dangling from her lips. The view of her silhouette, filtered through the green netting, was pure romance, the sort of thing you might find in an Edo woodblock print. In fact, years later, when nets like these had become scarce, I lent one to the Kabuki actor Kunitaro for a performance of *Yotsuya Kaidan* in Kyoto. *Yotsuya Kaidan* is a ghost story, commonly performed in summer to give the audience a 'chill', and the ghostly green netting with blood-red borders is considered an indispensable backdrop.

One night I brought a Japanese friend over to visit. When our taxi pulled up in front of Tenmangu, all the lights were off in the house, and there was just the sound of wind and waterfall. Diane was standing in the doorway dressed in a black kimono, her long blonde hair falling over her shoulders. In her outstretched hand she held a rusty old candle stand, over which spiders crawled. My friend took one look, shuddered, and hastily returned to the station in the same taxi we had come in.

In the evening, Diane and I would light a candle and sit out on the verandah talking, while watching the spiders spin their webs. Diane had a talent for vivid bons mots, most of them as politically incorrect as they could possibly be. Some prey on my mind even now. 'Tea ceremony,' she once said, 'is aesthetics for unaesthetic people.' What she meant was that tea ceremony tells you what to do about everything – where to put the flowers, which art objects should be displayed and how to use even the tiniest division of space. This is very comforting for people who have never thought about such things and have no idea what to do on their own.

Another time, she said, 'Zen is profundity for shallow people.' That is the sort of comment which the old Zen master Ikkyu would have loved. What sticks in my mind most of all, however, is when Diane said, 'You know, Westerners with their full-blown personalities are infinite in interest as human beings. But Western culture is so limited in depth. The Japanese, on the other hand, so restricted by their society, are limited as human beings. But their culture is infinitely deep.'

In retrospect, the late 1970s in Kyoto were the turning point of an era. Diane, David Kidd, many of my other foreign friends and I were all living in a dream of ancient Japan, because in those days it was still possible to believe in the dream. Around Tenmangu was wilderness and rice paddies, and the streets of Kameoka were still lined with wooden houses and the big *kura* of saké-makers, lending it the feel of a feudal castle town. The mountains had yet to be covered with steel pylons, and the wave of concrete and plastic had yet to overtake the town. Our actions at the time may have been a bit eccentric, but they still had some air of reality. It was possible, as we sometimes did on summer nights during the seminar at Oomoto, to walk all the way through town back to Tenmangu wearing kimono and *hakama* (trousers). To do so today would be so divorced from modern Japanese surroundings as to seem wholly ridiculous.

Time passed, and the early 1980s saw the renovation of Tenmangu advance steadily. I wired the house for electricity, swept away the cobwebs and installed glass doors along the verandah. With the exit of the spiders, Diane did not feel quite at home anymore and she moved out as well. I turned my attention to the *doma*, an earthen-floored room used as the kitchen, which took up about a third of the floor space in Tenmangu.

First, the head priest of Kuwayama Shrine, my landlord, performed a Shinto purification ritual for the old earthen oven and the well – fire and water. Then my friends and I set about transforming the *doma* into a studio space by removing the oven and capping the well. I put in a long table where I could do calligraphy, and mount and back paintings. The other rooms of the house had ceilings, but the *doma*, in order to allow smoke from the oven to escape, was open all the way up to the rafters, like Chiiori. But the rafters were so crammed with lumber and old sliding doors that it was impossible to see them. We carried out the detritus, and swept down one hundred and fifty years of accumulated soot, enough to fill ten large garbage bags. In doing so, a wide expanse of rafters and crossbeams magically appeared. This airy room is now my workspace.

Though the age of mosquito nets, candles and kimono has ended, a special world lives on at Tenmangu even now. This is a very simple thing: nature. When I return to Tenmangu after a trip to Tokyo or abroad, I always find that the cycle of the seasons has shifted a bit, and new natural phenomena await me. According to the old Chinese calendar, the year is divided into twenty-four mini-seasons, with names like 'Clear and Bright', 'White Dew', 'Great Heat', 'Little Cold' and 'Squirming Insects'. Each has its own flavor.

The god of Tenmangu was originally a tenth-century courtier named Michizane, famed for his love of plum blossoms; as a result, the thousands of Tenmangu shrines across the country invariably have a plum tree planted in the grounds. The mystique of plums is that they bloom at the end of winter, when snow is still on the ground. Soon spring comes, and the old cherry tree in the garden blooms, along with azaleas, peaches and wildflowers. But my favorite season comes later, around the end of May or the beginning of June, when the rainy season starts. The frogs in the surrounding paddies start croaking, and my friends calling from Tokyo are amazed to find that they can hear them even over the phone line. Little emerald gems, the frogs hop about and ornament the leaves and stepping stones. Then lotuses burst into bloom, and the heavy rain drums pleasantly on the roof of my bedroom. Sleeping during the rainy season is always a joy.

Then one evening, a lone firefly appears in the garden. With a friend, I climb down behind the garden to the creek bed below, and we wait in silence in the darkness. After a while, from the thickets on either side of the ravine, glowing clouds of fireflies come floating out. In the summer, the village children come to swim in the pool below the waterfall. My cousin Edan, a little blonde imp, spent a whole summer playing under the waterfall. From my living room I can hear the children's voices as they dive into the pool. The trees on the mountain slope beyond sway in the breeze, and a black kite lazily spreads its long wings high above. The end of the summer brings typhoons and autumn's crimson maple leaves, yellow gingko, ruby nandina berries and, at the end, hanging onto the bare branches of winter, orange persimmon fruit. On winter days, frost descends on the garden, and each blade of grass sparkles like diamonds in the morning sun. Frog emeralds, frost diamonds, nandina rubies – these are Tenmangu's jewel box.

But these seasonal changes are being slowly erased from today's Japan. For example, in most cities it is standard practice in autumn to cut off the branches of trees lining the streets, in order to prevent falling leaves. To modern Japanese, falling leaves are not a thing of beauty; they are messy and to be avoided. This accounts for the stunted appearance of the trees which one encounters in most public places in Japan. Recently, a friend here told me, 'Just going to look at the mountain wilderness – what a bore! It is only when you have something to do that nature becomes interesting. You know, like golf or skiing.' This may explain why people feel compelled to bulldoze so many golf courses and ski slopes into the mountainsides. My wilderness remains that of the Chinese poets, my nature that of Basho's haiku. A frog jumps into an old pond; just that sound brings me joy. Nothing else is needed.

When Diane was living at Tenmangu, the house had almost nothing inside of it. However, in time, Tenmangu became the setting for my growing art collection. Japanese gold screens, Chinese carpets, Tibetan mandalas, Korean vases, Thai Buddhas, Burmese lacquerware, Khmer sculpture – all things Asian were crammed into every inch of the house. 'Crammed' is not, I realize, the most aesthetically pleasing of expressions; it hardly conjures up images of elegant refinement. But the artworks of every country and every historical period of Asia made up a jungle of such luxuriance inside Tenmangu that the foliage outside was almost outclassed: it was a greenhouse of beauty. One friend called it 'Aladdin's Cave'. On arrival, visitors would see a dilapidated old house which looked not much different from the Tenmangu I found in 1977. Then they would enter the foyer, and – 'open sesame!' – colorful screen paintings, thick blue-and-yellow rugs, and the luster of polished quince and rosewood met the eye.

In recent years, the novelty of owning all these things has worn off a bit and I have cleared out Tenmangu considerably. The rugs and the furniture are still there, but taking a hint from old households which used to store their possessions out of sight in the *kura*, I have loaned most of the screens, statues and paintings to museums. Now I keep just a few favorite things, and rotate them as the mood strikes me. I suppose I will keep removing more and more, until eventually the house will come full circle and there will be only a bare tatami room looking out onto an open garden.

In the meantime, even with a much smaller number of objects on display, Tenmangu still has an Aladdin's Cave feel about it. I think it has something to do with color, one of the things I learned about from David Kidd in the days of my apprenticeship. To digress slightly, I once read an account of life in Tibet before it was invaded by China, when Tibetan culture still flourished. One day, the author met a group of Tibet's high-ranking statesmen traveling in a convoy across the steppe. They were a blaze of color: even the horses were draped in gorgeous silk and handwoven blankets. The statesmen wore garments of yellow brocade on which blue dragons, purple clouds and green waves danced wildly, and in their hair they wore beads of turquoise and coral.

In today's world, people's sense of color has faded considerably. Just think of the drab suits of modern politicians and you'll see what I mean. This lack of color is especially true of Japan, where all lighting is fluorescent, and most household items are made from aluminum and synthetic materials. However, Tenmangu is alive with rich, deep hues. It is a striking contrast to the ash-gray color of life in Tokyo. First, there is gold, a color which, as Tanizaki pointed out in *In Praise of Shadows*, does not generally go well with a brightly lit room; this may be why gold is hardly seen in modern Japanese life. But in Tenmangu there is the gold leaf of screens, the gold of Buddhas, gold lacquer – many different kinds of gold. Within gold, there is green gold, red gold and alloyed gold, which tarnishes with time. In addition to gold, there are painting pigments, especially the vivid green seen in Tibetan mandalas. Then there is the deep red of lacquerware, the pale blue of Chinese celadon, and the somber and cloudy oranges and tea greens of Japanese brocade.

As a calligrapher, living in Tenmangu could not be more propitious. I feel as though I receive direct inspiration from the deity of the shrine. Although I am not a Shinto convert, I have a secret belief in the god of Tenmangu, who has been worshipped since antiquity as the god of scholarship and calligraphy. Sometimes, I step out to the shrine, ring the bell and say a prayer. Actually, 'prayer' is too strong a word; it's more like an informal greeting. When high-school and college-entrance exam season rolls around, students come to pray at the shrine before class, and their prayers probably have a little more urgency than mine. The early-morning ringing of the bell often wakes me up, serving as Tenmangu's alarm clock.

There are many gods in Tenmangu. First of all, there is the household altar above the studio room. In the center sits a figure of Michizane, and to the left and right of him are paper charms, talismans from shrines and temples, and rosary beads. Above the entryway there sits a small, blackened, wooden statue of Dai-koku (god of prosperity). The statue is only about twelve centimeters high, but it radiates power as though it were carved by the sculptor Enku. Of all the things that were in the house when I first moved in, this is the only one I've kept, and I think of it as the true guardian of Tenmangu. On the central pillar is pasted a charm from Kuwayama Shrine, and a likeness of Marishi-ten (god of contests) seated on a chariot of swiftly moving wild boars. In the living room, a *tanzaku* plaque by Onisaburo Deguchi hangs on the pillar of the *tokonoma*. In the innermost room is a Thai Buddha, and next to that a small altar to Shiva. This may seem an extreme sort of superstition, but I am only following the typical Japanese religious pattern: not wanting to be bound to a single religion, I subscribe to them all – Buddhist, Shinto, Hindu. Gods and Buddhas float ceaselessly in the air of Tenmangu, and their warm breathing fills the house.

Living in the countryside brings with it a number of inconveniences. Foremost among these are the insects. From the time of 'Squirming Insects' around the middle of March, legions of mosquitoes, moths, bees, ants, centipedes, spiders and helmet bugs sally forth. Doing battle with them is quite a chore. When Diane lived here, she had a thirteen-stringed *koto* which she kept on one side of the living room. Once, late at night, the sound of the instrument suddenly broke the silence. Strumming chords floated gently across the room – *chiri chiri chiri zuru zuru zuru* – but Diane and I were under the mosquito netting, alone in the house as far as we knew. Taking a candle, we went over to the *koto*, but there was nothing to be seen. Even as we watched, ghostly fingers continued to play and *chiri chiri chiri zuru zuru zuru* cascaded through the house, while Diane and I clung to each other in terror. Finally, I could bear it no longer and turned on all the lamps in the house, to find that a large moth had got itself trapped under the strings of the *koto*.

Ghost concerts I could live with, but mosquitoes were another matter. Mosquito netting is strange stuff: while not actually having any holes, it always seems to let some mosquitoes in. In the end, as a result of the mosquito problem, I finally put up glass doors against the garden, installed air-conditioning and effectively divided inside from outside. However, one hundred and fifty years have passed since Tenmangu was moved to its present spot, and as the result of a succession of typhoons and earthquakes, all the pillars lean and there is not a single right angle in the entire house. Insects manage to find a way through the gaps, and I don't think Tenmangu will ever be completely liberated from them.

Another problem is the length of the commute to Kyoto and Osaka. In truth it is not really all that long: twenty-five minutes to Kyoto by train, and one-and-a-quarter hours to Osaka by car. But for city dwellers, the distance to the countryside feels wider than the Sahara, and it is not easy to get the courage to cross this desert. I once got a call from an art collector in Amsterdam. 'I'm going to Japan next month. I'd love to visit Tenmangu,' he said. A month later, when he arrived in Tokyo, he called again, 'I'm going to Kyoto tomorrow. I'll see you the day after.' The next day, a call came from Kyoto, 'I'm looking forward to seeing you tomorrow.' Then, on the morning of the appointed day, he called to say, 'I'm sorry. I can't go to Kameoka. It's just too far.'

At the turn of the century, the Comte de Montesquiou ruled the Parisian social world with an iron hand; nobody ever turned down an invitation to one of the Comte's soirées. But one day Montesquiou moved from the east side of the Bois de Boulogne to a larger palace on the west side. It meant only a two-kilometer drive through the park, but from the day the Comte moved, high society tossed him aside without a qualm, and Montesquiou lived out the remainder of his days in isolation.

Certainly visitors to Tenmangu are not numerous. It's bad for the art business, but I don't feel particularly lonely. On the contrary, the distance from Kyoto and Osaka screens me from casual visitors, so that most of my guests are good friends. As a result, having guests over to my house is always pleasantly relaxed and enjoyable.

Over the past eighteen years, Tenmangu has seen a stream of Japanese friends who have lived here with me or taken care of the house. They all shared one thing, which was not an interest in art, nor a love of nature, as you might think. Their aim was to escape from Japanese society. There are very few places in Japan where you can escape from the constraints of this society. It is nearly impossible to 'drop out' and live a hippie life in the countryside: the stranglehold of complex rules and relations is at its most severe in the rice-growing countryside. On the other hand, in the big cities life is so expensive that it is all one can do to just pay the rent. In Tokyo, people who want to work in an environment that is free of Japanese social constraints typically try to get a job with a foreign company; but working in one of these offices is a rat race that brings its own strains and hardships. So the relaxed life at Tenmangu seems like a peaceful haven for such people, at least until the next step, which usually involves leaving Japan.

A Japanese friend once said to me, 'I always associated old Japanese houses with an image of poverty. When I saw Tenmangu I realized for the first time that one could live well in an old house.' The key to the destruction of the city of Kyoto lies in this comment. In the eyes of the city administration, rows of old wooden houses look 'poor'; they are an embarrassment, and should be removed quickly. This is not only true of Kyoto – the same feeling lurks deep in the hearts of people all over Japan. If this were not so, the rampant destruction that has occurred here would have sparked a strong public outcry; but until recently there has been hardly a peep of protest.

Kameoka has already been completely transformed, for the wave of 'uglification' that threatens all of Japan is advancing here as well. Every year a few of the rice paddies surrounding Tenmangu are torn up to become parking lots or golf driving ranges.

Fortunately, the grounds of Tenmangu are spacious and the mountain behind the garden is shrine property, so for a while, at least, we should be safe.

There is a framed calligraphy in the foyer of Tenmangu which reads 'Nest of Peace and Happiness'. It was written by an Edo-period literati and harks back to the house of one of the Sung scholars who revived Confucianist philosophy in the twelfth century. Though he did not have much money, he surrounded himself with books and scrolls in his small cottage. He invited friends over to his 'nest', and there they laid the grounds for a revolution in thinking. For me, the true charm of Tenmangu lies in its air of relaxation. My friends and I may be plotting revolution, but due perhaps to the quiet surroundings, or to the 'black glistening' of its four-hundred-year-old pillars, whoever enters Tenmangu quickly succumbs to its relaxed atmosphere. The visiting businessman, the type who always rises punctually for breakfast meetings, inevitably oversleeps at Tenmangu, or forgets to fax or call his office. It is quite common for a guest who planned to stay only a single night to lose track of time and stay for several days.

The visitor to Tenmangu soon finds himself becoming inexplicably drowsy. It is not because I have put something in the wine, but because the pace of life has suddenly slowed down. While talking or listening to music, my guest gradually begins to slouch to one side. From a chair, he moves over to the soft silk cushions on the *kang*, and lies down. Soon he is unable to prop up his head any longer, his face sinks down onto the pillow and he slips off to sleep. The 'nest' has worked its magic again.

Chapter 8

Trammell Crow

The Bubble Years

At the end of 1983, I visited Dallas, Texas, for Christmas. I was invited there by Trammell S. Crow, an old Yale classmate. Trammell S., with his long hair, bright orange jumpsuit, sports car and elfin grin, was one of my wilder college friends. He had promised to meet me at the airport, but when I arrived I couldn't find him. Then I realized with a shock that the clean-cut businessman in a blue suit holding out his hand to greet me was Trammell S.; I only recognized him by his grin. When I asked what had happened to him, he told me that he had gone to work for his father, Trammell Crow.

As our car approached downtown Dallas, Trammell S. pointed at the skyline ahead, and said, 'That forty-story skyscraper on the right is ours, and that fifty-story building under construction is also. And the hotel we're passing – Dad let me design some of it myself.' I realized then that I really knew nothing about his father. Trammell S. began to tell me something about him.

Trammell Crow was a Texan, born in Dallas, and until the age of thirty-five he was an ordinary bank employee. However, one day he had a sudden inspiration to buy an old warehouse. He remodeled it, found tenants to rent it, and then bought up two or three warehouses nearby. He remodeled them, and rented them out also. He continued for forty years, expanding from warehouses into trade marts, office buildings, apartments, hotels and every other imaginable form of real estate. Eventually, the Trammell Crow Company became the largest real estate developer in the world.

The next day, Trammell S. took me to his father's office. Expecting to see dull, corporate Americana, I felt for a moment that we had mistakenly stepped into a museum: as far as the eye could see was a treasure house of Asian art. Khmer sculpture stood in the corridors, and Chinese jade carvings sat casually next to computers and on top of filing cabinets. 'Dad loves Asian art,' Trammell S. said. 'He likes using his collection to decorate the office, so his employees can enjoy it too. I'll introduce you to him.'

Trammell Crow sat at a long table covered with blueprints, in conference with his architects concerning the design of a new city. 'Dad, I want you to meet a friend,' said Trammell S, but his father did not even lift his head. 'He studied with me at Yale.' Still no interest. 'He majored in Chinese and Japanese Studies.'

At this, Trammell Crow jumped up and said excitedly, 'Chinese and Japanese? Wonderful!' He grabbed a jade carving from the shelf nearest at hand and asked me, 'What do you think of this?' 'It has the squared barrel shape of an ancient Chinese Song jade, but I don't think it could be so old,' I answered. 'The style of the characters was popular at the end of the nineteenth century, so I would guess it's probably a nineteenth-century scholar's reconstruction.'

'What?' Trammell shouted. 'The folks at Sotheby's guaranteed that this was a genuine ancient artifact!' I tried to mumble an apology, but he brushed it aside. 'How would you like to work for me?' he suddenly asked. 'We've recently opened a business in Shanghai, and I could use a manager there.' Taken aback by the sudden change of topic, all I could say was, 'I'm very flattered, and there is nothing I would rather do than live in China for a while. But I've spent my whole life studying nothing but culture and art, and I have absolutely no knowledge of business. I'm sure I would make a mess of it, so I really can't accept.' Trammell replied, 'No business experience? Fine. At any rate, let's make you an employee. Starting today.' And he turned to his secretary and said, 'Send Mr Kerr a thousand dollars every month as a consulting fee.'

'Thank you very much, but what's this fee for?' I asked. 'Don't worry. You go back to Japan, and think about it. Then you write me a letter and let me know what you're going to do for me.' And with an abrupt 'Good-bye', he turned back to his desk and the waiting plans. The entire exchange took only ten minutes.

I went back to Japan, and sure enough a payment of $1000 arrived in my bank account each month; but I was at a loss as to what I could do for Trammell Crow. Since my specialty was art, all I could think of was art collecting. So I wrote him a letter proposing that if I acted as his agent at the Kyoto auctions, he could develop a collection of Japanese art very affordably. Trammell liked the idea, and soon I was buying an enormous volume of screens and scrolls for him. To pay for them, he wired me sums of money far greater than I had ever dealt with before. I soon reached the limits of my old informal mode of operations: taxes had to paid, screen-repair expenses ballooned, employees had to be hired and the accounting became complicated. I had no choice but to establish a company, so in the fall of 1984 Chiiori Ltd was born. I took the name from my house in Shikoku, but Chiiori Ltd's focus was far removed from the romance of Iya: it was all about taxes, accounting and the filing of official documents.

Trammell seemed satisfied with the artworks I was choosing for him, and would occasionally invite me to Dallas. I later learned that he was regarded as a maverick in American business. According to one famous anecdote, when he was asked during a speech to the Harvard Business School what the secret of his success was, he simply answered, 'Love.'

Before meeting Trammell, all my efforts to understand Japan were filtered through the medium of classical literature and traditional arts such as Kabuki. In my opinion, business was a sideline from which there was little to be learned. But one day, Trammell said to me, 'Alex, what you need is some lessons in reality!', and he invited me to sit in on business meetings when I was in Dallas. One such meeting involved the representative of an Italian company from which Trammell Crow was ordering marble for the face of a new office building. Negotiations over the price were heated: first the Italian side named a unit price of thirteen, then Trammell proposed nine, and eventually the price was set at ten. The marble company representative was about to leave when Trammell stopped him, 'You brought the price down to ten for us,' he said, 'but that gives you very little profit and you'll be unable to return home feeling good about this. Let's make it eleven. In exchange, I expect you'll put extra effort into this for us.' And the marble salesman went home happy.

In the summer of 1986, I received a fax from Trammell S., telling me that the Trammell Crow Company was planning on jointly developing a wholesale mart in Kobe with the Sumitomo Trust Bank, and that I was required to meet with the manager of the development section of the bank in Osaka. Digging a little-used suit out of the back of my closet, I fearfully made my way there. Except for when I founded Chiiori Ltd, I had never spoken to a bank manager before, so I was extremely nervous.

The manager of Sumitomo Trust's development section was a man named Nishi. Looking back now, I see that Nishi was emblematic of the so-called 'bubble' of the 1980s. At heart an entrepreneur like Trammell rather than a staid banker, he had become involved in the Kansai area's mega real estate developments early on, and was the mastermind behind projects such as the Nara Technopolis. Riding the wave of the real estate boom, Nishi had realized enormous success. Brimming with excitement, he explained that Sumitomo Trust had won the bidding for a contract to develop Kobe's Rokko Island, a large plot of landfill in the middle of the harbor. It was not, of course, open bidding: the city, as is customary in Japanese construction, had made a cozy deal with Sumitomo Trust, but one of the conditions was that a wholesale fashion mart be constructed on the site. The largest mart facility in the world at that time was Trammell Crow's Dallas Market Center, so Sumitomo Trust wanted to link up with Trammell Crow to develop the Kobe mart.

Thus began a long interchange between Sumitomo Trust and the Trammell Crow Company. The project manager assigned from Dallas was Bill Starnes, a big Texan with genial manners belying a killer business instinct. My job was to interpret, but it was very rough because the financial terminology being used was lost on me in both English and Japanese. For instance, Starnes kept talking about something called IRR (internal rate of return). This calculates the overall profit that a real estate venture is going to earn, incorporating debt repayment, annual rental income and the projected rise in land value. In America, IRR is the standard measure for all real estate developments, and so naturally Starnes put great emphasis on it. But I had no idea what he was talking about. There was nothing for it but to follow Starnes back to his hotel each evening, where he gave me a crash course in IRR and general real estate know-how. Before joining Trammell Crow, Starnes had been a professor at Rice University, so he made a good teacher. He bought textbooks for me to read, drew up lists of vocabulary and even gave me mathematics homework to do.

There were many points of controversy between Sumitomo Trust and Trammell Crow, but the most memorable of all had to do with this IRR calculation. After some time I finally got to the point where I understood IRR, but I soon discovered that the Sumitomo bank officers I had been in such awe of had no idea what it was! 'We don't need IRR in Japan,' they told Starnes. 'Who cares about rental income? The main thing is that land prices will always go up. Japan is different from America.' 'In that case,' Starnes replied, 'you must have some other method of calculation in order to evaluate real estate projects here?' And slowly the strange truth emerged: Sumitomo had precise criteria for establishing mortgage rates or determining collateral for loans, but they had absolutely no method of evaluating the aggregate merit of a new real estate venture. They had never needed one. For forty years since the war, land and rents in Japan had risen uninterruptedly. If one just had enough money to acquire land, everything else would go smoothly. Large banks like Sumitomo Trust, protected and coddled by a financial system which stifled both domestic and foreign competition, had had a particularly easy time of it.

In Trammell Crow's swashbuckling youth, real estate moguls had simply made deals which felt right and had then sealed them with a handshake. But after suffering the consequences of several disastrous real estate booms and busts – the so-called 'real estate cycle' of America – they had called in experts to run their companies for them, and the experts had brought tools of analysis like IRR with them. Japan, however, had not made this adjustment, and there were no brilliant analysts like Bill Starnes in the Sumitomo Trust Bank. The management of large financial institutions had become soft, because they had failed to learn the next generation of real estate know-how that had become common knowledge in the rest of the world. The fact that the bank did not understand IRR should have been a danger sign to us; from that alone we could perhaps have predicted the impending crash.

In 1987 the long year of negotiations came to an end, and Sumitomo Trust and Trammell Crow finalized a joint-venture contract. Until then I had only been working part time, but from that autumn I came to work at the planning office in Osaka as a full-time employee. I put Tenmangu in the hands of a student caretaker, and rented a house in Okuike, in the hills of Ashiya between Kobe and Osaka. Every day I would commute into Osaka, joining delegations of experts from Dallas in meetings with prospective tenants, architects and so on. IRR was not the only communications gap I experienced. Once, in a conference about floor space, a Dallas expert burst out, 'We're talking about square footage here. We don't even know yet how many tenants we'll have; isn't it a bit premature to bring up soup bowls?' 'Soup bowls? Nobody said anything about soup bowls,' answered a bewildered Sumitomo architect. The offending word turned out to be *tsubo*, the standard unit of land measurement in Japan.

When the Kobe Fashion Mart opened, it was the largest building in Kansai – and its financial planning, design, leasing and negotiation had been my 'business school'. During that lengthy process, Trammell's purchases of art had slowed, my art dealing had faded into the background, and I had devoted myself full time to the mart. Every once in a while I would receive an encouraging phone call from Trammell, saying, 'Business is fun, isn't it!' And it was. One of the reasons was Trammell's personal charm, including his colorful Texan turn of phrase. One time I was escorting a group of Singaporean bankers around the Dallas headquarters. Trammell saw them off at the elevator, and then turned to me and said, 'Now you take care of those men, Alex. They have money in the bank and cattle out west!'

In 1988 we lost our energetic overachiever Nishi. He collapsed from overwork, and was replaced by a traditionalist from the Sumitomo Trust staff. At the same time, Dallas assigned an American manager to the project. The antagonism between the American manager and the Japanese staff was a sight to behold. As the buffer between them, it was fairly rough on me, but it was also a great learning opportunity. Until the American manager's arrival, I had always thought of workplace relations in the US as being equal, and those in Japan as hierarchical. But the Japanese-division chief guided his subordinates with a very gentle hand. Nishi, for instance, would frequently say to Starnes, 'I understand your point, but until I can convince my subordinates, I can't move. Give me time.' Of course, this was often no more than a negotiating ploy, but I noticed that Nishi really did consult with his staff, and often left important decisions up to them. The American corporate structure, on the other hand, is far more authoritarian. It's modeled on boot camp: the manager gives commands, and his subordinates carry them out. In terms of company organization, the Japanese way is much more democratic.

In January 1989, I quit working on the Kobe mart. Flying to Dallas, I helped Trammell to publish a book on his jade collection, and then briefly returned to my art business. In the meantime, the clash between Japanese and American management styles reached a crescendo. Sumitomo offered to buy out Trammell Crow's share of the mart, and after a few months of negotiations the two sides gracefully parted ways.

However, the bubble was still going strong. The Crow Group's financial division, Trammell Crow Ventures, was introducing development deals to Japanese investors, who were pouring vast sums of money into US real estate. The Crow Company at that point was the recipient of hundreds of millions of dollars of Japanese investments and loans, so it became necessary to set up a liaison office in Tokyo.

In the fall of 1989, I became Trammell Crow Ventures' representative in Tokyo. My friend Mrs Chida, who had worked for years as secretary to the Egyptian Ambassador, happened to be free at the time, and came to work as my office secretary. I entrusted the management of my art business to a friend, rented an apartment in Akasaka in downtown Tokyo and commuted to Kameoka on the weekends. And so began the most interesting period of my business career. Trammell Crow Ventures' clients were mostly large financial institutions, such as life insurance companies and banks, but we also did deals with construction companies and developers. That autumn, the Tokyo stock market climbed above 37,000 yen, and money was cheap. There was euphoria in the air, and the Japanese were convinced that they were about to take over the world; words like 'a billion dollars' and 'ten billion dollars' rolled off people's tongues, and Japanese investment in US real estate appeared to be growing without limit.

However, in January 1990 the bubble began to burst. Japanese stocks nosedived, and by the summer of 1995 they were hovering at 18,000 yen. The American real estate business also entered one of its periodic recessions: Donald Trump and other major players were declared bankrupt one after another, and the industry went into meltdown. The fact that the Trammell Crow Company was about ten times larger than Trump only made its problems ten times larger; Trammell's trust in young people like myself clearly had some drawbacks to it. After some very painful years, the Crow Company is slowly climbing out of the slump, but the structure of the company has become more traditional. Trammell S. has left the company, and the legendary Trammell Crow no longer exerts much influence over its policy, which is guided by his son Harlan and the Crow Company president.

During my Tokyo years, I noticed a number of things. Japan's *Wall Street Journal* is the *Nihon Keizai Shimbun*, commonly called the *Nikkei*. At first I read the *Nikkei* religiously, but I gradually got the queasy feeling that the real state of things was not being reported. When the stock market first began to drop, the news was nowhere to be seen in the *Nikkei*. Somewhere on the bottom of page five, in tiny print, one might find a headline saying, 'Stock Market a Bit Unwell'. However, on buying a copy of the popular tabloid the *Evening Fuji*, front-page headlines ten centimeters tall would be screaming 'CRASH!'. The English-language papers, while not so sensational, were also far more accurate than the *Nikkei*. This was my introduction to Japan's controlled press. In every field, whether it is business or crime, Japan's reporters belong to 'press clubs', where they depend on news handouts from government bureaucrats or the Police Agency. As a result of these cozy relationships, newspapers like the *Nikkei* verge on being a kind of government propaganda organ. Tabloids like the *Evening Fuji*, however, are cut off from this system, and are therefore rarely privy to any important inside information. They are unreliable for any but the broadest sort of economic data – like the daily stock market average, made public to all. At the same time, they are free to criticize business and government in a way the large established dailies rarely do.

While the *Nikkei* was still reporting the stock decline with words like 'market a bit under the weather', Mrs Chida brought my attention to a humorous article in the *Evening Fuji*. It was about a banker who had disappeared because of stock market debts, and the headline was '*Yappari deta!*', or 'Now It's Out!'. At that moment I heard the warning bells ringing. I had accumulated a large debt from the thatching of Chiiori and from buying artworks, but from that day I began to pay it back. One of Trammell's sayings was 'Debt is the road to fortune', and this was very much the spirit of the 1980s bubble era. If I had read only the *Nikkei*, I might have let my loans stand, and would later have been wiped out. But thanks to the *Evening Fuji*, I paid everything off before the bubble completely collapsed.

The bursting of the bubble was an opportunity to observe the different responses of America and Japan. In the 1970s there was a real estate slump in the US. At that time, the Trammell Crow Company was in even more trouble than it is now, coming perilously close to bankruptcy. However, Trammell rode it out, and made it into the period of rapid growth in the 1980s. It is now conventional wisdom in the US that real estate goes through cycles. Trammell's son-in-law, Henry Billingsley, used to explain the cycle like this: 'Here, at the bottom is farmland; that's where Trammell Crow buys in. Here, a building gets developed; that's where US real estate investors buy in. Here, at the top, too many buildings have been developed, and as a result of oversupply, values are going to drop.' And pointing to a spot about twice the height of the top of the curve, Henry would say, 'This is where the Japanese buy in.'

The reason the Japanese bought in such a way was that there had never been anything which could be called a cycle in Japan. After shaking off a brief 'oil shock' in the 1970s, the vocabulary of Japan's stock and real estate industries was limited to 'onward' and 'upward'. The universal attitude was just what the people at Sumitomo Trust told Starnes: 'This is Japan. Land and stock prices only go up.' There were people predicting that the stock market would rise to 60,000 yen, or even 80,000 yen, even though price-to-earnings ratios at those levels would be so small as to be almost zero. So the shock when land and stock prices dropped was severe: when it came time for the *Nikkei* to print the announcement of the stock decline, the *kanji* for words like 'drop', 'fall' and 'crash' were not to be found in the typesetter's box.

Not everything I learned in the Tokyo office had to do with economics. The only employees were Mrs Chida and myself, and the floor space was barely seventeen *tsubo*. Even so, visitors would often comment, 'How spacious. It has that nice foreign look.' Mrs Chida and I racked our brains to figure out what it was that gave us that 'foreign look', and we could only think of one possible reason: the lack of clutter. For some reason, Japanese businesses cannot get the hang of managing office space. Even when the building and office are brand new, heaps of documents cover the desks and boxes jam the corridors. Our office looked different because we kept only what we were using on view; everything else was filed in the appropriate spot.

A pure tatami room, empty but for a single flower in a vase, is an almost archetypal image of Japan. Such spaces do exist, but only in tearooms, temples or formal meeting rooms – locations where people do not live or work. Anyone who has spent time in a Japanese home or office knows that they are usually flooded with objects. From the old farmhouses of Iya to the apartments of modern Tokyo, living in a pile of unorganized things is a typical pattern of Japanese life. In my view, this is what led to the creation of the teahouse. In the Muromachi period, tea masters grew weary of a life crowded with junk, and created the tearoom: one pure space with absolutely nothing in it. It was where they escaped from the clutter. The culture of the Japanese is bracketed by the two extremes of 'clutter' and 'emptiness'. But when it comes to the middle ground of 'organized space', that is, space with objects organized for daily use, their tradition fails them.

Well organized though our office was, its days were brief. By the early 1990s, Japan's real estate investment in the US came to an abrupt halt. Trammell Crow Ventures' Tokyo office became unnecessary, so at the end of 1991 I moved back to Kameoka, and ran everything by fax and phone from my office there. By 1993, even that operation ended, and so the curtain fell on my ten years of working for Trammell Crow. Meanwhile, the art business began to look interesting again, as artworks made unaffordable during the bubble days dropped in price.

In retrospect, my business career with Trammell Crow exactly spanned the bubble era. During that period I had plenty of chances to 'learn about reality' whether I liked it or not. I gained a perspective on Japan's present difficulties that tea and Kabuki could never have given me.

The fall of the Japanese stock market was the biggest loss of wealth in the history of the world, yet the stock markets in New York, London and Hong Kong were completely unaffected, and have continued to rise regardless. Such is Japan's influence today. In the 1980s, everyone thought that Japan would become the center of the world; but in the 1990s, with the economies of China and ASEAN booming, Japan is being bypassed in many important fields.

The root of this decline lies in the telltale word 'cozy'. Cozy non-public bidding of the sort which awarded Rokko Island to Sumitomo Trust, cozy press clubs and other such systems are endemic in Japan. For decades they served to keep order at home and build up a competitive edge abroad. But meanwhile, rigidity set in: rocked in the cradle of its closed domestic systems, Japan failed to learn. Bankers did not master basic mathematics, such as IRR, and as a result, while Japan's banks make up eight of the world's ten largest institutions, in 1995 they ranked between eight hundredth and nine hundredth in profitability. Stockbrokers did not acquire tools of analysis vital in the business today. The Construction Ministry did not learn about ways of protecting the ecosystem while shoring up rivers – knowledge that has become standard in the developed world.

The only way to move forward is to dismantle these closed systems, but large businesses are too dependent on them, and so Japan is paralyzed. This paralysis affects culture as well as business, and how Japan breaks out of it will be the single biggest issue as the country enters the twenty-first century. The stock market exemplifies this paralysis. Since 1991, the government has kept the stock market from dropping below around 16,000 yen in order to protect banks, whose capital depends on the value of their stock portfolios. But because the market has not been allowed to drop to realistic levels, there have been almost no new issues. In other words, Japan's stock market is no longer fulfilling the main function of a stock market: raising capital. It has been effectively shut down for four years.

Another area where Japan is being bypassed is in the fashion world. Ten years ago, the leading fashion designers of Tokyo (including Issey Miyake, Kansai Yamamoto, Rei Kawakubo, etc.) got together to create the Council of Fashion Designers (CFD). They thought Tokyo's CFD would supplant Paris as a world fashion center, but the rigid organization of the domestic fashion world undermined them. The CFD was not open to foreigners, nor to new faces in Japan, and certainly not to the up-and-coming

Asian designers. It was too comfortable and predictable, so international fashion editors lost interest. Rei Kawakubo dropped out; Kansai Yamamoto has not shown in Tokyo in several years. In 1995, the CFD mailed invitations to its spring collections to dozens of foreign fashion editors; almost none attended. And so it was back to Paris.

The Japanese film industry, once led by giants such as Kurosawa, has not produced an internationally successful movie in over ten years. The movie industry is dominated by two giant production companies, Shochiku and Toho, which also own most of the movie theaters. This means that the films of smaller independent producers have very little chance of being seen. Shochiku and Toho pre-sell their films to large companies, which buy up blocks of tickets to give to their employees as company benefits. The purpose is to avoid risk, to avoid having to suffer the verdict of the marketplace. As there is no need to appeal to the public, Japanese movie producers have grown completely out of touch. So the public flocks to foreign films.

One of modern Japan's great mysteries, which almost every foreign observer puzzles over, is how can the citizens of the world's richest country have such a poor lifestyle? The Japanese live in houses a quarter the size of the French or the English. And those houses are made of cheap, flimsy materials (as was graphically demonstrated by the Kobe earthquake). The variety of produce available in the food markets is a fraction of that which can be found in most large cities of the world. There are only eight TV channels (including satellite), versus dozens elsewhere, or even hundreds in America. There will soon be more channels available in upper Burma than in Japan.

The answer to the puzzle lies in those comfortable systems. Japan maintained 'peace in the marketplace' by supporting cartels which set prices high, to the disadvantage of the consumer. It avoided competition in communications or the film industry by restricting the number of companies involved in service industries. And through every possible means, the impact of the outside world was kept to a minimum: foreigners were not allowed to run companies here, to design or construct buildings here, to make movies here, etc. It worked all too well. Because of the high wall of regulation and the cozy systems which exclude them, foreign firms are now giving Japan a miss as they move into the rest of Asia. The president of a firm specializing in computer services based in Dallas recently told me that his company is considering Vietnam, Thailand, China and Malaysia – but not Japan. 'It's not worth the brain damage,' he said.

As with other over-regulated systems, in time the conflicts with reality multiply, and cracks begin to show. To prevent collapse, further restrictions become necessary. In the end, it becomes harder and harder to move – hence, the present paralysis. For instance, one reason for the poor state of Japanese housing and related industries (furniture, interior design, etc.) is the high cost of land. But when land prices began to drop after 1989, the government panicked because the Japanese banks were awash with red ink from bad loans to real estate developers. The amount of their non-performing loans now tops one trillion dollars, dwarfing the savings and loan crisis in America.

Rather than auctioning off non-performing real estate, which would have lowered the price of land, the government found ways for banks not to sell. This was done through a trick of accounting, whereby real estate assets can be shown on the books at purchase value until the time of sale. As long as a business does not sell its land, it need not show a loss on its books, and so there is no incentive to sell. On the other hand, no one is buying in an inflated market, so the real estate market has remained frozen for the last five years.

The situation is serious, and the mid-levels of almost every Japanese institution are filled with people in their thirties and forties who are extremely dissatisfied. They are questioning the slowness and inefficiencies of Japanese life and showing anger in a way never seen before. This was reflected in the recent mayoral elections in Tokyo and Osaka, when voters rejected all the established parties to elect two non-politicians, both of them former TV comedians.

Above is the massive weight of decades of regulation by bureaucrats; below is rising desperation on the part of a generation that has some knowledge of the outside world and realizes that Japan is falling behind. The situation is a prelude to revolution. There is a small possibility that the volcano will erupt, and that true revolutionary change will come.

Revolutions have occurred twice in Japan over the last one hundred and fifty years. The first was the so-called Meiji Restoration of 1868, sparked by Commodore Perry's opening of Japan. Overnight, Japan discarded a millennium of rule by shoguns and feudal lords, and established a modern nationalist state. The second revolution, led by the US Occupation after World War II, was the basis for the postwar rebuilding of Japan. Military dictatorship, Emperor worship, dominance by agrarian landlords – the entire edifice of the Meiji state was in turn discarded in favor of a bureaucratic industrial complex: 'Japan Incorporated'.

Japan's third revolution, if there is one, will have to be led from within. No one is seriously trying to open Japan's markets anymore. No one outside of Japan cares that Shochiku and Toho don't make good movies. Nor will they object if the Construction Ministry covers the whole country with concrete. There will be no Perry or MacArthur: the Japanese will have to do it themselves.

Trammell once told me, 'Success comes when you realize that no one is going to help you.' But Japan has trained its citizens for fifty years to be obedient and docile, to quietly await the bureaucrats' bidding. The revolution will not come easily.

Chapter 9

Kyoto

Kyoto Hates Kyoto

It was only after I had lived on the outskirts of Kyoto for eighteen years that I managed to enter the home of one its great old families. Kyoto is that kind of city. Restaurants and geisha houses routinely refuse entrance to the *ichigen* ('first look'); that is, a customer who has not been introduced. A foreign acquaintance once made the mistake of trying to make a booking at Doi, a lavish restaurant in the eastern hills. When he called, the owner asked, 'Do you know anyone who eats here?' 'No.' 'In that case,' she murmured in her soft Kyoto dialect, 'I must respectfully advise you to . . .' and here she slipped into English, 'forget it!'

Kyoto is unfriendly, and it is unfriendly for a reason: it is an endangered species. A way of life was built up in Kyoto which has miraculously survived all the changes of the nineteenth and twentieth centuries to make it into our time. It had relatively little to do with the city's famous monuments, such as the Gold Pavilion, the Silver Pavilion, Nijo Castle and the Hall of the

Thousand and One Buddhas, crowded though they are with tourists. The monuments stand unchanged from the past, but the Kyoto way of life is nearing its last gasp as modern development sweeps over it, and so the guardians of Kyoto culture are nervous. Their way of life is fragile, like a dying person who mustn't be allowed too many visitors lest he becomes overexcited. Only the few who really loved him can understand the world of significance in each feeble gesture and whisper.

The day I first visited that great house was in summer, during Gion Matsuri – a festival which takes place in the old neighborhoods in the heart of the city, bounded by Gojo, Oike, Kawaramachi and Karasuma streets. Over the course of the year, prominent houses in this district store wooden frameworks and decorations that are brought out into the streets for the festival and assembled into floats. The decorations, some of which are centuries old, include metalwork, lacquer, woodcarving, brocades and rugs. During the week of Gion Matsuri, hundreds of thousands of people, many dressed in summer kimono, mill through the streets, looking into the open windows of shops and houses decorated with folding screens and artworks. In the evening, children striking chimes sit in the upper balconies of the floats, beating out the slow hypnotic rhythm of the Gion music. On the final day, the floats parade through the city.

My guide was flower master Kawase Toshiro, who grew up next door to Rokkakud-o, the temple where ikebana was born, and is a Kyotoite down to his fingertips. Kawase is mostly active in Tokyo these days, so he was seeing the Gion festival for the first time in a few years; I had not attended in maybe ten years. How the city had changed! Where there were once rows of wooden houses, each hung with lanterns, most had been replaced with shopfronts of glass and aluminum. The narrow backstreets were impossibly crowded because little *yomise* (stalls) selling food, souvenirs and goldfish for children stood in front of most of the buildings. '*Yomise* are fun enough, I suppose,' said Kawase.

'They are what you see everywhere throughout Japan during the summer. But this is Kyoto! When I was a child, the main attraction was looking at the neighbors' artworks, and then playing in the streets with fireworks. We didn't need *yomise*!'

Kawase took me and a couple of friends to two houses. The first was an old Kyoto *machiya* (town house). Taxes used to be levied according to frontage, so the old houses of Kyoto tend to have narrow street entrances, and stretch far back into the interior of the block. The building's paper-and-wood sliding doors had been removed for summer, and replaced with doors made of reeds, *sudare* (bamboo blinds) and gauze hangings – all more or less transparent. As we walked through the house, the blinds and hangings revealed ever-changing vistas, with room after room, separated by gardens, disappearing into the distance. On the floor were blue Nabeshima rugs, each the size of one tatami mat.

Tradition in Japan demands a sweep of empty tatami mats, against a row of stark pillars made of white wood, and that is mostly what we see in modern versions of old architecture. But the residents of Kyoto overlaid the mats with coverings of blue and brown, and hung the pillars with bamboo blinds and gauze. Of course, being Kyoto, where only the suggestion of a decoration counts as true decoration, they did these things in moderation. They did not cover the whole floor with rugs; instead, they put Nabeshima on only a few mats where guests would sit. Most of the blinds and hangings were rolled up, allowing freedom to move around, and giving just the impression of blinds and hangings.

As we filed through the house, Kawase said, 'This house is old, of course, but it has been largely redone in the last few years. They Japanized it. They did an excellent job, and I'm glad it's here. But now let me show you the real thing.' We pushed our way through the crowds again, at last arriving at a complex of buildings and *kura*, surrounded by a long wall extending back a full block. This house, Kawase told us, was the last great house of inner Kyoto. The owners had almost lost the land a few years ago, and there was a plan to tear the house down and turn it into an apartment block. But a group of Kyotoites joined forces with the owner and saved it.

It was one of the houses that store the Gion float decorations, and the gateway was thronged with people coming to view the metalwork and brocades on display inside. Just beyond the gateway was a walkway, with a bamboo barrier at one end. Kawase pushed the barrier aside and motioned for us to step into the entranceway. The elder daughter of the house, dressed in a yellow kimono, bowed at the edge of the steps, and invited us in.

The din of the crowds outside faded away. Ahead of us was the foyer, decorated with long leaves of *susuki* grass in a vase. The *sudare* blinds were rolled up and secured with dangling ribbons of purple silk. Beyond the foyer was a small room looking out onto a garden of moss, one of the Kyoto *tsubo-niwa* ('gardens in a bottle'), encased by a high wall. You could see bits and pieces of the garden through oddly placed Mondrianesque openings – a square window at ground level covered with bamboo lattice, or an open wall hung with *shina-sudare* (bamboo blinds from China covered with pictures of birds and flowers, created by winding silk threads over each thin slat of bamboo).

From there, we entered another room, and then another, each separated by different types of doors or gauze hangings. There were a variety of floor coverings: blue and pale-orange Nabeshima, or a three-mat expanse of shiny brown paper dyed with persimmon juice, giving the room a crisp, cool feeling. I noticed a stone at the entrance to one of the inner gardens, with two straw sandals set neatly beside it. Beyond the stone was an inviting path leading through the moss to another part of the complex. As I was about to step into the sandals, Kawase stopped me. 'The sandals are arranged to the side of the stone, not on top of it. That means, "Don't go here".' He was alerting me to the subtle sign language of Kyoto life.

After centuries of political intrigue and relentless scrutiny by tea masters, the people of Kyoto have developed the technique of never saying anything. In conversation, the true Kyotoite waits patiently for the other person to figure out the answer for himself. Once, when I was staying overnight at a temple, I tried to ask the abbot how much it was going to cost. Guests stayed there all the time, and I knew there was a standard fee. 'Oh, you pay what you like,' the abbot began. My heart sank, and sure enough, it took almost two hours of tea drinking to drag the answer out of him. In fact, he never did tell me. He just kept giving me hints until I provided the answer myself.

Kyoto is full of little danger signs that the uninitiated can easily miss. Everyone in Japan has heard the legendary story of *bubuzuke* ('tea on rice'). 'Won't you stay and have some *bubuzuke*?' asks your Kyoto host, and this means that it is time to go. When you become attuned to Kyoto, a comment like this sets off an alarm system. On the surface, you are smiling, but inside your brain, red lights start flashing, horns blare *Aaooga, aaooga!* and people dash for cover. The old Mother Goddess of Oomoto, Naohi Deguchi, once described how you should accept tea in Kyoto. 'Do not drink the whole cup, 'she said. 'After you leave, your hosts will say, "They practically drank us out of house and home!" But, don't leave it undrunk, either. Then they will say, "How unfriendly not to drink our tea!" Drink just half a cup.'

The four of us sat down on rugs laid out by the *tokonoma*, while the two daughters of the house brought out tea, saké and, to my surprise, a small dinner. (This had involved yet more subtlety. 'I thought there might be food served,' said Kawase, 'when they asked me how many would be coming in my party.') 'Dinner' is not quite the right word. It was just a few small peeled potatoes, some slices of beef and some beans – providing the feeling of dinner rather than dinner itself. It was what they call in Kyoto 'one bite and a half'. Each serving was arranged in a bowl or tray of unpretentious white pottery or orange lacquerware.

Every detail was lovingly attended to, down to beads of dew on the green chopsticks made of freshly cut bamboo, which had been set in the freezer to chill. I could see in this 'feeling of a meal' the origins of *kaiseki*, the formal Japanese cuisine found in expensive restaurants. The difference is that *kaiseki* tends to be a heavy-handed, elaborate affair, with dozens of dishes and lots of little decorative devices. This meal, while elegant, was as simple as it could be. 'The food served in a Kyoto house,' remarked Kawase, 'should stop just short of being the kind of dinner you feel you should write a thank-you letter for. Any more than that would be ostentatious.'

Evening began to fall. 'The Gion music will soon begin,' said the elder daughter. 'I can't imagine living any place where I would be out of earshot of the Gion music in summer.' That rules out the rest of the world, and even most of Kyoto, other than a few square blocks. As she sat there in her yellow kimono, one hand resting in her lap like the hand of a Buddha, the other lying with fingers bent backwards on the tatami, it struck me that we were talking to a princess. Keeping a precise distance from us, seated at just the right angle on the tatami, she chatted politely but with an occasional flash direct to the heart. I could see the origin of tea ceremony: the combination of politeness and the appeal to the heart. But so often in tea ceremonies the politeness is suffocating; here, it was like fresh air.

The room grew dark. The two sisters brought Japanese candles on tall bronze stands from behind *sudare* hangings, and set them out in a row before a wall lined with folding screens. We sat entranced, watching the silhouettes of the two women flickering in the candlelight. Tea was served, and I thought, 'It was all leading up to this. I'll just sit here for a moment, relax and enjoy this while it lasts.' But it was not to be. 'Tea,' whispered Kawase, nudging me, 'that means it's time to go.'

Such was the life inside the houses of old Kyoto. However, for all their refinement, the people of Kyoto were not aristocrats (with the exception of a handful of *kuge* nobles living around the palace), nor did they run big enterprises like the merchants of Osaka. Kyoto was and is a city of shopkeepers. Power moved from Kyoto to Tokyo (then called Edo) at the beginning of the 1600s, and Edo boasted feudal mansions ten times larger than the Kyoto *machiya*. Removed from real power and big money, Kyoto became a backwater, the center of crafts such as silk weaving and dyeing, woodwork and lacquerware. It was the interlinked world of thousands of craftsmen that defined the city.

My favorite craftsman is my mounter, Kusaka, who was my guide to the Kyoto antique auctions. His studio is in another old area of the city, not far from the geisha district of Gion. As you approach Kusaka's studio, you pass a store selling beans. It is typical of the intense specialization of old Kyoto: in front of the shop are four trays, displaying black, white, red and purple beans. That is all. On arriving at Kusaka's studio, the first thing you notice is the display window. On a red lacquer stand is a gourd-shaped vase, and from its neck there gracefully stretches a single flower. By its side hangs a scroll with a whimsical painting of a sparrow. This window is old Kusaka's playground: he seeks out flowers, selects just the right scroll to match them, and arranges a display to please the passing townspeople.

Inside the shop, Kusaka sits surrounded by a mountain of folding screens and hanging scrolls. I have brought a calligraphy scroll with me to be mounted. So far, I've found no one who can decipher it, but Kusaka reads the archaic forms without hesitation. 'It is one of the "Eight Scenes of Omi Province",' he informs me. Then the talk turns to its mounting. 'This calligraphy was made for tea ceremony, so the cloth strips at the top and bottom should be made of Takeyamachi silk,' he says, and brings down from a shelf a piece of Takeyamachi fabric he bought twenty-five years ago. It is white silk gauze, interwoven with flowers made of gold paper threads. The conversation broadens, moving on to the other types of material which will frame the piece, the shape and lacquering of the roller ends, and so on. Along the way, Kusaka tells me about the 'Eight Scenes of Omi Province', which turns out to be the Japanese version of the Chinese 'Eight Scenes of the Xiao and Xiang Rivers'. Kusaka, now in his nineties, is a true scholar.

Master that he is, Kusaka is only one of Kyoto's many expert artisans. Observing the process by which a folding screen is made illustrates the way the Kyoto craft world works. First, Kusaka has a wooden framework made to order at the carpenter's. On this he glues paper from Mino, with glue made by the glue-maker near Nijo Station. With a wide brush bought from the brush-maker on Teramachi Street, Kusaka smooths and flattens the paintings, and backs them with more glue and paper. He stretches them on drying boards coated with persimmon juice purchased from the persimmon-juice brewery near the Kyoto Hotel. About a month later, he uses a bamboo spatula carved by the bambooware-maker to peel the paintings from the drying boards. He takes the paintings to the restorer, who uses gold leaf from the gold and silver shop on Oike Street, and ground mineral pigments from the paint store behind the Tawaraya Inn. Next, Kusaka glues the paintings onto the screen, and frames them with mounting brocades ordered from the weaver, which he has dyed with colors from the dye-maker. Lastly, Kusaka has the lacquer specialist paint the edges of the outer frame, and adds metal fittings supplied by the bronze-ware shop. If this were a hanging scroll, then he would still need to have a box-maker craft a paulownia-wood box for it, and to then request a tea master to do the calligraphy on the box.

I include the tea master among the 'artisans' here because it is a fact that all of Kyoto's arts are unified by tea. Folding screens and hanging scrolls are made to the dictates of tea masters, to harmonize with their gardens and flowers. Kusaka's store window, at first glance, seems to convey nothing much to do with mounting. Yet because it reveals a tea aesthetic, it is a true window to the artisan's world.

In its prime, Kyoto was a city that had mastered the art of relaxation. Many traces of this remain, notably the outdoor restaurants set up on high pilings over the river in summer. People sit in the night air fanning themselves, a rare sight in Japan, which has very little in the way of street cafés or outdoor restaurants. In the winter, I sometimes go with a friend to Imamiya Shrine, to the north of the city, where two old *aburimochi* (grilled rice cake) shops stand facing each other. The shops are rather out of the way so tourists rarely venture there. The rice cakes are put on bamboo skewers, covered with sweet miso sauce and then grilled over charcoal. Entering one of the rickety old shops, we sit in a tatami room and leisurely eat our sweet rice cakes while talking of this or that. Outside is the cold Kyoto winter; inside, the atmosphere is warm and cheery.

The rice-cake restaurants are hardly the most glamorous of spots. The tatami are old and tattered, the gardens are not neatly kept, and the overall air is shabby, even 'poor'. They are in striking contrast to today's Japan, where the smell of money everywhere is overwhelming, and everything has been polished and made perfectly neat and sterile. But beauty is not limited to brand new tatami and pure white wood: somewhere deep in people's hearts 'poor' brings with it a sense of relaxation and ease.

Another word for 'poor' would be *wabi* – the rallying cry of tea ceremony. It means 'worn' or 'humble', and refers to the use of rough, simple objects and a lack of ostentation. Not only did *wabi* transform tea ceremony, but it was perfectly adapted to the city of Kyoto, whose residents could not afford the luxuries of Edo or Osaka. Poverty-stricken *kuge* nobles and middle-class shopkeepers used *wabi* as a weapon to establish their cultural superiority. It was a form of deceit, carried to the level of art. A crudely fashioned brown tea bowl was held up as superior to the most elaborately decorated Imari platter, and nobody ever dared ask why. Bamboo blinds disguised small rooms and shiny paper covered worn tatami. *Wabi* was Kyoto's unique achievement: a rug, a bamboo hanging, a meal of 'one bite and a half' – all were manipulated to create an effect superior to the gold-leafed halls of feudal lords.

But aside from a few relics like the *aburi mochi* shops at Imamiya Shrine, *wabi* is no longer alive and well in Kyoto today. This is because the city of Kyoto is, unfortunately, quite ill. Go visit the headquarters of the various schools of flower-arranging and tea ceremony. The hereditary grand masters of these organizations are revered as the guardians of *wabi* and other sacred principles of Japanese art. But what do you find? Marble lobbies with gleaming chandeliers. If even the guardians of culture have forgotten their roots, then the sickness of Kyoto is far advanced.

Kyoto hates Kyoto. It is probably the world's only cultural center of which this is true. The Romans love Rome. Beijing suffered greatly during the Cultural Revolution, but most of the damage was wreaked by outsiders, and the citizens of Beijing still love their city. But the people of Kyoto cannot bear the fact that Kyoto is not Tokyo. They are trying with all their might to catch up with Tokyo, but they will never come close. This has been going on a long time. I first noticed the malaise shortly after moving to Kyoto. I asked a friend, 'When did the unhappiness set in?' and he answered, 'Around 1600.' In other words, the people of Kyoto never forgave Edo for usurping its place as capital. When the Emperor moved to Tokyo in 1868, that was the final blow to Kyoto's self-esteem.

While Nara and other cities have also been uglified, this was mostly the result of thoughtless city planning. In Kyoto, however, the destruction was deliberate. People coming to the city for the first time are shocked by the sight of the needle-shaped Kyoto Tower standing by Kyoto Station. This tower was built in 1964, at the urging of the city government, expressly to break the line of old tiled roofs, which were thought to look old-fashioned. The city was trying to tell visitors, 'We are modern, we have nothing to do with all this old stuff around us.' Despite the fact that tens of thousands of people signed a petition opposing the building of the tower, the city pushed it through.

It was the symbolic stake through the heart. The construction of Kyoto Tower was followed by the rapid destruction of most of the old town, leaving only temples and shrines untouched. Each step of the way was marked with open attacks on the city's heritage by the municipal administration. The most dramatic attack came quite recently with the rebuilding of Kyoto Station. A competition was held, to which both foreign and Japanese architects submitted a number of plans, some of them incorporating traditional features such as sloping tiled roofs. There was a super-modern design by the architect Tadao Ando in the shape of a great gate, reminiscent of the gates that used to stand on the edge of the city. But the selection committee rejected them all and chose the one plan that denied Kyoto's history in every way. Designed by the leading architect at Kyoto University, it is a huge box faced with glass which looks rather like an airport lobby. There could be no greater proof of Kyoto's hatred of Kyoto.

As the city has degenerated, the monks in their temples, living in a world divorced from the life around them, have also lost track of what they are preserving. I used to always take guests to Entsu-ji, a quiet temple far to the north of Kyoto, which has a sublime example of 'borrowed scenery'. You enter from a narrow corridor, and suddenly the scenery opens out before you. The garden beyond the verandah is a carpet of moss in which are placed long flat stones. You raise your eyes, to be met with a long hedge at the far side of the garden. Look higher and you can see a grove of bamboo appearing from behind the hedge, and beyond that is Mt Hiei, rising between two trees like a painting framed in pine. The scenery of the inner garden and the outer world are in marvelous harmony. I have visited Entsu-ji many times, sat on the verandah and spent light-hearted hours looking out at that scene. However, when I brought a friend there recently, I realized that even Entsu-ji has been infected with the Kyoto malaise. The view was as beautiful as ever, but the 'quiet' verandah was not so quiet. A taped explanation of the garden by the head priest was being noisily broadcast over a public-address system. My friend felt ill at ease, and we left quickly.

I always recommend three travel items to friends who visit Japan: slip-on shoes to go easily in and out of Japanese buildings; loose pants or dresses so as to be able to sit comfortably on the floor; and earplugs to block out the noise at Zen temples. Ryoan-ji, site of the famous rock garden, was notorious for its taped announcements, although it has cut them back recently due to frequent complaints from foreign tourists. On the back of the admission ticket to Ryoan-ji is written: 'Quietly open your inner mind, and converse within the self'. Clearly, the people in charge of the temple have forgotten what this means.

The garden at the Daisen-in temple in the grounds of Daitoku-ji is one of Zen's great masterpieces. It begins with a landscape of jagged rocks from which a river of sand flows – reminiscent of Ni Tsan's mountain wildernesses. As you walk along the verandah, you come across a stone in the shape of a boat in the river of sand. You can feel your point of view being drawn closer. Then you round the corner, and the river of sand opens wide, with just two mounds of sand in it. You are now so close you are looking at the ripples themselves. And finally, there is only flat sand, the world of *mu*, or 'nothingness', which is at the core of Zen. But what do you see at that point? A large metal sign with red lettering saying 'Daisen-in. Cultural Property. HITACHI'.

At last count, Daisen-in features four signs saying 'HITACHI', and you will find them in front of most other historical monuments. Why the Cultural Ministry decided to make Hitachi advertisements a part of Japan's cultural heritage is a mystery. In Paris, you don't find a sign saying 'Notre Dame. RENAULT', or in Bangkok, 'The Emerald Buddha. THAI CEMENT'. In fact, at such cultural sights, you don't see advertisements at all.

The end result of decades of purposeful destruction is that today Kyoto consists of very well-preserved temples and shrines, situated in an urban conglomeration of electric wires, metal and plastic. The monks fill their gardens with signs and loudspeakers; the centers of traditional art fill their headquarters with polished granite. In the modern city there is no place for kimono, screens, scrolls and most of the other traditional crafts, all of which are in terminal decline. For students of history, this is fine. They will push their way through the urban jungle to the Gold Pavilion, and be pleased that it is Muromachi period; and then they will go to the Hall of the Thousand and One Buddhas, where they can learn about Kamakura-period sculpture. But for everyone else, for people who simply want to take a stroll and enjoy the atmosphere of a place, Kyoto no longer satisfies. So it is being replaced by a totally new type of cultural attraction: European theme parks. There are several of these in Japan, the largest being Shima Spain Village, in Mie Prefecture, and Huis ten Bosch, the Dutch town near Nagasaki. Already, the total number of visitors to these places is approaching the number who come to Kyoto, and within a few years will outstrip it. In particular, travelers from Southeast Asia are flocking to Huis ten Bosch.

When I first heard about Huis ten Bosch I was baffled. What interest could a reconstruction of a Dutch town possibly have, when in Kyoto and Nara, Japan had its own traditional cities? I went to visit Huis ten Bosch on behalf of a Japanese magazine, intending to write an exposé of this cultural travesty. But what I found there took me completely aback. It is perhaps the single most beautiful place I have seen in Japan in ten years. There are no signs, no wires, no plastic, no loudspeakers and no HITACHI. All the buildings are faced with rough-surfaced bricks and natural materials; the interiors, as well, are decorated with the most sensitive attention to color and lighting. Even the embankments along the sea are made of piled-up rocks, instead of concrete, in order to preserve the ecosystem of the shore. In my modern hotel in Huis ten Bosch, I sat on a wooden deck built out over a canal, and listened to the birds chirp while I ate my breakfast. In Kyoto, something like this might be possible in one of the remaining old inns, but it is completely out of the question in any of Kyoto's dreary modern hotels. Huis ten Bosch was everything the new Kyoto is not – namely, peaceful and beautiful. To my great embarrassment as a lover of Japanese art, I could hardly bear to leave the place.

The future of Japan, and possibly of all East Asia, is going to be theme parks. As living cities like Kyoto decay, they will be replaced by copies. For example, even as the Chinese are leveling vast stretches of the old city of Beijing, there are plans to build a new 'old Chinese city' of thousands of homes just outside town. In Japan, the most popular copies at the moment are of European cities, but the time is not far off when the Japanese will begin copying themselves. In the town of Ise, for example, a large tourist village built in pseudo-traditional style has been developed near the gates of the Grand Shrine of Ise.

Tamasaburo said recently, 'Kyoto is beyond preservation. The next step will be re-creation.' In some ways this will be a good thing, especially if it results in buildings such as the first *machiya* that Kawase took us to. But if it is just a matter of the look of things, then Kyoto will probably never do it as well as a well-planned theme park. The sad thing is that copying the past is not necessary. There are many ways of bringing *wabi* into the modern world. For example, buildings made of untreated cement slabs, pioneered by Japanese architects, are an attempt to use rough, simple materials in a sophisticated way – contemporary *wabi*. There are some rare modern masterpieces in the city, such as Ando Tadao's Times Building, where Ando incorporated the Takase River into the overall design. Architecture like this takes the spirit of Kyoto's tradition and translates it into modern media. Ando's building points the way to a middle road between the use of wood and paper, and the use of shiny marble and plastic. That road, rather than simply endlessly guarding the past, would have been the most exciting one for Kyoto. But it was the path not taken.

Kyoto's great treasure did not lie in its temples and shrines, nor in the outward look of its streets. It lay in the intricately complex customs and elegant life of its citizens. They were proud people who felt they were above common pleasures like the *yomise* stalls which everyone else enjoys in summer. Over the centuries, they spun for themselves a gorgeous web of *wabi*, with all its artifice, snobbery and artistic refinement. This still survives, but barely. When it goes, I will move to Huis ten Bosch.

Chapter 10

The Road to Nara

Follies

I am often asked to show guests around Kyoto and Nara. Typically, we start with Kyoto, but after a few days or so there comes a moment when I can see my guest beginning to grow weary. The intense refinement and detailed conventions of Kyoto life become oppressive. Of course, no one ever goes so far as to voice the word; most people are not even conscious of the feeling, but its presence shows clearly in the glazed look of their eyes. This is when we leave Kyoto for Nara.

Japan's first capitals in the sixth and seventh centuries were situated on the Yamato plain, southwest of Nara. The capital moved frequently, gradually working its way up to present-day Nara in 720, and then northwest to Kyoto in 794. The moving capital left temples, shrines, palaces and tombs in its wake, scattered over a huge area on the plains and in the mountains surrounding Nara – Yamato, Asuka, Yoshino, Koya and Uji. Later rulers piously continued to support these relics, and so the building and rebuilding of Nara went on long after power had moved elsewhere. 'Nara' is thus much larger than simply the city of Nara or the period when Nara was capital. It encompasses the entire region between Kyoto and Wakayama, built up over a thousand years between the sixth and sixteenth centuries.

Until the sixth century, Japan's history is cloudy: only archaeological digs indicate what life before that time was like. But in the sixth to eighth centuries, Japan adopted Chinese writing, architecture and Buddhism, and the basic framework of Japanese culture emerged from the mist. Ancient Shinto, Imperial power, esoteric Buddhism, the role of the court nobles, early poetry and arts of wood and stone took primal shape. These were the rough timbers which Kyoto culture was later to refine into polished and squared wood.

Kyoto culture stops at around Kyoto Station: in my view, everything south and east of the train station belongs more to Nara than to Kyoto. So my guests and I start out from the station, driving south along the foothills of Kyoto's eastern mountains. Here stand Sennyu-ji, Tofuku-ji and other temples, nestled in enormous tree-filled grounds along the hillsides. There are very few tourists, and the atmosphere is expansive and relaxed. Inside Tofuku-ji, there is a small deck jutting out from the main temple, above a ravine overhung with maple trees. Standing on that deck, looking out over leaves rustling in the wind and a small wooden bridge far below, one feels deep in the hills, although the temple is only ten minutes south of Kyoto Station.

Much has been written about the way Japanese buildings harmonize with nature, but there is another side to this: the strong tendency to bind and restrict nature. The gardens of Kyoto developed from this tendency, with every tree carefully pruned and set amongst discreet rectangles spread with white sand. Once I was seated on the verandah of a Zen temple in Kyoto and I praised the shape of a particularly well-formed pine branch. 'Well, it's not quite right,' apologized the abbot. 'It's taken about one hundred and fifty years to get it to this point, but I'd say another seventy, no, eighty years, and it will be perfect.'

I personally appreciate the desire to bring order to a garden, having spent years fighting the weeds and vines at Tenmangu and Chiiori; if you turn your back for a minute, all is immediately overgrown with unruly greenery. So when the early Japanese built a temple or a palace, the first thing they did was to make a clearing in the woods and spread it with gravel. This was called the *saniwa*, or 'sand garden', and important acts of government took place there: criminals were judged, and shrine maidens went into a trance and delivered the oracle of the gods. In later times, under the influence of Zen and martial discipline, the *saniwa* became the basis of the Zen rock gardens that exist in Kyoto today.

The rock garden of Ryoan-ji in Kyoto is known worldwide, and much ink has been spilled describing the layout of its rocks, the raking of the sand and even the surface texture of the surrounding wall. But nobody ever talks about the shady trees behind the wall. This is like talking about fish while ignoring the sea. The garden at Ryoan-ji lives because of the surrounding trees. Problems arise when the roots of a tradition like the *saniwa* are forgotten, and it expands beyond its native environment. Golf, as practiced on the rounded grassy slopes of Scotland, was a benign sport, combining the pursuit of leisure with enjoyment of the outdoors. But the courses being built all over the world today, which require drastic alterations to deserts, forests and mountains, have wreaked untold environmental damage. Likewise, the sand gardens of Kyoto worked because they existed within the surroundings of the rich, native forest. As the forests disappear, or are replaced with stands of industrial pine, there is less and less need for sand gardens. Applied indiscriminately to modern urban surroundings, the tradition of raked sand creates only sterility. Sometimes I think the aim of Japan's ruling bureaucracies is to turn the entire nation into a *saniwa*, in which patches of greenery exist only as slight variations in a sea of white concrete. This is the modern context for the deck at Tofuku-ji, where the maple branches spread out unrestrained and the little bridge in the ravine is the only sign of human presence.

Just south of Tofuku-ji is Fushimi-inari Grand Shrine, also built along the eastern hillside. It is the main shrine of the Inari cult, dedicated to the god of rice (and therefore money and prosperity), and the god's messengers, foxes. There are numerous Inari shrines in Japan, but this is the largest and oldest of them. The Japanese rarely bring foreign visitors here because the shrine has little in the way of architecture or gardens of historical importance. Also, the hundreds of small shrines in its precincts devoted to fox spirits and magical stones smack of animism and superstition.

The gardens of Kyoto, in addition to being highly controlled, usually have fixed spots such as verandahs from which to view them. There is a strong sense that these gardens are 'art', with particular points of view from which they must be seen. But Fushimi-inari is not one site to be viewed from one angle; it is an experience that you must pass through, like dreaming. At the entrance is an enormous cinnabar-red *torii* gate, and beyond that, an outdoor stage and main hall. Before the main hall are two large fox statues: one with its mouth open, the other holding a key in its teeth. (Foxes are considered to be magical creatures, with the ability to bewitch human beings.) Above the entrance is a banner with another symbol of Inari, a flaming jewel, which also represents occult power. Behind the main hall is a procession of several hundred red *torii*, lined up so close together that they make a tunnel. Most visitors walk through this row of gates, then return home feeling a little disappointed. But they have turned back at the entrance to the dreamworld.

If you continue walking up the hill beyond the first row of *torii*, you find another row of red gates, much larger than the first ones, and another row beyond that; in fact, a procession of tens of thousands, maybe hundreds of thousands, of *torii* wind ever deeper into the mountains. Each *torii* bears the name of the business that donated it. Many businesses in Japan have a red Inari *torii* somewhere, either on their premises in a small altar or in the grounds of an Inari shrine.

Few people venture up into this quiet vermilion world. You climb up over knolls and into dells, gradually making your way deeper into the hillside, but looking back or looking ahead you see nothing but rows of red *torii* encased in a green forest. Vermilion is the color of magic. It was the color of Chinese Taoism, and since the Shang dynasty thousands of years ago it has been revered as being sacred to the gods. In the *Analects*, vermilion signifies noble qualities. Confucius said, 'How regrettable when purple usurps the place of vermilion' – meaning, 'when the vulgar usurps the place of the noble'.

From Taoism, vermilion entered Buddhism, becoming the color of temples and, later, palaces. Most of the ancient structures of Kyoto and Nara were once brilliant red, but the color faded as the temples aged. Meanwhile, Kyoto developed its culture of *wabi*, in which all color was watered down and muted. In the process, 'art' took over and 'magic' faded along with the vermilion. But at Fushimi-inari, the color is still alive, evoking ancient Taoism.

After walking for a while, you come upon groups of small altars, known as *tsuka* (mounds). Here, repeated in miniature, are the Inari themes first seen at the main shrine: each altar features a pair of animals, a stone stand and a magical stone behind the stand. There may be banners or carvings with the flaming jewel on them. On the stone stands you will find offerings of five or six grains of rice, one-yen coins, rows of tiny red *torii* and mini-bottles of saké, of the sort sold in vending machines. You will also find Japanese-style candles burning on the altars, with twisting fire rising from their wicks, echoing the motif of the flaming jewels. The atmosphere is more akin to Hinduism than to anything usually associated with Japan.

Some *tsuka* are higher than head height, others lower than one's knees. They stand alone or in knots of tens. Foxes predominate, but there are also horses, snakes, squirrels, dogs, cats and even crocodiles. You are looking at Shinto's animist and occult roots. The repetition, large and small, of a few basic themes – the flaming jewel, the red *torii*, the foxes – creates a hallucinatory atmosphere. I think this inevitably happens in places where a set of forms is endlessly repeated, such as in Venice (canals, bridges, lions, Gothic windows).

You can wander for hours under the *torii* and through the collections of stone altars, and as you do so, it's easy to become completely disoriented. I once went walking with Diane along Fushimi-inari's upper paths, and we lost our way. It began to grow dark, and the flickering candles made the scene utterly fantastical. We caught sight of someone coming towards us, but when we drew near, we found that he had become a stone fox. In the end we practically ran down the mountain, terrified of losing our wits amongst the foxes.

It is interesting to compare Fushimi with the Grand Shrine of Ise; with its pale wood and simple angular designs, Ise is often held up as Shinto at its purest. Unpainted and unadorned, the brute strength of its buildings conjures up a sense of awe, as if you are in the presence of a great divine power. There is nothing at Fushimi to even approach this. However, as for 'Shinto at its purest', I believe that Ise has strayed a bit from the true origins of Shinto. The fences enclosing the grounds and buildings are neatly laid out with perfect symmetry, their concentric rings demarcating inner precincts of increasing sacredness. In this arrangement can be seen the influence of Chinese palace architecture. But pure Japanese style in art and architecture has always involved the staggered, even higgledy-piggledy, placement of things. Apart from Kyoto and Nara, which were modeled after Chinese capitals, no Japanese city shows an ordered plan; Edo, the Shogun's capital, was the most haphazard of them all. In China, the ruler's palace was square or rectangular, with a central avenue leading up to it, and gates located north and south. The palace precinct in Edo, however, was an amorphous blob, surrounded by a zigzag of moats and ramparts, with no grand avenue, and no order to the gates or interior buildings.

Chinese axial symmetry has great power, but Japan's zigzag arrangement of things can also be very pleasing, as a walk along the rear of the palace moat in Tokyo still proves. The zigzag approach led to the complicated crisscross of spatial arrangements found in tea ceremony, as well as the slashing diagonals found in paintings on folding screens, and the design of woodblock prints – almost everything traditional or modern which looks 'Japanese'. The origins of this style can be seen in the chaotic layout of the *tsuka* at Fushimi-inari.

From Fushimi, I take my guests south to Byodo-in, the Phoenix Pavilion, which is known to everyone in Japan because its image is on the back of the ten-yen coin. It was built at the height of the Heian period by a Fujiwara prime minister, and is one of only a handful of surviving Heian-period temples in Japan. Its design is unique: there is a central hall, on either side of which are two outspread wings with raised eaves, facing a lake. The building looks like a phoenix alighting on the lake; hence the name. Byodo-in belongs neither to the Kyoto that was built after military rule began in the twelfth century, nor to religiously devout early Nara. It is an air pocket, a survivor from a realm we know little about today: the world of the idle Heian aristocrats.

Byodo-in is simultaneously a temple and not a temple. Only the central hall, which enshrines Amida, Buddha of the Western Paradise, is a temple; the rest of the building appears to be almost entirely useless. For instance, from the rear of the main hall projects a building that corresponds to the tail of the phoenix; other than simply representing a tail, it has no apparent function. Then, looking at the wings springing from either side of the main hall, you notice that the first floor is nothing but a high colonnade.

The upper level is also open to the air, with neither walls nor sliding doors. The lintels are lower than human height, making it difficult for people to even enter. It is hard to imagine what the upper level was ever used for, although one guess is that orchestras sat and played music there, while the aristocrats boated on the lake.

I was once invited to an old estate in England, and while taking a walk around the grounds, I came across a garden surrounded by high hedges. In the middle of the garden was a tiny round temple straight out of Greek myth. On asking the owner of the estate what this building was for, she told me it wasn't for anything; it was simply a 'folly'. Follies exist all over England, but they are hard to find in Japan. The most luxurious buildings and gardens, such as the Katsura Detached Palace, were all created with distinct functions in mind. The ultimate luxury – complete functionlessness – is absent. Zen, in particular, is a serious affair: *mu* (nothingness) is a virtue, but *muyo* (functionlessness) is a sin. Zen gardens are designed with a specific aim in mind, to serve as aids in meditation or as guideposts on the way to enlightenment. In other words, gazing at a Zen garden does not come free: there is a spiritual bill to be paid for the pleasure. In contrast, Byodo-in is a perfect folly, born from the caprice of the Heian aristocracy. Gazing at it, you feel a sense of lightness, a desire to fly up into the heavens together with the phoenix. In post-Heian Japan, strictly ruled by military overlords, such caprice was almost unthinkable. Byodo-in is one of the few places in Japan that breathes the air of freedom.

After Byodo-in, I take my friends to the city of Nara. Just before we enter Nara Park, where the most famous temples are preserved, we stop at Hannya-ji Temple. Rarely visited by tourists, it is dedicated to Monju, the Bodhisattva of Wisdom. Its gate is another bird-like construction, with wide eaves flung upwards into the sky. Inside is a garden of the type found only in Nara: a tangle of wildflowers, mostly cosmos, growing in profusion

alongside the paths and on the base of the temple's tall stone
pagoda.

In Kyoto, and most other places in Japan, such wildness would
never be tolerated. I recently visited the site of the reconstruction
of a large Zen temple in Takaoka on the Sea of Japan coast, and
was astonished to hear the supervisor, a senior official of the Cultural Ministry, say with pride, 'The central courtyard of this
temple used to be filled with *keaki* and pine trees hundreds of
years old. So we cut all these unsightly trees down, and now we
will be able to spread the entire courtyard, a full one thousand
tsubo, with raked white sand.' Such is the vision of Japan's Cultural Ministry! But at Hannya-ji, wildflowers still grow untamed.
Inside the temple, a charming statue of Monju, seated on his
lion, gazes out over the sea of cosmos flowers and contemplates
the flow of the centuries undisturbed.

From Hannya-ji, my guests and I descend into Nara Park, our
destination being Nandaimon, the Great Southern Gate of
Todai-ji Temple. For most visitors, the main attractions of the
park are Todai-ji's Hall of the Great Buddha and Kasuga Shrine,
with its walkway lined with hundreds of stone lanterns. Nandaimon is seen as no more than something you have to walk under
to get to Todai-ji. However, for me, Nandaimon is the one perfect
structure in the park. Built during the thirteenth century, when
timber was plentiful, its huge pillars soar almost twenty-one
meters into the air. The towering figures of two wrathful temple
guardians are Kamakura originals, with furious faces and
immense power in their bulging muscles. But most breathtaking
of all is the massive roof, with eaves flung outwards and upwards
like a bird taking flight.

The bird analogy recalls Byodo-in and Hannya-ji, and this is
because all three buildings were built under the influence of Song
and Yuan China. During this period, the Chinese experimented
with architecture as fantasy, piling up multiple pavilions decorated with curling eaves. Almost every one of these buildings has

perished in China, and only a very few remain in Japan, most of them in the area surrounding Nara. Ancient Chinese roofs from the old heartland in the north were originally straight A-frames. But gradually, a new influence began creeping up into China from Southeast Asia. As can still be seen today, the eaves of Thai and Burmese buildings transform into flame shapes as they extend downwards, then swoop back up into the sky. By Sung and Yuan times, the Chinese were experimenting with rising eaves, and this style was transmitted to Japan.

Japan was on the receiving end of influences from all over Asia and the Pacific, and, as a result, it had a wonderful variety of roofs. In addition to Sung and Yuan flaring eaves, there were palm-thatched stilt-houses from the south, with the upper half of the roof expanding outwards, Polynesian style. Another type of roof can be seen in the pit dwellings of the Yayoi period – holes cut into the earth, with a round, tent-like roof dropping almost to the ground. Indigenous Japanese roof styles mingled with those imported from the mainland and the islands of the South Seas to create the widest range of styles found in any nation in East Asia. As a result, Japan's old cities, particularly Kyoto and Nara, had truly spectacular roof lines.

Rising eaves create a feeling of uplift and release, which can hardly be explained away as just a trend in architecture. The Taoist scholar John Blofeld once said to me, 'In ancient Southeast Asia, the very raising of a building was considered taboo. Sinking pillars into the ground and setting a roof above them was believed to be a sin against Mother Earth. So they took the eaves that pointed down towards the earth and turned them back up towards the heavens. By doing this, they were absolved of having broken the taboo.'

The upswept roof became a part of Japanese architecture, and even in the thatched roofs of Iya, extra rice straw was added under the eaves to give them a little lift. However, the extreme upsweeping of eaves as in Nandaimon, or the gate of Hannya-ji

Temple, is rare in Japan. In the Edo period, there was even a movement away from rising eaves when tea masters designed their pavilions to be very low, with straight roofs of many angles mixed in a jumble. It was a return to the 'zigzag' approach to life visible at Fushimi-inari, and it developed as part of a playful type of architecture known as *suki*.

Suki was the final destination of the *wabi* of Kyoto. Typically, art movements go through three phases: 'early', characterized by strength and simplicity; 'classical', when all elements reach harmonious maturity; and 'baroque', distorted and elaborate. *Wabi* followed a similar pattern. In its early period, it could not have been simpler, the purest *wabi* composition being Murata Juko's tea garden (circa 1500) in the temple of Shinju-an in Kyoto: a little strip of moss running along a temple verandah, with three rocks, five rocks, seven rocks. That is all. Later, when tea ceremony came into its own in the seventeenth century, *wabi* entered a classical period, resulting in dramatic creations like the Katsura Detached Palace, where villas and tea pavilions stretch over acres of artificial hills and ponds. The scale is large and the designs are complex – alternating squares of blue and white paper pasted onto sliding doors, rock pathways inset with a mixture of long rectangles and small squares.

In the eighteenth century, the decorative conceits of Katsura went one step further, resulting in *suki*: proof that in the hands of architects and designers even the simplest art can become baroque. It was an architecture focused on details: a window here, a verandah there. The emphasis was still on natural materials, but now they were combined in fanciful and elaborate ways, with curved pillars in the *tokonoma*, lattices of unusual woods, and antique roof tiles and the bases of old columns placed for effect in moss gardens. In roofs, it produced a mix of thatch, tile, bark and copper, with eaves projecting every which way.

In East Asia the roof is everything – whether flared or projecting. Stand in front of the massive Higashi Hongan-ji Temple in

Kyoto, and you realize that fully three-quarters of the total height of the building is roof. Think about the Forbidden City in Beijing, or the Royal Palace of Bangkok, and you will find that you are thinking almost exclusively of roofs. Thus, when the administrators of Kyoto and Nara set about destroying these cities, they began with the roofs. In the case of Kyoto, they built Kyoto Tower and dealt a mortal blow to the city's roof line. In Nara, the jutting concrete ridges of Nara Prefectural Office had the same effect. Ever since its completion in 1965, generations of tourists have had to screen its unsightly concrete spears out of their photographs. It was as strong an attack on the roof line of Nandaimon and its neighbors as could be imagined. Luckily, however, Nara does not suffer from the self-hatred which afflicts Kyoto, so subsequent developments in the park are more promising. A large civic building, recently completed, has sweeping tiled roofs very much in the spirit of Nara architecture.

The traditional roof styles of East Asia face a mixed future. In Japan, most cities have already been turned into a jungle of concrete blocks, and the process is far advanced in Bangkok and Beijing as well. Swooping, curving and flaring roofs have turned out to be one of the most difficult cultural traditions to integrate with modernism. There was a period in prewar Japan, and in 1950s China, when large modern structures were capped by wide tiled roofs. But no self-respecting modern architect would be caught dead doing this today.

While extravagant roof lines are dying out in Japan's city centers, they live on in the suburbs and countryside, and newly built houses in these areas commonly feature the complex joints and ridges of *suki*-style roofs. In general, however, Japanese architects have almost completely failed to integrate their own traditions into contemporary urban life. The only reason why interesting roofs survive in the suburbs is because residential architecture is considered a secondary area in Japan and has been ignored.

In the West, postmodern architects awoke from half a century of relentless modernism and rediscovered the traditions of the arch, the dome and the column, and they succeeded in incorporating these into a new modern idiom. Thailand, because of its thriving tourist industry, has seen imaginative experimentation with traditional-style roofs in modern architecture. Hotels such as the Amanpuri in Phuket or the Sukhothai in Bangkok are particularly successful examples. In Japan, however, the elite architects concentrate on building square office towers; sometimes, the more daring of them will incorporate arches and columns in the Western postmodernist manner.

The modernism which swept the West in the 1950s and '60s is still clung to with almost religious fervor in Japan. In this, one can see Japan's conservative habit of clinging to outside influences long after they have been discarded in their country of origin. For example, high-school students in Japan still wear black military uniforms with high collars and brass buttons, a style imported from Prussia in the nineteenth century.

A taste of Japan's resistance to change and fear of departing from Western models was provided by the 1995 Venice Biennale. The government decided to entrust Japan's exhibition to an art expert named Ito Junji, who proposed organizing the entry around modern *suki* design. Although still minor in influence, *suki* has undergone a renaissance recently, inspiring a group of younger contemporary artists and architects. There was a huge outcry from the 'traditionalists'; that is, the old-style modernists. A leading photographer dropped out in protest against this unwarranted intrusion of 'Japaneseness'. Ito was raked over the coals by art critics who warned that 'Japanese artists will no longer be able to eat at the main table of contemporary art'.

The old-fashioned 'modern' architecture jamming Japanese cities is in touch with neither Japan's cultural roots nor the new standards of environmental harmony and human comfort that have developed recently elsewhere. Unfortunately, the traditionalists for whom Ito's proposal came as such a threat include most of the bureaucrats whose building requirements ultimately determine trends in urban architectural design. In their view, cubes with elevator shafts and air-conditioning boxes on the roof are satisfyingly 'modern', and therefore preferable to the fantasy of Byodo-in, the soaring wings of Nandaimon or the playfulness of *suki* houses. I cannot help but think, 'How regrettable when purple usurps the place of vermilion.'

Chapter 11

Outer Nara

Secret Buddhas

A friend of mine studied the art of *bonkei*: she learned how to place curiously shaped rocks and bonsai plants on a tray spread with sand to create a miniature landscape. But as she slowly worked her way up the hierarchy of *bonkei* technique, the final secret eluded her: no matter what she did, her sand never held together in the perfect waves and ripples of the master's precisely arranged grains. Finally, after many years and payment of a high fee to obtain her license as a *bonkei* professional, she was to be told the answer. She bowed at the feet of the master, and he spoke. 'Use glue,' he said.

Japan is fascinated by secrets. They are the defining feature of the way traditional arts are taught and preserved. They cause problems for government and business, since different departments of the same organization tend to guard their knowledge jealously and not speak to one another. In museums, the finer an artwork, the less it will be shown to the public – which is why you will often find that the National Treasure you traveled so far to view is actually just a copy. The real piece stays in storage, and is shown only to a chosen few curators.

This tradition goes back to ancient Shinto, when the objects inside shrines, typically a stone or a mirror, became invested with mystical secrecy. At Izumo, Japan's oldest Shinto shrine, the object has been hidden from view for so long that its identity has been forgotten; it is referred to merely as 'the Object'. At the Grand Shrine of Ise, the object is known to be a mirror, but no one has laid eyes on it for at least a thousand years. When asked about Ise, the nineteenth-century Japanologist Chamberlain replied, 'There is nothing to see, and they won't let you see it.'

In Esoteric Buddhism, secrecy manifested itself in mandalas (diagrams of spiritual truth). A mandala can be a painting made up of squares and circles with Buddhas at strategic corners; equally, it can be an arrangement of statues, the layout of a building or a temple circuit followed by pilgrims. The largest mandala of all covers the whole island of Shikoku, which is made sacred by a ring of eighty-eight temples founded by the monk Kukai. Iya Valley, as it happens, lies right at the heart of this great mandala – appropriately, since the heart of a mandala should be inaccessible and secret. Buddha statues with great power became *hibutsu* (hidden Buddhas), and were displayed only once or twice a year. Important *hibutsu* could be seen only once every few decades, and there are some that have stayed in hiding for centuries at a stretch.

The ultimate cauldron of secrecy was the area around Nara, where ancient Shinto grew up and Esoteric Buddhism flourished. Over time, the mountains ringing Nara evolved into one vast mandala, made up of overlapping sub-mandalas, and every peak and valley was imbued with romantic and esoteric overtones.

A good example is Mt Yoshino, which lies south of Nara and is famed for its cherry blossoms. Going to view cherry blossoms at Yoshino would, on the surface, appear to be no different from making a similar excursion to anywhere else in Japan during spring. But for people familiar with Kabuki, the cherry trees here are the backdrop for *Yoshitsune Senbon Zakura*, a famous play which centers around the ill-fated warrior Yoshitsune's exile in Yoshino, his beautiful wife, Shizuka Gozen, and a magical fox which has disguised itself as one of his retainers. Yoshino is also celebrated as the center of the Southern Court, a group of exiles who fought a guerrilla war here in support of the legitimate Imperial line against the Shogunate for much of the fourteenth century. So for the historically minded, the cherry trees stir thoughts of this brave band of loyalists and a long sequence of Imperial visits to view the blossoms. And from a religious perspective, Yoshino is important because it was the headquarters of the Yamabushi sect of mountain mystics. To someone familiar with Esoteric Buddhism, the cherry trees lining the ridge at Yoshino mark the border between two huge sub-mandalas covering the mountains to the east and west.

The interest of a place like Yoshino is therefore not something you can see easily with the naked eye: it is veiled by heavy overlays of history, literature and religion. As a result, although they are only an hour or two's easy drive from Osaka or Kyoto, the outer mountains of Nara are among those least accessible to the public, and are more distant psychologically than even the so-called 'Three Hidden Regions'. Other than during cherry-blossom season, the public by and large ignores this area; but over the years, these mountains became my playground.

Mt Koya lies between Osaka, Nara and Ise at the core of one of the area's mandalas. Founded in the ninth century by Kukai, it is a complex of temples and monasteries built on a plateau in the mountains of Wakayama, southwest of the city of Nara. It is the sacred ground of Esoteric Buddhism. For a long time I hadn't had a chance to visit it, but at last I was invited to join some friends on a pilgrimage to the mountain.

A Tibetan lama once gave me the following instructions about how to explore a mandala: never rush headlong to the center. The proper way to contemplate a mandala is to first train your thoughts on the Buddhas guarding the gates along the periphery. Having entered, you gradually work your way into the interior, going round and round in ever tighter circles until you arrive at the center. Taking this advice to heart, we spent three days driving around southern Nara and the Yoshino range before approaching Mt Koya. As we finally neared the peak, the mountains grew higher around us, and the winding road to the summit was nothing short of spectacular. I could well imagine the feelings of pilgrims to this sacred place, far from the 'dust of the world'. Our excitement built as we speculated on what esoteric wonders unknown to Nara and Kyoto lay at the heart of the mandala. But on arriving at the summit, our hoped-for realm of wonder was nowhere to be found. The temples of Koya make up a small town; this in itself was no surprise, but it was the sort of town you see everywhere in Japan. The 'dust' had penetrated even here.

Koya turned out to be a series of such letdowns, for the interest lay entirely in the approach and never in the central object. For instance, the forest path leading to the grave of Kukai is lined with stone stupas marking the burial places of famous historical families. Walking along the dim, tree-shaded path, the flavor of history grew stronger as our eyes passed over one great legendary name after another carved in mossy stone. But when we arrived at Kukai's grave, we found that it had been obscured by a shiny, steel-reinforced Hall of Lanterns, which jarred against the backdrop of moss, stones and ancient conifers.

As we made our dutiful round of the temples in this disappointing town, I reassured myself that we had only just entered the mandala. There was much more to explore before we reached the center: the Konpon Daito ('Fundamental Great Tower'). A round tower with a square roof, the Konpon Daito symbolizes the center of the universe. In Esoteric Buddhist temples throughout

Japan, one finds a square table before the high altar, its sides marked off with string, and flowers, bells, vases, cups and dishes geometrically arranged on its surface. This array, called a *goma*, is a three-dimensional mandala made up of ritual utensils. The word '*goma*' comes originally from India, and the mandala represents a map of the heavenly capital. At the center is sacred Mt Sumeru, identified as Mt Kailash in Tibet, which is said to be the great Shiva lingam of the universe. The concept of the 'heavenly capital' spread throughout East Asia, and can be seen in the layout of Angkor Wat and in Thai palace architecture. In the case of the Japanese *goma*, one often sees a small tower at the center of the table of implements. This tower, the symbol of Mt Sumeru, is the Konpon Daito, modeled after the large tower at Mt Koya.

When I was translating for the Oomoto traditional arts seminar, one of the modern masters of Zen, Abbot Daiki of Daitoku-ji Temple in Kyoto, paid a visit. A student asked the abbot, 'What is Zen?', and Daiki Roshi replied, 'Zen is the Konpon Daito of the universe.' As a fledgling interpreter I was completely at a loss. Not knowing all the symbolism involved, I couldn't figure out why a Zen monk was referring to a building at Mt Koya.

At long last we approached the Konpon Daito, and I could see this mysterious tower with my own eyes. However, it turned out to be not the least bit mysterious! The original building had burned down, and the present tower was a Meiji-period reconstruction with no magic about it at all. In *goma* arrangements, the Konpon Daito is set apart by string and flowers, but at Mt Koya, the Konpon Daito just sits alone in the midst of an empty space.

With that, I gave up on Mt Koya. That evening, we stayed at Kongo Sanmai-in, one of the sub-temples that offer rooms to pilgrims and travelers. We arrived at our lodgings at around half past four. One of the monks asked us if we would like to see the

Buddha in the main hall, but we were all exhausted. After an early supper, I went to my room to read a book and relax for a while. That night, on my way to the bath, I passed a monk in the hall. 'Good evening,' he said pleasantly. 'How fortunate for you to have come here today. You were able to see our great Buddha of divine power.'

'Well, actually we were planning to see it tomorrow,' I said. The monk shook his head. 'I'm afraid that won't be possible. Sanmai-in's Buddha is a *hibutsu*. Mt Koya's other statues are sometimes put on display, or even lent to other temples and museums. But this one has never left the mountain. This is the first time it has ever been shown to the general public. It's called a "five-hundred-year *hibutsu*". The doors closed at five o'clock today, and you'll have to wait another five hundred years if you want to see it.'

This was my greatest failure ever as a travel guide. I was so embarrassed that I could not bring myself to confess to my friends, and to this day I don't believe they realize that they missed seeing a five-hundred-year *hibutsu* by only thirty minutes.

Faubion Bowers, my friend and mentor in Kabuki, once told me this story about Greta Garbo. One day he was walking with her in New York, when a fan approached the actress for her autograph. The fan begged with tears in her eyes, but Garbo coldly turned her down. When the woman had left, Faubion turned to Garbo and said, 'That's a cruel way to treat your fans! What would it have been to you to give your signature to that woman? She would have treasured it all her life.' Garbo retorted, 'If I'd given her my autograph, she would've grown bored and put it aside in a week or two. But because I refused, she'll treasure my autograph until the day she dies.'

Thinking back on it now, I realize that had I actually seen the five-hundred-year *hibutsu*, I might not have been all that moved. It could well have been as uninspiring as 'Use glue'. But thanks to the *hibutsu* I never saw, Mt Koya was transformed into a mystical realm, and among Japan's countless Buddhas, the secret Buddha of Sanmai-in remains for me without peer. My joy lay in the discovery that behind the desolate Konpon Daito and the harsh steel Hall of Lanterns, Mt Koya still has places that are dark and hidden. In a sense, Mt Koya is a model of all Japan: there are still mysteries hidden within.

In Nara, unless you have done considerable historical research, the names of the gods, even the reasons why the temples exist, are a closed book. The name of the god of Omiwa Shrine, Yamato no Omononushi Kushimikatama no Mikoto, is an arcane rush of syllables which are completely meaningless to Japanese ears today. Ancient Shinto and Esoteric Buddhism are populated with unseen gods and spirits, not meant to be understood by the average person. In this lies the fundamental distinction between Kyoto and Nara: Kyoto, for all the philosophy underlying Zen, *wabi*, *suki* and so forth, is a city of art; Nara, however, is a realm of religion.

Even within tourist-clogged Nara Park there are places that possess this religious appeal. Entering the Sangatsu-do Hall, next door to the Hall of the Great Buddha, you find a quiet room far removed from the flurry of people in the park. In this dim space, there towers a magnificent gilt statue of the Fukuken-saku Kannon Buddha, surrounded by a mandala arrangement of statues of guardians, the Sun and the Moon, and other bodhisattvas. From the halo behind the Buddha's head project gilded rays, gleaming in the darkness. Tourists come into Sangatsu-do talking and laughing, but they soon fall silent in the presence of Fukukensaku Kannon's fearsome light. None of them, including myself, has the slightest idea what the significance of Fukukensaku Kannon is. It doesn't matter – those beams of light are enough.

But Sangatsu-do aside, for me the real Nara lies outside Nara Park; so when I take friends to Nara, after a quick circuit of the park, we head out of the city. Our goal is the southern and eastern mountains, via the temples and relics scattered over the surrounding plain.

Our first stop is Akishino Temple. Its statue of Gigeiten (the god of art) is one of the finest masterpieces of Japanese sculpture. In the delicacy of the face and slightly turned neck, the S-curve to the body and the gracefully bent fingers, the figure of Gigeiten seems to condense all the pure beauty conjured up by Tamasaburo's dance into a single sculpture. It almost seems that the statue is swaying slightly as you watch it. As is to be expected from a truly Esoteric work, it is easy to believe that the soul of the god of art actually resides within this sculpture. In Nara, you often feel that you have not seen a statue, but that you have *met* a statue.

After leaving Akishino Temple we head southwards, keeping to our left the Yamanobe no Michi (the Path at the Foot of the Mountains), a historic road running along the foothills. I often make detours to explore the little farming villages at the base of the hills. To the right is the Yamato plain. Birthplace of Japan's religion and culture, it is now a vast web of power lines, lit up by the imposing glass and neon palaces of *pachinko* parlors.

Pachinko is a mild form of gambling. The player sits in front of a vertical pinball machine, in which a stream of ball bearings descend through circles of pins. When a ball falls into the correct slot, the player gets a jackpot of hundreds of ball bearings. If the player has any ball bearings left over when he has finished, he takes them to the counter and receives cigarettes or candy in exchange. These are then taken to a booth outside the premises, where they are traded in for money.

There being no such thing as sign control or zoning in most of Japan's neighborhoods, *pachinko* parlors have developed a uniquely garish style: enormous rows of neon lights, several meters high, flashing every color of the rainbow, and roofs capped by dramatic floodlit towers in the shape of the Statue of Liberty, spacecraft or dinosaurs. I recently took a European architect to visit Shikoku and Nara. I had intended to show him temples, houses and natural scenery, but the only things to catch his eye were the *pachinko* parlors. He explained, 'The old temples and shrines are just dead ruins. Looking at what is happening to Kyoto, it's clear that these things have no relation to today's Japanese. On the other hand, they don't seem to have mastered true modernism. The layout of new office buildings and apartments is very out of date from the point of view of the rest of the world. Only the *pachinko* parlors are luxurious in their own way, creatively and fantastically built. Of course they're tasteless, but isn't it exactly this poor taste which defines modern Japan? Because *pachinko* parlors have perfected this taste, they are the most consistent and interesting examples of contemporary Japanese design.'

Though depressing, I realized that this was a very keen observation. When you look at the cultural remains of a historical period, you are able to perceive its dominant ideology. In the Nara and Heian periods there were Esoteric temples; from Kamakura through to the end of Edo there were Zen temples and teahouses; and in Meiji the great monuments of the time were train stations. What about the present? When you travel through the countryside of Europe or Southeast Asia, you notice that the highest point of any village is always a church steeple, a mosque or the soaring eaves of a Buddhist temple. In the Japanese countryside, however, the tallest and most ostentatious building is invariably a *pachinko* parlor.

Sitting in front of a *pachinko* machine is the modern form of meditation. The circular arrangement of the pins inside the machine is today's version of the mandala, and the old model of thoughts flowing from the circumference of the mandala towards its center has become the flow of balls from top to bottom of the machine. The overwhelming hold of *pachinko* can hardly be exaggerated. In some rural districts, it accounts for up to twenty per cent of disposable household income. *Pachinko* is now the single largest industry, outpacing cars and computers, and Japan's richest man by some calculations is a man whose company produces most of the machines. *Pachinko* has developed its own style, consisting of brightly colored rooms laced with constructions of chrome and neon, and oversize plastic statues of animals or gods of good luck. It has become the preferred style of Japanese entertainment: you find it everywhere, from restaurants and bars to the sets of most popular TV programs. It influences architecture, and is the inspiration behind many a glitzy hotel lobby. Kyoto Tower is very much in this *pachinko* mode.

Pachinko style has even colored industrial design. Recently I spoke to an official of the Japan Design Association. 'A decade ago, Japan was a leader in world industrial design, producing simple classics like the Walkman,' he lamented. 'But today the mainstream in modern design is pink toasters in the shape of pigs. What happened?' The answer, of course, is *pachinko*. With all the energies of the economy and culture flowing into *pachinko* parlors, they have become Japan's modern Konpon Daito.

Back to showing my visitors around. After driving south for about twenty minutes from Nara, we arrive at two large burial mounds: the tomb of Emperor Sujin and the Kushiyama mound. Many old tombs can be found in the Osaka, Nara and Asuka regions, some of them hundreds of meters in circumference. The tomb of Emperor Nintoku, on the outskirts of Osaka, is said to be the world's largest. Typically, these tombs are built in a keyhole shape, with a raised hill in the center surrounded by a moat. Imperial mounds are under the supervision of the Imperial Household Agency, and so it is forbidden to excavate or even walk on them; thus, little patches of virgin forest have been preserved in suburbia.

The tombs are not far from the road, but they nestle in the eastern foothills and have national parkland as their backdrop. The nearer of the two is the grave of Emperor Sujin, surrounded by a wide moat of still water, before which stands a majestic *torii* gate. To either side are rice paddies, and farther back rises the Kushiyama mound. Visitors are rare here, so it is always quiet. In summer, the paddies are awash with green, the leafy boughs of the trees on the mounds reach far over the water in the moat and high up into the sky, while the air pulsates with the droning of cicadas. It is not known who is buried in the Kushiyama mound, and I have no idea who Emperor Sujin was, but walking around the moats I feel as though I have been transported back to Shinto's legendary 'Age of the Gods'. Accompanied by the throbbing sound of the cicadas, my heart roams in the distant past. Breaking out of my reverie with a start, I realize we have been standing in front of the graves for over an hour.

Tearing ourselves away from the 'Age of the Gods', we drive further south. As part of the spirit of Nara's secrecy, lovers of this region frequent hideaways unknown or preferably not open to the general public; the writer Yukio Mishima's occasional visits to the aristocratic abbess of Ensho-ji Nunnery were rooted in this cult of secrets. I too have a secret temple, situated in the mountains to the east of Yoshino and Mt Koya. My temple is called Seisen-an. The drive there is very pleasant, and the road winds past famous temples such as Hase-dera and Muro-ji. Deep in the mountains between these temples lies the town of Ouda. There's nothing special to see in this region, so travelers are scarce. Around 1978, Abbot Daiki of Daitoku-ji found and remodeled an old village headman's estate near Ouda. He slowly built up a complex of sub-temples and worship halls, one of which is Seisen-an – a farmhouse from deeper in the hills that was dismantled, moved to Ouda and restored.

The abbot of Seisen-an is an American disciple of Daiki Roshi named John Toler. In 1973 while I was staying at David Kidd's house, a man with a completely shaved head came to visit. This man was John Toler. He had been working as a writer for the Dentsu advertising agency, but had quit to become a Zen monk. I sat listening to John until late at night, as he explained all about

Zen catechism and life as a monk in Daitoku-ji, including the mis-understandings that arose between him and his family in Lubbock, Texas. His mother once came to visit, and after a few days of touring the Zen gardens of Kyoto, she turned to John and said, 'I'm sorry, John, I'm a little confused. Would you please explain again? You say you *worship* these gardens?'

John spent four years in meditation at Daitoku-ji as a layman, and then entered its special practice hall for four more years as a monk. In 1980, his master, Abbot Daiki, sent him to Ouda. I recently discovered that John had first shaved his head only the day before I met him! As a result, I missed seeing him with hair by just one day. The five-hundred-year *hibutsu* missed by thirty minutes, John's hair by a single day – I seem to have bad karma with Buddhism. Perhaps it is punishment for the years I have spent working for Oomoto, a Shinto sect.

When I take friends to Seisen-an, John comes out to greet us dressed in monk's robes. He shows us around the meditation hall, and then when dusk falls we sit around the living room talking to the other guests. Seisen-an, while remote, is a gathering place for artists, dancers, writers and other monks, so you are always bound to meet somebody interesting there. Just like when I first met John twenty years ago, we talk of Zen, art and life until late at night. Once I got John very drunk and tried to wheedle out of him the answer to the first Zen *koan*: 'You know the sound of two hands clapping. What is the sound of one hand?' John refused to tell me, saying that the answer was not worth knowing, and the whole value of the *koan* lay in the process of figuring it out. But I insisted, plying him with more cups of saké. And finally he told me. The answer was clear as a thunderclap, before which all other reasoning is useless. But John was right: just knowing the answer did me no good whatsoever. It would seem that the entire point of secrets lies in not knowing them. At Seisen-an I sleep at the foot of a folding screen on which is written Su Tung-p'o's 'Red Cliff Ode'. My favorite line is right by my pillow: 'I gaze at my loved one in a corner of the sky'. It seems the perfect theme for the mountains of Nara, filled with distant and unobtainable things.

The best time at Seisen-an is morning. Generally, I am a night person and mornings are hard to face, but at Seisen-an I always get up early. The other residents are up at the crack of dawn ringing the temple bell or reciting *sutras*, so I feel guilty to be the only one sleeping in. I sit in a rattan chair on the temple verandah, and look out at the garden while drinking a cup of coffee. The neatly raked gravel stretches before me like a sheet of pure white paper. Around the gravel are trees, and beyond them, blue mountains trail off into the distance, range after range. There is no sign reading, 'Seisen-an HITACHI', nor any taped explanation. Just me, alone, with time to think.

While staying at Seisen-an, I enjoy taking drives to the surrounding mountains. Japan's ancient faiths sprang from the mountains. A well-known example of this is Omiwa Shrine, a few kilometers south of the tomb of Emperor Sujin. Here, there is nothing hidden inside the shrine as the object of worship – the mountain behind the shrine is the sacred object. The hills behind many shrines and temples are sacred, and so special sanctuaries, called *oku no in* (inner sanctuary), were built on the slopes behind the main halls. A particular favorite of mine is the inner sanctuary at Muro-ji, and if there is time I always try to take friends there. I was once talking to the curator of a museum in Nara, who said, 'Muro-ji is a litmus test. If you ask someone, "What are your favorite spots in Nara?" and they answer "Yoshino" or "The Yamanobe Road", that is fine. But if they say "Muro-ji', then you can tell they truly know Nara.'

While I wouldn't go so far as to say that Muro-ji is a litmus test of familiarity with Nara, it certainly is a singular place. Located in the mountains to the east of Ouda, Muro-ji is not far from the border with Mie Prefecture, on the very outer edge of the Nara region. Until the 1880s Mt Koya was completely closed to women, but Muro-ji welcomed them. It became known as 'Mt Koya of Women', and is the center of its own mandala, balancing Koya's yang with Muro-ji's yin.

As you follow the road to Muro-ji along the edge of a gorge, a fifteen-meter-high stone Buddha carved into the cliff face springs into view. This is a *magai-butsu* (cliff Buddha), a common sight in China but rare in Japan. The *magai-butsu* near Muro-ji is of Bodhisattva Maitreya, the Buddha of the Future, and was carved in the thirteenth century by a sculptor from China. But why a Maitreya Buddha out here in the middle of nowhere? There must have been some symbolic necessity for carving it. Maybe a Maitreya was required to fill this position in the larger mandala of the region; or perhaps the carver sensed geomantic power in this particular cliff face. In any case, the retired Emperor Go-Toba came all the way from Kyoto to attend the ceremony of opening the Buddha's eyes, from which we can see that the carving of this Buddha was a national undertaking.

Muro-ji's grounds form a natural mandala. First, you enter the temple precincts by a bridge over a river. This is a pattern often seen in ancient shrines and temples, but the bridge to Muro-ji is particularly effective in conveying the message: from here on is sacred ground. A sign saying 'Mt Koya of Women' reminds you that this experience will be one of yin rather than yang. Then, passing through the gate, you climb the Armor Slope, so-called because from below you can only see wide rows of steps capped by the roof of the main hall above, looking like a helmet over a ribbed suit of armor. This stairway leads you upwards through the woods to halls of increasing mystical importance, culminating in the main hall, where you visit the Buddha of the Future enshrined within. Then you stroll over to the charming five-tiered pagoda, so small it seems almost doll-like. This tower, which is very feminine in atmosphere, is Muro-ji's Konpon Daito. Finally, you climb up a narrow stairway of four hundred stone steps, rising through clumps of ferns and thousand-year-old cedar trees.

When you clamber up the last step and see the inner sanctuary ahead of you, it is with the sense that you have arrived at the very end of the earth.

Here, you stop. Looking around at the thousand-year-old cedar forest, you drink deeply of mountain air. You are standing at the heart of a mandala.

Chapter 12

Osaka

Bumpers and Runners

Like many countries, Japan is bipolar. In China, power has swung periodically over the millennia between the north, the center of government, and the south, source of the nation's wealth. In the USA, the clear divide between the East Coast and the West Coast is so strong that at the Oomoto seminar, the biggest culture shock is not when Americans encounter Japanese, but when Californians meet New Yorkers. In Japan, the two poles are the Tokyo area (known as Kanto) in the east, and the four cities of Osaka-Kobe-Kyoto-Nara (called Kansai) in the west.

While Tokyo, as capital, draws the choicest international events, it is considered politically important to give Kansai its due. So, after the 1964 Olympics, when Japan announced to the world that it had recovered from World War II and intended to become a global industrial power, it hosted an international event in Osaka: Expo 70, held the summer I hitchhiked around Japan and discovered Iya Valley.

The Expo fairgrounds outside Osaka were centered around sculptor Taro Okamoto's 'Tower of the Sun'. The tower took Japan by storm, and its image on posters and on TV followed me everywhere that summer. It was a concrete and metal construction, with a cone-shaped base, two outstretched flipper-like arms and a round Picasso-esque head; it looked like a giant creature from outer space put together in a kindergarten art class. The statue can still be seen as you drive along the Meishin Expressway between Kyoto and Osaka. Once as I was driving past it with David Kidd, he remarked, 'There is the ugliest thing ever made by the hands of man.'

Welcome to Osaka. Few major cities of the developed world could match Osaka for the overall unattractiveness of its cityscape, which consists mostly of a jumble of cube-like buildings and a web of expressways and cement-walled canals. There are few skyscrapers, even fewer museums and, other than Osaka Castle, almost no historical sites. Yet Osaka is my favorite city in Japan. Osaka is where the fun is: it has the best entertainment districts in Japan, the most lively youth neighborhood, the most charismatic geisha madams and the most colorful gangsters. It also has a monopoly on humor, to the extent that in order to succeed as a popular comedian it is almost obligatory to study in Osaka and speak the Osaka dialect.

Osaka people are impatient and love to disobey rules; in that spirit, the best way to approach the city is to dispense with preliminaries and go straight to the heart of the mandala, which in Osaka's case is Tsutenkaku (the 'Tower Reaching to Heaven'). Tsutenkaku is another of the towers which, like Tokyo Tower and Kyoto Tower, were built in every major city after World War II. Wartime bombing had almost completely obliterated Osaka's old downtown area, so the city redrew the streets in a huge burnt-out district, and built Tsutenkaku in the middle of it. The tower stands in the center of a rectangle covering about twenty square blocks called Shinsekai ('New World'), which is filled with restaurants, shops and theaters. Roads radiate from the arches under the tower like the avenues emanating from the Arc de Triomphe in Paris. However, all resemblance to Paris, or even the amusement districts of other Japanese cities, ends here. Once the mecca of laborers, such as the farmers of Iya who flooded the cities in the decades after the war, Shinsekai has become a slum. In clean, organized and law-abiding modern Japan, this is an exceptional phenomenon.

Most people visiting Shinsekai enter via Janjan Yokocho, an arcade stretching from Imamiya Station into the district's interior. The minute you get out of the train station, you realize that you are in another country: drunks and homeless people stagger by, and young men are more likely to be wearing wide laborer pants and boots than the latest fashions from Tokyo's trendy Harajuku area. You pass a street market where you can buy second-hand underwear or a single shoe. Janjan Yokocho is dark and dingy – you see the occasional rat scurrying across from one building to another – but it is crowded with people. They are coming to eat at the *kushikatsu* restaurants lining the street, which feature cheap meals of pork, chicken, onions and eggs, deep-fried on wooden skewers and washed down with plenty of beer and *shochu* (vodka made from rice). Interspersed among the *kushikatsu* restaurants are *shogi* halls, where people sit in pairs playing Japanese chess, watched through open latticed windows by knots of people gathered on the street outside.

When I visit Shinsekai, I go to the barber before heading off for dinner. He offers a haircut for 500 yen, about one-fifth of the going rate elsewhere, and uses buzz shears, which are considered unfashionable in Japan nowadays. This was very convenient when my cousins Edan and Trevor were staying with me. They were very particular about their hair: Trevor liked his shaved up the sides, with a long Mohican strip at the top, and the fancy barbers in Kameoka and Kyoto never seemed to get it right. When I asked the barber in Janjan Yokocho if he thought he could handle hair like this, he replied, in English, 'Okeydokey. I cut the hair of the American soldiers after the war. I know exactly what to do.' He whipped out the buzz shears, and the work was over in a minute. The effect was exactly what the boys were looking for. The theme of Shinsekai is Cheap and Easy; in other words, this is not Japan.

Not far from Tsutenkaku is a small theater with a sign outside saying 'Japan's Cheapest Theater!' It's also one of the best. Entrance is 200 yen (50 yen extra for a cushion), and traveling troupes of popular Kabuki perform here. These troupes, centered around one or two families, are the remnants of the hundreds of troupes that roamed the country before World War II. After the war, most of the smaller troupes went out of business, and the better known performers were consolidated into the Grand Kabuki we see today in Tokyo. But a handful of these families survived by adapting Kabuki to modern tastes. They dance not to *samisen* and shoulder drum, but to *enka* (modern pop songs). Their kimonos are made of pink gauze and gold lamé, and their wigs may be red, purple or silver.

First, there is a love-and-loyalty play, and then some dances. The audience show their appreciation by placing cases of beer and cartons of cigarettes on the stage or stuffing five-or ten thousand-yen notes into the sashes of the performers. Then there will be an announcement: 'Ladies and gentlemen, we introduce the sexy, curvaceous Baby Hanako!' And with a roll of drums, a little girl of about four steps up to the microphone and belts out a song at ear-splitting volume. The children of these troupes start singing and dancing before they can read or write. My favorite at the moment is a boy of eleven named Bakudan Yuki (Yuki the Bomb), who can sing and dance better than any of the coddled children of the families of Grand Kabuki. In Grand Kabuki it is no longer necessary to appeal to the hearts of the public, but Yuki the Bomb immediately knows the effect he is creating by the amount of money stuffed into his sash. At the end of the performance, the troupe gathers outside on the street and waves good-bye to the audience.

A few blocks away from Shinsekai is Tobita, Japan's last *kuruwa*. In Edo days, prostitution was strictly regulated, and the courtesans lived in small walled towns within the cities, which had gates and closing times. These cities-within-the-city were known as *kuruwa* (enclosures). In Kyoto, the old gate to the *kuruwa* of Shimabara still stands, although Shimabara itself is defunct. The largest *kuruwa* was Yoshiwara, near Uguisudani Station in Tokyo. Within the walls of Yoshiwara, there was a lattice of streets lined with pleasure houses, a scene familiar in the Kabuki theater, where such streets form the backdrop of many love plays. The entrance to each pleasure house featured a banner with the name of the house on it; inside, women wearing gorgeous kimonos were on display. Today, Yoshiwara is still in business, but the boundaries, the street grid, the houses and the banners have been replaced by a jumble of streets sprinkled with love hotels and saunas, with the result that it looks not much different from most of the other places in Tokyo. If you can't read the signs, you might not realize the nature of the neighborhood. Tobita, however, survives almost completely intact. There are no walls, but there is a precise gridwork of streets lined with low tile-roofed houses. In front of each house is a banner, and inside the entrance a young woman and the madam sit side by side next to a brazier. This is as close to Kabuki in the modern age as you can get.

A word of caution: it is best not to stroll around Shinsekai or Tobita without a Japanese friend if you are a foreigner, as you might be accosted by a gangster or an unfriendly drunk. I usually go there in the company of an Osaka friend, Satoshi; he looks so tough that once, when he was on his way to a wedding dressed in a black suit and sunglasses, the police picked him up on suspicion of being a gangster. Many Japanese are afraid to enter the downtown neighborhoods of Osaka. There is one area in particular that taxi drivers will not go into at all because of the *atariya* ('bumpers'), who make a living from bumping into your car and then screaming that you have run over them. The whole neighborhood rushes out to support the *atariya*, threatening to act as witnesses in a lawsuit against you until you pay up. Even so, this pales in comparison to what can happen in New York and many of Europe's large cities. The gangsters of Osaka and Kobe, known as Japan's most vicious, keep largely out of sight, and in general, violent crime is rare. One of Japan's greatest achievements is its relative lack of crime, and this is one of the invisible factors that makes life here very comfortable. The low crime rate is the result of those smoothly running social systems, and is the envy of many a nation – this is the good side of having trained the population to be bland and obedient. The difference in Osaka is only one of degree; the streets are still basically safe. What you see in Shinsekai is more a form of 'misbehavior', rather than serious crime. People do not act decorously: they shout, cry, scream and jostle one another; in well-behaved modern Japan, this is shocking.

Osaka does not merely preserve old styles of entertainment, it constantly dreams up new ones. For example, Osaka premiered the 'no-panties coffee shops' with pantyless waitresses, that later swept Japan. In other places, the boom remained limited to coffee shops, but in Osaka they now have 'no-panties *okonomiyaki*' (do-it-yourself pizza) and 'no-panties *gyudon*' (beef-and-rice bowls). The latest, I hear, is 'breast-rub coffee', where a topless waitress, on delivering coffee to the table, rubs her customer's face in the way the name would suggest.

The entertainment is by no means limited to the sex business. Osaka pioneered a new type of drive-in public bath at Goshikiyu, near the Toyonaka interchange on the expressway. In general, public baths are slowly dying out in Japan, as the number of homes with their own bath and shower increases. However, an Osaka bathhouse proprietor of an entrepreneurial bent promoted the idea that an evening out at the public bath was the perfect family entertainment. He built a multistoried bathhouse with a large parking lot to service Japan's new car-centered lifestyle. Inside, he installed restaurants, saunas and several floors of baths with every type of tub: hot, cold or tepid; with jacuzzi, shower or waterfall. On a Saturday night you can hardly get into Goshikiyu's parking lot; the place is jammed with families with small children.

Fashion in Osaka is not like fashion elsewhere. Tokyo is the home of trends: all the businessmen wear the same blue suit, housewives wear the same Armani, artists wear the same pastel shirts with high collars, and the young people hanging out at Yoyogi wear whatever the latest craze happens to be. Kyoto people are afraid to do anything that might make them stand out, so they dress rather drably – like Tokyo on a bad day. But Osaka is a riot of ill-matched color, tasteless footwear and startling hairdos. Satoshi puts it this way: 'In Tokyo, people want to wear what everyone else is wearing. In Osaka, people want to shock.'

Japan's national problem is homogeneity. The school system teaches everybody to say and think the same thing, and the bureaucracies restrict the development of new media, such as cable TV, the information superhighway and even movie theaters. As a result, no matter where you go, from Hokkaido to Kyushu, all the houses look the same, the clothes look the same, and people's lives center around the same humdrum activities. With everyone so well behaved and satisfied with their mediocre lives, Japan specializes in low-level pleasures. *Pachinko* is the perfect example. Why has *pachinko* swept Japan? It can hardly be the excitement of gambling, since the risks and rewards are so small. During the hours spent in front of a *pachinko* machine, there is an almost total lack of stimulation other than the occasional rush of ball bearings. There is no thought, no movement; you have no control over the flow of balls, apart from holding a little lever which shoots them up to the top of the machine; you sit there enveloped in a cloud of heavy cigarette smoke, semi-dazed by the racket of millions of ball bearings falling through machines around you. *Pachinko* verges on sensory deprivation. It is the ultimate mental numbing, the final victory of the education system.

In a department store in Tokyo recently, I saw a girl at the Shiseido cosmetics counter who summed this up. She was seated demurely at the counter, while the attendant did something with her make-up kit. The girl's head was tipped forward, and her long black hair hung around her on all sides, completely obscuring her from view. Her hands were folded with eternal patience in her lap; her down-turned head faced the table. The passivity, the way in which her hair shut out the outside world – it was a distinctive posture which I have seen in Japan so many times. Sensory deprivation? Passive silence? Fear of the world? I wish I could find the right words for it, but Japan is becoming a nation of people like this.

Donald Richie, dean of the Japanologists in Tokyo, once made this observation to me: 'The people of Iya were not the only ones who escaped regimentation during the military period. There was one other group: people living in the downtowns of big cities like Edo and Osaka. The merchants in these cities were a different breed from the farmers, with their need to cooperate in rice growing, and the samurai, with their code of loyalty and propriety. The samurai despised the merchants as belonging at the bottom of the social totem pole, but at the same time, the merchants had the freedom to enjoy themselves. The brilliant realm of the "floating world" – Kabuki, the pleasure quarters, colorful kimono, woodblock prints, novels, dance – belonged to the old downtowns. Even today, people from these neighborhoods are different from ordinary Japanese.'

This is especially true of Osaka. The downtown neighborhoods of Tokyo, while they still exist, have largely lost their identity, but Osaka maintains a spirit of fierce independence which goes back a long way. Originally, Osaka was a fishing village on the Inland Sea called Naniwa. The writer Ryotaro Shiba maintains that the colorful language and brutal honesty of Osaka people can be traced to Naniwa's seaport past.

Osaka dialect is certainly colorful. Standard Japanese, to the sorrow of Edan and Trevor, has an almost complete lack of dirty words. The very meanest thing you can shout at somebody is *kisama*, which means literally, 'honorable you'. But Osaka people say such vividly imaginative things that you want to sit back and take notes. Most are unprintable, but here is one classic Osaka epithet: 'I'm going to slash your skull in half, stir up your brains and drink them with a straw!' The fishwife invective and the desire to shock produced the playful language that is the hallmark of Osaka dialect. When Satoshi describes a visit to the bank, it's funnier than the routines of most professional comics. It begins with the bank, and ends with the dice tattooed on his aunt's left shoulder. Free association of the sort he employs is called *manzai*, and it is Japan's most popular form of humor. Osaka people have *manzai* in the blood. That's why comedians have to come here to study.

During the early Nara period, Naniwa was Japan's window to the world, serving as the main port of call for embassies from China and Korea. Osaka was so important as the seat of diplomacy that the capital was based there several times in the seventh century before finally being moved to Nara. In the process, numerous families from China and Korea emigrated to the Naniwa region, and Heian-period censuses show that its population was heavily of continental origin. In the late sixteenth century, Osaka's harbor shifted from Naniwa to Sakai, a few kilometers south. As Chinese silk and Southeast Asian ceramics flooded into Japan, the Osaka merchants grew rich; among them was Sen no Rikyu, founder of tea ceremony. For several decades Osaka was again Japan's window to the world, and outshone Kyoto as the source of new cultural developments. During the Edo period, the Shogunate closed the ports and three hundred years of isolation set in. But Osaka continued to thrive, its merchants establishing themselves as wholesale rice brokers and moneylenders. Certain unique occupations grew up, such as 'runners', who still exist even today; their job is to visit one wholesaling street and jot down prices, then dash over to the next street to report them to competitors – and then do the same thing in reverse.

The mercantile ethos in Osaka resulted in many of Japan's largest businesses being based there, such as Sumitomo and the trading house Itochu, which did more volume of business in 1995 than any other company in the world. Osaka's good fortune lay in the fact that the government left the city almost totally free of control. In Tokyo there was the Shogun; in Kyoto there was the Emperor; but in Osaka there was nobody on top, except a skeleton staff of the Shogun's officials holed up in Osaka Castle, pitifully unprepared to join in a battle of wits with wily Osaka merchants. The ratio of samurai to population was so low that people could go their whole lives without meeting one. In Edo, the Shogunate built bridges; in Osaka, private businessmen built them. In other words, in Osaka, the people ran their own lives.

In recent years, the fact that certain areas like Shinsekai have became slums has acted as a protection, scaring away the developers and investors who raised land prices and transformed the face of Tokyo. Osaka preserved its identity, which goes right back to the old seaport of Naniwa. So when friends ask me to show them the 'true Japan of ancient tradition', I don't take them to Kyoto: I take them to Osaka.

However, Osaka today stands at a critical juncture. It has preserved its local dialect more successfully than any other city in Japan, and much of the brash insouciance of its people has survived; but TV and modern education are beginning to succeed where a thousand years of samurai government failed. Osaka people are becoming well behaved, and with their newfound good manners, they are becoming just like everybody else. In a classic case of misguided urban redevelopment, the city, ashamed of Shinsekai's reputation as a slum, is planning to tear down Jan-jan Yokocho and replace it with the sort of colorless arcade seen everywhere.

A different option for the revitalization of Shinsekai is illus-trated by Amerika-mura ('America Town'). This is a district of several blocks of import shops and novelty stores which was developed in the 1980s. No civic administrator decided to estab-lish Amerika-mura; it's not even known when the district acquired its name, now commonly shortened to Ame-mura. It just grew up, as young entrepreneurs started selling American jeans and boots on the streets behind the Nikko Hotel. Around the time of the Osaka Expo, a woman named Higiri Mariko opened a café-bar called Loop in the neighborhood. Loop caught on, and in 1976 Hijiri expanded her operations into Palms Disco, to which Osaka's young people flocked. More cafés, discos and shops opened, and today Amerika-mura boasts hundreds of stores and is always crowded with young people day and night. Leaving it up to the people themselves is the traditional Osaka way, but it is the one option least likely to occur in modern Japan.

As it turned out, Taro Okamoto's 'Tower of the Sun' was just as ill-fated as the 'Tower Reaching to Heaven'. Until Expo 70, Osa-ka's last shining moment, the four big cities of Kansai held their own in the contest of power with Tokyo. However, one of the core developments during Japan's period of rapid economic expansion was massive involvement by government agencies in trade and technology. As all these agencies are located in Tokyo, it became essential to be based there; as a result, Tokyo's dominance is near total, and Kansai is slowly falling off the map. There could be no better indication of this than the incredibly slow response of the central government to the 1995 earthquake in Kobe. As people in Osaka and Kobe remarked at the time, 'Would the prime min-ister have waited half a day to send in help if a disaster had occurred in Tokyo? No, the mismanagement on the part of the government was because the earthquake was in Kansai.'

In the 1990s, developments in the art world bypass Kyoto and Nara; trade and business ignore Osaka and Kobe. Even giants like Sumitomo and Itochu, which are officially registered in Osaka, are managed out of their headquarters in Tokyo. Osaka has been relegated to the position of Branch Office of Japan Inc. The only hope for the city's regeneration is to make it once more an international port, and there is much talk of turning Osaka into the 'gateway to Asia'. Unfortunately, the chances of this happening are slim, as bureaucracies such as the Transport Ministry maintain their stranglehold on harbors and airports; for instance, the recently completed Kansai International Airport is so expensive and over-regulated that most international airlines shun it. For a moment there was a golden opportunity for Kansai to establish itself as the airline hub of East Asia, but the initiative has been lost to South Korea, Hong Kong and Singapore.

The future of Osaka as an interesting place is in doubt. It is the last bastion against the sea of ordinariness sweeping over Japan, and when it goes there will be many who miss it. In the words of Tamasaburo, 'The decline of Kyoto I can live with. But please, please, Osaka never change!'

Chapter 13

The Literati
Doing Nothing

As the Chinese monk Lin-chi, founder of Rinzai Zen, lay dying, his disciples tried to reassure him by saying, 'We will pass your wisdom on to future generations.' 'Then all is lost,' cried Lin-chi. 'My teachings will die with you, a pack of blind mules!'

At the temple of Manpuku-ji, south of Kyoto, there is a large plaque over the Founder's Hall, and on it is written, 'The eyes of a blind mule'. The plaque is in the hand of Ingen, a Rinzai monk who fled from China to Japan after the fall of the Ming dynasty. At that time, Zen in Japan was in a state of decadence: teaching at the head temples of Daitoku-ji and Myoshin-ji in Kyoto had lost all rigor, and Zen was becoming a mere formula. When Ingen arrived in Nagasaki in 1654, he created a sensation. Tall, white-haired and austere, Ingen stood for no nonsense. 'With a wild blow from my stick, I show who will live and who will die', reads one of a pair of plaques by him at Manpuku-ji; on the other side, it says, 'With a fierce *Katsu!* I shout who is dragon and who is snake'.

Soon, several senior Myoshin-ji monks converted to Ingen's Zen, and one of them invited Ingen to Kyoto, aiming to have him installed as abbot of Myoshin-ji. This sparked an anti-Ingen demonstration within Myoshin-ji by monks who disliked the idea of their institution being taken over by a foreigner. Just at that juncture, the young Shogun Ietsuna heard of Ingen and invited him up to Edo. The eighteen-year-old Shogun was completely taken by Ingen, and offered him something even better than Myoshin-ji: hundreds of acres of land south of Kyoto, where he could build a Chinese Zen temple, and establish his own sect, known as Obaku. With the full resources of the Shogunate behind him, Ingen imported shiploads of teak logs from Thailand and Burma and marble column bases carved in Beijing, and he built his Manpuku-ji Temple completely in the Chinese style. The Shogun and his warlords went on to support the building of hundreds of Obaku temples throughout the land.

Ingen brought with him not only Zen, but Ming-style calligraphy and *sencha* (Chinese tea ceremony). Meanwhile, back at Myoshin-ji, the 'Ingen shock' lasted for decades. The monks revived the *zendo* (meditation hall), copying the one built by Ingen at Manpuku-ji. The anti-Ingen faction leaders shouted '*Katsu!*' even louder and struck even more fiercely with their sticks; the disciples of the anti-Ingen group included such great masters as Hakuin and Takuan, and Myoshin-ji Zen came alive again. In this way, both by action and reaction, one Chinese monk succeeded in revolutionizing Japanese Rinzai Zen.

Manpuku-ji still stands largely unchanged from Ingen's day. The entrance is a three-tiered gate, designed after the *pai-lou* decorative gates of China. Inside, corridors of teak columns and swastika-patterned balustrades surround a courtyard planted with pine trees. On every gate and over every building is posted calligraphy by Ingen and his disciples. Manpuku-ji is pure Ming China.

Japan is like an oyster. An oyster dislikes foreign objects: when even the smallest grain of sand or broken shell finds its way inside the oyster's shell, the oyster finds the invasion intolerable, so it secretes layer after layer of nacre upon the surface of the offending particle, eventually creating a beautiful pearl. However, while pearls may vary slightly in size or luster, they all look very much alike. In the process of coating, not a trace remains of the shape or color of the grain of sand inside. In like manner, Japan coats all culture from abroad, transforming it into a Japanese-style pearl. The finished pearl is a thing of great beauty – often, as in the case of tea ceremony, more refined than the original – but the essential nature of the original is lost. This is why Japan, which has hundreds of thousands of Italian and Chinese restaurants, has almost no genuine Italian or Chinese food. Ingredients are altered and watered down, and there is even a brand of olive oil that bears the label 'Specially Reconstituted for Japanese Taste'.

While foreign influence is welcomed, the cardinal rule is never to delegate responsibility to foreigners themselves. This was one of the principal points of friction between the Trammell Crow Company and Sumitomo Trust. Sumitomo Trust avidly sought Trammell Crow's know-how, but strongly resisted allowing the manager from Dallas to run the office in Japan. This, more than any other factor, led to Trammell Crow's decision to sell out to Sumitomo Trust and withdraw from the Kobe Fashion Mart project before its completion.

In my business days, I often met foreign staff who had been brought in to help out at the head offices of Japanese banks or insurance companies. Sometimes we would go out for a drink after work, and I would invariably be treated to a tale of woe. Elite stockbrokers from New York or London saw wealthy Japan at that time as the ultimate career opportunity. They arrived expecting to carve a niche in the booming Tokyo business world, only to find that their companies never gave them any authority or listened to their advice; the longer they stayed, the greater their unhappiness. Meanwhile, Japanese executives would confide, 'You can't rely on foreigners. We bring them into the office, show them everything, and then they leave us for another company.' The reason, of course, is that in most cases a position given to a foreigner in a Japanese company is a career dead end. This is now a very real problem in Southeast Asia, where the Japanese have invested massively and have a great need for well-educated local staff. However, these are the very people who object to being kept in low-level positions, and they soon leave.

For most of its recorded history, Japan has succeeded in keeping foreigners out. The biggest exception was in the decades before World War II, when thousands of Overseas Chinese moved to Yokohama and Kobe, and hundreds of thousands of Koreans were forcibly brought over to Japan as laborers. The descendants of these settlers form large and vocal communities today. Most of the other well-known cases of foreign presence in Japan, especially those involving Westerners, disguise failures rather than successes. For instance, during the Edo period, the Dutch were allowed to trade from the island of Dejima in Nagasaki harbor. Heavily guarded, the island was connected to the mainland by a narrow causeway, which was closed after hours; traders could only venture onto the mainland with special passes for a limited length of time. The noteworthy thing about Dejima was that it was not a device to let the Dutch in – it was a way of keeping them out.

Kobe's *ijinkan* ('alien residences'), a group of grand houses inhabited by foreign traders in the late nineteenth and early twentieth centuries, are a popular tourist destination. Guidebooks describe them as an example of Kobe's internationalism, but the houses actually represent a failed community. The families who once lived there have disappeared, and the number of foreign residents in Kobe is shrinking year by year; in the 1980s the American Consulate moved to Osaka, and in the 1990s Kobe's international schools are struggling to survive.

The history of keeping foreigners out is inextricably bound up with Japan's smoothly functioning social systems – which is why Japan has not allowed in large numbers of foreign workers or students, even though its industry needs the cheap labor, and Japan's future partly depends on its success in training a corps of foreign engineers and business people educated here. Allowing people of many races, creeds and philosophies to move too freely in Japanese society is viewed by conservative government offi- cials as destabilizing. For the time being, therefore, the doors stay open only a crack.

Manpuku-ji, however, was another matter. The young Shogun delegated real authority to Ingen and welcomed his disciples and a large Chinese trading community which was based in Naga- saki. When Ingen died, his disciple Mokuan, who had come over with him from China, succeeded him as leader of the Obaku sect. Twenty-one generations of Chinese abbots (with the exception of one or two Japanese) presided over Manpuku-ji for one hun- dred and twenty-three years, until Japanese abbots finally took over due to a lack of Chinese immigrants. At this point the coat- ing process began, and the temple is slowly being turned into another pearl. But even so, Manpuku-ji never abandoned its Chinese identity; it is the single most successful and long-lasting venture initiated by foreigners in Japanese history.

But all this is incidental to the real importance of Manpuku-ji: it was the center of Japan's literati. Since they first appeared on the scene in Japan in the sixteenth century, the literati have exerted an immense influence, and they still exist today in their thousands. However, in a world that equates Japanese culture with Zen, the literati are almost completely unknown.

Japan is the land of the 'Ways' – the Way of Tea, the Way of the Sword, and so forth – and all these Ways seem to involve the utmost seriousness. The emphasis is on martial discipline; there is little room for free spirits. But in the process of art collecting, I discovered objects divorced from such Ways. These included the calligraphy scrolls of Edo-period scholars and the implements of *sencha*.

In the Edo-period calligraphy scrolls was a playful point of view completely at variance with the rigid rules of the Ways I had encountered. One scroll I found early on was by the great Confucianist Ichikawa Beian. It read: 'The lover of wine is ashamed of nothing under heaven or earth'. This didn't sound like a very serious Confucianist to me. Beian and his circle were Japanese literati. They traced back to a long line of Chinese literati, called *bunjin* in Japanese, which means literally, 'man of literature'. Soon I began to see their presence everywhere.

One of the utensils popular in *sencha* is the fly whisk, called a *hossu*. I found a variety of these: flowing tufts of horse or yak hair fixed on staffs of red lacquer, woven bamboo or gnarled branches. In old books illustrating scholars' gatherings, they could be seen hanging next to the *tokonoma*. I found that *hossu* whisks went back to the Chinese Taoist sages of the fourth century, who used them to brush away flies as they engaged in *seidan* ('pure conversation') with their friends. In time, the whisks came to symbolize brushing away the flies of care. Hanging one nearby meant that you were going to engage in 'pure conversation'.

In Tenmangu I keep a collection of *hossu* on one wall by the sofa, indicating 'this space is for pure conversation'. Of course, most of my guests are wholly unaware of this – they probably just think I have a bad problem with flies! On the opposite wall is a pair of scrolls, a conversation in the form of calligraphy. The first, by a Kyoto potter of the 1930s, reads, 'With the *hossu*, I brush away all worldly desires'. Next to it is the reply by the Zen abbot Nantenbo: 'I brushed away everything, but the dust won't move!' From scrolls such as these and implements like the whisks I surmised the existence of the Japanese literati; but there are no illustrated books about them, no museums devoted to their art, and no hereditary schools dedicated to passing on their wisdom. It was only because of an experience at Oxford that I knew what to look for.

It was during my third year at Oxford that I first met John Sparrow, Warden of All Souls College. Of the forty or so colleges making up Oxford, All Souls is the most exclusive. Over the centuries, it raised its admission standards so high that about two hundred years ago it stopped taking new students altogether; now there are only dons at All Souls. They are not required to conduct research or teach – all they have to do is think. All Souls is the original 'think tank'.

John Sparrow had been Warden of All Souls for decades, and was in his last year before retirement. He was an avid book collector, a prolific writer on obscure literary topics, and friend to many of the better-known British writers and artists of the twentieth century. In his long life of leisure, he had cultivated a peerless wit, so fine as to be almost transparent: with a word he could make you smile, although later you could hardly recall what it was that he had said. Sparrow took me under his wing, and during my last year I went to live in All Souls. It was a dreamlike opportunity. In the late afternoon, I would join him in his study for tea, and we would pore over old letters to him from Edith Sitwell and Virginia Woolf.

Sparrow and his friends were erudite and proud of it. However, as knowledgeable as they were, the hallmark of their talk was the light touch. Academic explanations were forbidden. If asked to explain something, they would divulge their meaning in a gesture or a phrase succinct as a haiku. One day Lady Penelope Betjeman, wife of the poet laureate Sir John Betjeman, came to lunch. She was describing her travels in Nepal, when someone asked her what she meant by a Tibetan prostration; Penelope, a dignified woman in her sixties, rose from the formal dining table and cast herself flat on the floor to demonstrate. Another of Sparrow's friends was Ann Fleming, widow of '007' author Ian

Fleming. She would rise at about one o'clock in the afternoon, and come downstairs in a pink nightgown to stroll with us on a lawn surrounded by rosebushes. Waving her ivory cigarette holder, she told us stories of her friend Evelyn Waugh, who was hard of hearing and used an ear trumpet. Once at a dinner party, in the midst of an argument with Ann, Evelyn began to pretend he couldn't hear what she was saying. So Ann reached over, stuck her cigarette holder into his ear trumpet and rattled it noisily about inside. This got his attention.

Ann Fleming with her pink nightgown and ivory cigarette holder, the lawn sparkling in the afternoon sun, the eyes of John Sparrow as he laughed – it was truly a world of exquisite indolence. At that time I had no very clear concept of 'literati', although through Sparrow I had already entered into that world. They were people whose whole lives were devoted to art and literature, but for whom nothing was too exalted to question or laugh at. They were free spirits.

I returned soon afterwards to Japan to start work at Oomoto, resigned to the knowledge that I would never meet people like John Sparrow and his circle again. However, the learned but witty comments I found on old calligraphy scrolls and the concept of 'pure conversation' symbolized by the *hossu* whisks in my collection seemed suspiciously close to what I had seen at Oxford. It was clear that literati had once thrived in Japan, and I later found that they still exist today. However, when I delved further I found that the Japanese literati were very different from their counterparts in the West.

The roots of the tradition in Japan went back to the Chinese literati, who were a hybrid of Confucianism and Taoism. From Confucianism came the serious side, the basis of which was a love of learning, exemplified by the first line of the *Analects*: 'To study and at times put your learning into practice, is that not a joy?' The Confucianist scholar was expected to study the wisdom of the past, and in the process acquire a mysterious 'virtue'

that would influence all around him. This virtue radiated outwards, and according to ancient teachings, its mere possession
was enough to transform the world. That was the logic behind
the text I saw the first day I opened a book of Chinese philosophy
in the Kanda market: 'If you wish to rule the state, first pacify
your family. If you wish to pacify your family, first discipline
yourself. If you wish to discipline yourself, first make right your
heart.'

The first step was to discover how to make right the heart:
the answer, as it developed in China, was to practice the arts. In
addition to a wide knowledge of literature, the literati were
expected to master the Three Perfections of poetry, painting and
calligraphy. In time this grew to encompass all the fine arts
involved in the scholar's studio: bamboo work, ceramics, metalwork, stone carving, paper, ink, brushes, inkstones, and much
more.

The drawback to Confucianism, however, was the heavy
emphasis on virtue. Although we are taught that 'the virtuous
man is not alone', a life devoted solely to virtue does not seem
very appealing. This is where Taoism came in. Taoism was the
world of untrammeled sages walking in the hills. 'The sage has
his wanderings,' said the Taoist philosopher Zhuangzi; 'for
him, knowledge is an offshoot.' Taoists saw life as free as water or
wind – who cared about virtue? They loved mountains, waterfalls
and the moon so much that the poet Li Bo drowned one night at
a boating party, when he reached out over the water to embrace
the moon. They were hermits who wanted nothing more than to
withdraw from the dust of the world and enjoy 'pure conversations' with their friends.

In time, these two opposite images – the cultured scholar and
the free-spirited nature lover – coalesced into one ideal: the literati. By the Ming dynasty a clearly distinguishable literati culture
had grown up. It centered around the *inkyo*, or hermitage, where
the literati were supposed to live in semi-retirement. There were

clear guidelines for what the hermitage was to be like. According to one Ming writer's advice: 'It is best to live deep in the mountains. Then the rural countryside. Failing that, the suburbs. Even if you can't live among cliffs and valleys, the literati cottage must have an air of retirement away from the mundane world. Ancient trees and exotic flowers in the garden; artworks and books in the study. Dwellers in this house will not know the passage of years, and guests will forget to leave.'

The development of the literati up until the fifteenth century took place entirely in China; Japan, in the meantime, had become the land of martial, as opposed to literary, arts. Warriors ruled from the headquarters of the Shogunate, which was called the *bakufu* ('tent government'). Centuries later, when the Shogun lived in a magnificent palace in Edo dozens of times larger than the Imperial Palace in Kyoto, the word *bakufu* was still used, as a reminder that the country was basically under the administration of soldiers in tents.

This military ethos is still a dominant force in Japanese society. Before coming to Japan, Trevor and Edan asked me what life in Kameoka was going to be like. I answered, 'Like joining the army.' It turned out to be even truer than I suspected. The very first word of Japanese that Edan learned in third grade was *Kiritsu!* – 'Attention!' On arriving in class, all the students had to stand up smartly with their hands at their sides and bow in unison to the teacher, like soldiers on review. When you read the many books written by foreigners who played baseball in Japan, or practiced Zen, or worked for a stock brokerage, the army-style discipline is the one unifying thread in their experiences.

This was brought home to me in a visual way when I helped translate for a photographer involved in the production of the book *A Day in the Life of Japan*. To create the 'Day in the Life' series, several dozen photographers descend on a certain country to take photos during a twenty-four-hour period. When the book on Japan came out, there was an astonishing number of photos in which people were lined up in rows: police, students, department-store service attendants, businessmen.

Japan would thus seem to be the last place that the literati ideal could take root, but by the 1600s the centuries of warfare were drawing to a close. It became possible to enjoy a life of leisure, and leisure is fertile ground for the literati. In fact, it is indispensable – the literati will allow nothing to get in the way of their life of leisure. The 'exquisite indolence' of Ann Fleming and her friends was not a mere fluke of the British class system – it was an essential ingredient of literati culture, in both the East and West. Literati are rarely great academics, because their curiosity leads them into odd byways that tend to disqualify them from serious scholarship. Likewise, they may not be the greatest of artists or writers, because they rarely have the ambition to build reputations in society or establish themselves commercially. In short, they are amateurs, those whom the Chinese called *hogai* ('outside the system'). It is for this reason that they have been so little studied and are so hard to find.

The first literati to surface in Japan were the tea masters of the sixteenth century, sheltered from the war and turmoil of their age by the Zen establishments of Kyoto. They took the Ming ideal of the *inkyo* hermitage and developed *wabi* teahouses. The teahouse was a place to escape the mundane world, and in it were all the arts of the literati: calligraphy in the *tokonoma*, poetry, ceramics, bamboo, stone and iron. Tea came out of Zen, which has not only a pronounced military side but also a witty irreverent one, going back to Lin-chi and the shocking and humorous things he said to his disciples. The tea masters applied their wit to everything around them, producing a world of fantastically varied play. Oribe created offbeat tea bowls with twisted, lopsided edges; Enshu surprised his guests after a heavy downpour of rain by throwing a bucket of water into the *tokonoma* instead of setting out the usual flower arrangement.

By the early 1600s, literati culture stepped out from under the umbrella of Zen and a true flowering began. One of the first great literati was Ishikawa Jozan, a failed military commander who retired to Kyoto and built himself a hermitage, called Shisen-do, which still survives. He had absolutely no interests other than amusing himself inside his hermitage, and it is said that even when the retired Emperor Go-Mizunoo came to visit, Jozan refused to come out and greet him. To paraphrase Jozan's philosophy, 'At times I pick a garden flower; at times I listen to the cry of the geese. At times I sweep fallen leaves; at times I plant chrysanthemums. Climbing the eastern hill, I sing to the moon; at the northern window, I read books and recite poetry. Other than this, I do nothing.'

Soon there were hundreds and thousands of literati doing nothing the length and breadth of Japan. Doing nothing is only one step away from subversion. The Shogun had established a university at Yushima Confucian Hall in Edo, the purpose of which was to educate schoolmasters to train the nation in Confucian loyalty and good manners. The graduates of Yushima were expected to return to their native districts and set up academies in their native towns. However, the policy backfired, because many of these local scholars became literati, and the literati are loyal to no system. In their leisure they began to study ancient Shinto. Soon they were publishing books denouncing the Shogun and calling for the return of the Emperor, thus laying the groundwork for the fall of the Shogunate. Meanwhile they traveled constantly, exchanging letters, poems and calligraphy.

Right in the midst of all this ferment, Ingen arrived, bringing with him Ming calligraphy and *sencha* – Chinese-style tea ceremony, which was anything but *wabi*. *Sencha* involves ordinary green tea such as is still drunk in most places today, rather than the thick powdered kind used in Japanese tea ceremony, so it was much more relaxed and manageable. *Sencha* had a minimum of ceremony, and a maximum of play; it was tailored perfectly to the tastes of the newly wealthy Edo merchants, and it swept the nation. Today, there are dozens of *sencha* schools with tens of thousands of adherents, the national headquarters being at Manpuku-ji.

Two of the most remarkable of the Edo literati were Beian and Bosai, whose calligraphies I collect. As in China, the Japanese literati were an unstable combination of two opposites – Confucian scholar and free-minded Taoist – so they tended to lean to one side or the other. Beian and Bosai represent the two poles. Beian was a strict moralist who refused to teach dubious people like geisha or Kabuki actors, and as the result of his high standards of conduct attracted thousands of disciples, including many feudal lords. He was a great art collector and scholar, and wrote a book of calligraphy quotations that is still a standard text today. He wrote a crisp, classic style of calligraphy which he learned from a Chinese merchant in Nagasaki.

Bosai, sometimes called 'the literati of the downtown', was constantly drunk, and his calligraphy was completely unreadable. He loved to give parties, to which geisha and Kabuki actors came in great numbers. Bosai habitually walked around his home naked, even when guests were present, and he definitely did not get on well with feudal lords. Once he was called to the Shogun's palace for an interview with the chief minister, Lord Matsudaira Sadanobu. But Bosai was in the habit of buying his clothes second-hand, so the crests on his upper kimono did not match his lower kimono. Sadanobu dismissed him in disgust, and that was the end of Bosai's official career.

The first Japanese literati I met was Sawada Minoru, the tea master at Oomoto. Sawada grew up in a poverty-stricken farming village on the Sea of Japan coast, coming to Oomoto as a young man to work as a gardener. He was a wild youth, famed for once smashing all the windows in the headquarters on a drunken spree. One day, Sawada was invited to the residence of Naohi, the old Mother Goddess of Oomoto, and as he sat there talking, he had a cigarette. When he was finished, he looked around for an ashtray and found none. Luckily, nearby was a floor hearth, just like the ones he had grown up with in his village, so he stubbed his cigarette out in it. 'Don't you realize that is a tea-ceremony hearth?' scolded one of the other guests. Sawada was so ashamed of his ignorance that he decided to learn tea ceremony just to get the better of the man who had scolded him. Today, he is one of the famed tea masters of the Kyoto area.

Sawada's approach can be seen in the following story. The tea used in the ceremony is finely powdered green tea, carried in a lacquered caddy called a *natsume*, which is shaped like an egg with a flat bottom and top. One day, a student failed to support the body of the caddy, taking only the lid in his hands, and the caddy dropped from the height of about one meter directly onto the tatami. The powdered tea puffed up high into the air in a cloud, and tea settled in a green ring on the mat before our startled eyes. Everyone was petrified. In the silence, Sawada asked us, 'What is the appropriate thing to say at a time like this?' Nobody could answer. He said, 'You should say, "How beautiful!"'

And indeed, the ring of powdered green tea on the tatami *was* beautiful. Sawada told us to gather around and look at it. 'You may never see this again in all your lives,' he said. 'It's almost impossible for the caddy to land perfectly on its bottom like that. Look, and admire!' Then, after we had looked, Sawada kept us on for a lesson in how to clean the tatami, which involved painstakingly tapping the surface inch by inch to force the tea out of the grooves. We worked on that tatami for three or four hours.

Although it was created by the literati, tea ceremony has been overtaken by the militarist spirit and codified to the point where the wit and spontaneity have been largely stamped out. Tea masters are not usually very interesting people, bound as they are by a lot of rules and restrictions; someone like Sawada, who combines Confucian strictness with Taoist freedom, is very rare. It is my theory that only the badly behaved become truly great literati. You have to be the sort of person who would break windows or rattle your cigarette holder in Evelyn Waugh's ear trumpet.

In addition to tea, Sawada also plays Noh flute, wields the martial arts sword, writes professional calligraphy and carves seals. He has mastered not only Three Perfections, but six or seven. Sawada is often to be found around the Oomoto grounds, climbing trees, clipping hedges or heaving rocks into place to make a path. In these activities lies the critical difference between the literati of the East and West. The free spirits, the light touch, the indolence, the love of literature and the arts – these are universal literati traits. However, John Sparrow and Ann Fleming were essentially people of words, written or spoken. They appreciated the arts, but except for an occasional go at the piano, they did not practice the arts themselves. They enjoyed walking on the grass and admiring the roses, but they did not plant the roses or mow the grass themselves – they were truly 'people of literature'. But the Chinese ideal was much broader than just literature: from the Taoist side, it included an intense love of nature; from the Confucian side came the mastery of arts.

The Confucian influence can be seen clearly in Japan today, where it is expected that politicians, bureaucrats and business executives be reasonably proficient in some art. In my Trammell Crow days I was constantly surprised by the number of bankers and stockbrokers who turned out to be expert in kendo, judo or haiku. At the very least, people in positions of authority need to polish their calligraphy, as wherever they go they will be presented with brush and paper, and they cannot treat requests for autographs in the cavalier way that Garbo did. The number of people who are proficient in tea, poetry or some other art is staggering – there are millions of them. From this point of view, the impact of the literati has been enormous.

Probably the supreme literati alive in Japan today is a woman in her eighties named Shirasu Masako, who lives just outside Tokyo. She is a writer, an art collector and an expert on Noh drama, having begun her study of Noh very early, at a time when women were not allowed to perform on the stage with mask. But she managed to break through this barrier in the 1920s, to become the first woman in history to officially dance Noh.

Shirasu was the daughter of Meiji nobility, and her husband helped to write the Japanese constitution. But although she had a privileged upbringing, Shirasu is a strong-minded type, who does things in her own way. For instance, she was a friend of the legendary potter Rosanjin, active in the 1930s and '40s; everyone who knew him was in awe of Rosanjin's eccentric personality, except Shirasu, who took her fists to him when he overdid the design for her kimono. Once when I visited her, the subject of Rosanjin came up. 'If you really love ceramics or painting,' she said, 'then you will get angry about them.' When dinner arrived, and I admitted that I was not much of a gourmet, she smiled and said, 'You should get angry about food too!'

Shirasu has the ability to judge talent, having discovered artists such as the flower master Kawase Toshiro and the designer Issey Miyake when they were still unknowns in their twenties. Tough-spirited as she is, her conversation displays the literati's classic simplicity. Kawase once described to me an evening when he was visiting her house and the conversation turned to ceramics. He was asking her about shape, texture, the spirit of the potter, and so forth. She brought out a Momoyama-period Shino-ware cup, and filled it with whiskey. 'Drink,' she ordered him. He put it to his lips. 'And then,' said Kawase, 'I felt as though I had been pulled into a deep kiss. A sense of nobility rose from that cup, consuming my entire body. And Shirasu turned to me and said quietly, "That's ceramics."'

This is how the literati live and teach. The flavor is so subtle that there is almost no flavor at all. I think that might explain why the world of the Japanese literati is so little known nowadays – there are no comfortable definitions like 'Harmony, Respect, Purity, Solitude' that can sum it all up. Had I not known John Sparrow and his circle, I never would have known what to look for.

However, although the literati tradition may be little known, it has shown uncommon strength over the ages. In particular, the role of foreigners in Japan has been tied up with its fate. It would not be too much of an exaggeration to say that almost the entire thrust of Chinese influence between the fifteenth and early twentieth centuries involved the transference of literati thought to Japan; Ingen and Manpuku-ji were just one part of a process that lasted into the 1930s. The role of Westerners in Japan is also connected to the issue of literati; in the twentieth century, the two Westerners to have had the greatest cultural influence here were the writer Lafcadio Hearn and the art expert Ernest Fenollosa – both of whom were literati types.

The ideal of the literati was utterly incompatible with traditional Japanese culture, yet it took root and grew, resulting in a flourishing of the arts of the sort the world has rarely seen. This suggests that traditions such as Zen or tea ceremony may have an easier time of it in the West than one might expect. The people bringing these things to the West are a modern breed of literati such as Sawada, who has spent years traveling and teaching in Europe, America and China. Meanwhile, Japan's cultural decadence today is on a par with Myoshin-ji Temple at the time Ingen arrived. This is why so many leading Japanese artists, such as the conductor Seiji Ozawa or movie-soundtrack composer Ryuichi Sakamoto, are forced to base themselves abroad. The times cry out for fresh influences from outside, for someone with an international outlook to wave a stick and shout fiercely. The story of the interaction between literati and foreigners may be about to begin a completely new chapter.

But a literati would say, 'Who cares? The next generation are only a pack of blind mules.' It doesn't matter whether a particular tradition gets passed on or not, since the most important thing about the literati was the pleasure they took in the mountains and lakes, the moon, poetry, tea and talk. Their great achievement was the way they enjoyed themselves.

Chapter 14

Last Glimpse
The Moment after Glory

I'd like to tell an art-collecting mystery story.

Eight or nine years ago, I bought a pair of landscape ink paintings. They were extremely abstract: across an expanse of twelve panels of white paper there was only a slight amount of ink – a few dashes to indicate a rooftop, a mountainside emerging from a splatter of ink, as though 'thrown' from the brush. It was in the style known as *haboku* ('splashed ink'), popular in the Muromachi period.

Old screens rarely survive the centuries untouched; they almost always have been remounted once or twice. My screens appeared to have been repaired once around mid-Edo. By that time the abstraction of Muromachi had long since given way to the colorful 'floating world' of Kabuki and block prints. All that empty white space was seen as unsatisfactory, so the mounter brushed gold paint over the wide-open expanses in order to liven up the screens. At the same time, he erased the name of the original artist and wrote in the signature of Kano Tan'yu, a famous painter much in demand with Edo merchants. But there was no way that the screens could be by Tan'yu. Disguised by their layer of gold paint, they sat as a 'mystery piece' in a corner of my house for several years.

Eventually, curiosity got the better of me. I took the screens to my mounter Kusaka and asked him what he thought of them. He looked at the paper and said, 'These screens have been completely changed from their original intent. Just removing the gold ink is going to take two years. Perhaps you ought to leave them as they are.' By which, being a Kyotoite, he meant that they should be restored at once. He also suggested that we erase the spurious Tan'yu signature, which I agreed to on the spot; it came off easily with a sponge.

When the screens came back to me two years later, I got quite a shock: this was no ordinary ink landscape. The screens were almost identical in style to the work of the legendary fifteenth-century painter Sesshu, who first brought *haboku* from China to Japan. The wide, open white spaces of the painting were awash with the same air of meditative emptiness found in the classic Zen gardens of Ryoan-ji and Daisen-in.

I began to study *haboku*, but the research proved to be no easy matter. Sesshu's work is so famous that I expected to find that a great number of paintings had been done in this style, but I found that such works were surprisingly rare. *Haboku* was most popular between 1470 and 1550 during Muromachi, but by the end of Momoyama it was fading, and in mid-Edo it had died out completely. I looked for another screen done in the Sesshu style to compare mine with, but found only hanging scrolls, not screens. I began to wonder: was it possible that there existed only one *haboku* folding screen?

I consulted various scholars, but I could find no experts in *haboku* screens; people tend not to specialize in something of which there are no examples, or only one. The mystery remained.

As I delved further, I found that the history of *haboku* is connected to the 'Higashiyama Culture' of the mid-fifteenth century. In 1467, a battle between rival samurai clans known as the Onin War enveloped Kyoto. During the ensuing thirteen years of chaos, the capital was utterly destroyed, and as a result there are only a handful of buildings in Kyoto that pre-date this war. Once, at the Kaika teahouse in Kyoto, I met an elderly woman and we got to talking of antiques. 'My family used to have a wonderful collection of antiques,' she sighed, 'but they were all destroyed in the last war.' 'But I thought Kyoto escaped bombing in the war,' I began to say. Before I could expose my ignorance any further, the master of Kaika leaned over and whispered in my ear, 'By "the last war", she means the Onin War.'

The Onin War, still remembered five hundred years later, was a major shock in Japanese history, second only to the country's defeat in World War II. Kyoto was turned into a charred wasteland. Every Zen temple was razed, the *kuge* nobles fled to the provinces, and the Shogun abandoned the center of the city, taking up residence in Higashiyama's eastern hills.

From long before the start of the Onin War, the Zen teachings of 'nothingness' and 'void' had taken deep root in the hearts of the Japanese people. 'The world is the same as the Void. The Void is the same as the world' – so goes a famous line from the *Heart Sutra*, which even today many Japanese can recite from memory. But 'nothingness' had never been anything more than a literary conceit; with the Onin War, Kyoto's cultural elite had a shocking first meeting with the void.

The painter Sesshu left for China the year the war broke out, and when he returned he brought with him the technique of *haboku*. Its extreme abstraction and spontaneity perfectly matched the desperate tenor of the age. People wanted something simple, something fast. Instead of large-scale gardens requiring lakes and tall, exotically shaped stones, they created small sand gardens. The low, dark rocks scattered on sheets of white sand were the three-dimensional equivalent of 'splashed ink'. In flowers they favored *nageire* ('thrown flowers') dropped in a basket, rather than *tatebana* ('standing flowers') arranged formally in a vase. In time, the move towards simplicity gave birth to the idea of *wabi*.

The concept of 'the void' even influenced popular art forms such as Kabuki, where, in the play *Dojoji*, the lines from the *Heart Sutra* were rephrased for popular consumption: 'If you think it's not there, it is. If you think it's there, it isn't.' From the Onin War rose the culture of abstraction that defines Japanese art today. If Japan had nothing but the colorful side of its culture, there would be relatively little for foreigners to study here. Beijing's Forbidden City, Bangkok's palaces, Balinese dance – the rest of Asia is full of sights far more spectacular than anything found in Japan. But thanks to the 'meeting with the void', Japan developed arts of stark simplicity that have gone on to have a major impact on the rest of the world.

Back to the mystery of the folding screens. The style was more Sesshu than Sesshu himself, but the screens were not from his time. This placed them as a work of the Unkoku School. Sesshu built an atelier called Unkoku-an in the town of Hagi on the Sea of Japan coast, and his lineage came to be known as the Unkoku School. However, over the years the Unkoku painters gradually drifted away from Sesshu's spirit and created a wholly different painting style; I could not find a single Unkoku painting that resembled my screens.

Just at this juncture I met Hosomi Minoru. His father was an Osaka entrepreneur, a blanket manufacturer whose business was located south of the city near the old seaport of Sakai; he began collecting art in the years after World War II, and there are many stories told of his blunt Osaka ways. Once he learned of a fine screen in Nagoya which a dealer was offering for ten million yen. He drove all the way to Nagoya, and handed the dealer a packet containing eight million yen in cash. The dealer was so startled by the sight of all that money that he handed over the screen on the spot. Old Hosomi drove home with the screen, leaving the dealer to wonder what had happened.

Hosomi Minoru continued his father's work, and today the Hosomi Collection ranges from Nara-period Buddhist art to Edo Rinpa painting, and includes a great number of designated cultural properties. There are plans to build a museum, but for the moment Hosomi Minoru remains Japan's last great private collector. Aware that collectors often know more than museum curators, I went to ask Hosomi's advice. He knew a scholar, the highest authority on the Unkoku School, who identified the screens as the work of the early Edo painter Unkoku Totetsu (1631–1683). I also learned that *haboku* was almost exclusively executed in small formats. My pair of screens, it appears, are the sole extant Sesshu-style *haboku* screens.

Nevertheless, the mystery of the screens was not completely solved. There was now another problem: in Totetsu's time, the Muromachi period had already drawn to a close, and the prevailing culture was shifting to Edo mercantilism. How was it that Totetsu had managed to create a masterwork of Higashiyama culture, when the Higashiyama period was already a thing of the past? This led me to focus on early Edo, and I discovered that it was a period of summing up of former glories. There was a feeling that something had been lost, and with it came a desire to recapture the Muromachi spirit. The result was that early tea ceremony and the Katsura Detached Palace, while they belonged to early Edo, were vastly removed from the lively world of Kabuki and prints: they were more Muromachi than Edo.

Actually, they were better than Muromachi: nothing as perfect as the Katsura Detached Palace was built when Muromachi culture was still alive. Muromachi style was effortless, natural – if the rocks surrounding a temple were not perfectly aligned, no matter. But with the coming of Edo, this effortless Muromachi sensibility vanished and become a nostalgic dream. To turn

David Kidd's words around, this period was 'the moment after glory'. In order to recapture it, Edo artists had to become infinitely skillful, to the point that at Katsura, tea masters would meditate for years before setting each stone in position. Totetsu's work took place in this context.

There was another thing about Totetsu: he was the third son of the house. His older brothers went on to inherit the leadership of the Unkoku School, but Totetsu was forced out. Looking at a map of Hagi that dates from that time, you can see that Totetsu's brothers lived inside the castle walls, while Totetsu's house stood outside the moat. This explains why he did not follow the later Unkoku style that had been developed by his family. Rejected by them, he leapfrogged their tradition, and went straight back to the founder, Sesshu.

This was the history of my screens; now, back to the present. Until meeting flower master Kawase Toshiro, I had never been particularly interested in flowers. Ikebana is governed by strict rules – a central stalk rising upwards, with accompanying flowers bent awkwardly to the right or twisted to the left. The effect is thoroughly unnatural. Add to this the modern approach, which is to use heaps of flowers bent and twisted even more bizarrely, and the effect verges on the grotesque. Both old and new schools are afflicted with the ugliness that is modern Japan, and the vases they use and the environments they place them in are painful to behold.

Recently, a Japanese college student who attended the Oomoto seminar told me that he had been called in as temporary help to install an ikebana show at the Kintetsu department store in Nagoya. 'First we cleared the room, and then the ikebana masters made row upon row of arrangements on long tables. I overheard one lady say to another, "Your branch is leaning into my space. Would you please do something about it?" The other lady said, "I'm sorry," and without a second thought, clipped off the whole branch. If she could cut that branch off so easily, why had she arranged it there in the first place? It's clear that these masters had no thought-out policy about what they were doing. When the flowers were all laid out, we stood on the side and thought, "This room looked so much better when there was nothing in it!" '

But Kawase's flowers are different: they literally bring tears to the eyes. They have the dignity of classical-style ikebana, but the branches are not artificially bent or twisted to left and right. They spread elegantly, with a curve so natural they seem to say 'this is how we want to be'. Kawase's aim is to go back in time and re-create the spirit of Muromachi and Edo flowers. The implements he uses, whether antique or modern, are all works of art, and he chooses the sites for his flowers with the utmost care. As a result, Kawase's flowers radiate an otherworldly beauty.

As in the case of Kabuki dance, an exhibit or demonstration of flowers is called a *kai*. Recently, Kawase held a flower *kai* in Kyoto. He rented an old house, the last literati academy left in Kyoto, and completely transformed it. He covered the air conditioners with boxes made of rice paper, and had new *fusuma* sliding doors made because the hand-pulls of the old ones were not properly in literati style. Next, he borrowed handscrolls, *hossu* whisks and calligraphy utensils from friends, and decorated the room with silver folding screens and blue Nabeshima rugs. Finally, he arranged the flowers and invited the guests.

The most remarkable thing about this exhibition was the expression of amazement on the faces of the Kyotoites. They live in a city which gives every promise of beauty, but thwarts you at every turn; these are people who are starving for beauty. In Kawase's world, as carefully arranged as the Katsura Detached Palace, there was, for once, not a single jarring note. People were shocked to find a Kyoto they longed for but which they could hardly believe existed.

In addition to being an artist, Kawase is a philosopher. Listening to him discourse on *tatebana* (which according to him are phallic) and *nageire* (vaginal) gives you an entirely new point of view on something as seemingly innocent as flower-arranging. Unlike the ikebana masters in Nagoya, Kawase has a very clear idea of what he is doing. Once, he helped with one of the calligraphy *kai* I have given over the years. He offered to repair a flower arrangement, and I watched as he deftly turned the leaves and branches, transforming them into a thing of ineffable charm. 'Turn this leaf outwards,' he said, 'so that it faces the viewer. All Japanese things have a *men*' (a word meaning 'front' or 'face'). It was a simple comment, but one with huge ramifications for Japanese art. From gardens to tea bowls, all objects are designed to be seen from one particular point of view. I think of this every time I see a dining table set with a Western-style flower arrangement – to my eyes, a chaotic mass of twigs, leaves and flowers, lacking in drama because it looks exactly the same from any angle.

At the time of the Kyoto *kai*, Kawase said this to me: 'Showing something natural, in its native state, is not art. Artifice piled on artifice, giving you the illusion of the natural – that's art. If you are going to draw people into your dream, then you must make it completely convincing. If the dream is not perfect, then it will feel unnatural. Only the most perfect dream approaches reality.' What was so shocking to the Kyoto guests at Kawase's *kai* was the fact that at a time when Kyoto's culture has degenerated practically beyond hope, he showed them the 'dream' of Kyoto in perfection.

With its many wealthy institutions dedicated to preserving traditional arts, Japan will have no trouble maintaining outward forms. The Kintetsu department store will go on renting its exhibition hall to ikebana masters, and on the surface ikebana will appear to be well and thriving. In this sense, Japan is doing better than most other nations in East Asia. But the drastic decline in the quality of the environment – the mountains and rivers covered with wires and concrete, the old wooden houses replaced with aluminum and plastic – is having an effect: the fossilized forms remain, but people are forgetting the purpose behind them.

The other day I attended a rehearsal for a dance performance by a Kabuki actor. He was performing the dance 'Orochi', about a princess who turns out to be a serpent in disguise. There is a point where the princess dances with only the *tsutsumi* shoulder drum as accompaniment. Depending on how you strike it, the drum produces two notes: a deep *pon* and a light *ta*. The princess is listening to the sound of a waterfall in the mountains, and she brings her fan to one ear – *pon* – to the other ear – *pon* – and after a moment, she breaks into a flowing dance with rapid fan movements – *ta, ta, ta, ta, ta*.

The special appeal of Japanese music lies almost completely in its rhythms, which involve delicate variations and delays between notes, known as *ma* (spaces). *Ma* are everything. Traditionally, there were no musical scores; performers and musicians worked together and figured out the *ma* on the spot. But now there are scores, recordings and videos, and so the musicians have the *ma* all decided for them in advance. As a result, they do not need to think about why the *ma* are as they are.

The actor said to the musician, 'Would you please wait until just an instant after the fan reaches my shoulder – a moment while I am listening – before you strike *pon*? Another pause before the second *pon*. And then a longer pause – a yearning, almost unbearable pause – before *ta, ta, ta, ta, ta*.' But the musician simply could not do it: he was locked into a pattern he had learned without understanding its purpose. Later, the actor said to me, 'Have you ever been in the mountains and listened to the cuckoo? It says, *cuckoo, cuckoo*, with the slightest pause between syllables. It doesn't say *kuku kuku* like a metronome.'

The closeness with nature, the moment of unbearable yearning – this is what the whole performance is about. There is no particular value in preserving the art of the shoulder drum for historical and academic purposes alone. This is why the mass of the population has turned away from the traditional arts: whatever the scholars and experts may tell them, the people know in their hearts that these 'dead' arts have become a bore. Having lost their way, the practitioners of these arts rely on bombast to make them interesting again. Hence the popularity of *keren* acrobatic stunts in Kabuki, or masses of bizarrely twisted flowers in ikebana. Shirasu Masako has in her study a *tanzaku* calligraphy plaque which reads, 'Dogs and horses are difficult; demons and fascinating things are easy'. The idea is that painting dogs and horses is difficult because they are so ordinary; demons and grotesque objects, on the other hand, are quite easily depicted. The same applies to flowers: one camellia in a vase is infinitely harder to get right than a huge mass of modern ikebana.

It also applies to city planning. Japan is becoming a nation of monuments. The trend began back in the 1960s with Kyoto Tower and the Tower of the Sun at the Osaka Expo. In recent years, every city and town must have a museum or a 'multipurpose cultural hall', even though there may be nothing of importance to put into the museum, and not much use for the hall. Tens of billions of dollars have been budgeted for these monuments, of which, it is said, three or four open each week. In my own town of Kameoka there is a plan to build a multipurpose cultural hall, despite the fact that the city does not even have a municipal hospital.

'A multipurpose hall is a no-purpose hall,' says Tamasaburo. But in fact there *is* a purpose to these buildings, which is to assuage the conscience of civic administrators who feel they should be doing something, but don't know what to do. 'Dogs and horses' – that is, the quiet, invisible part of city planning – would be to establish zoning, regulate signs, bury telephone wires and restore the ecosystems of lakes and rivers. But instead, vast sums are squandered on 'demons and fascinating things': museums and halls designed by famous architects for which there is no use, but which symbolize culture.

As may be gathered from the fact that *pachinko* is Japan's largest industry, Japan is a nation in deep trouble. After fifty years of control by monopolies and bureaucracies, the problems experienced in Japanese music or city planning also exist in technical fields. For instance, Japan has lagged badly in jumping onto the information highway. The reasons lie in artificially high telephone charges, and in the tradition of secrecy which makes it so hard to get real information from government agencies or universities. But rather than deal with these fundamental 'dogs and horses' problems, the government is spending tens of millions of dollars to build 'experimental information centers' in provincial towns.

As a result of the 'demons and fascinating things' approach, Japan is losing the edge in fields where it was once expected to lead. It is falling behind in computer software, entertainment, advanced education, tourism, financial services, communications and medicine – that is, in almost every field that will grow in the twenty-first century. Meanwhile, traditional culture is in a state of crisis. Hosomi Minoru, Tamasaburo and Shirasu Masako are the last great figures of their respective lines. Many of the experiences I describe in this book come from worlds that are dead or dying. Even people who have lived in Japan for years may find these worlds unrecognizable. It's as if I were describing a trip to the moon.

The question is: what comes next? In ancient China, when the Mandate of Heaven passed from one dynasty to the next, the very first task of the new dynasty was to record the history of the previous one. Sung scholars wrote of T'ang, Yuan scholars wrote of Sung, and so on. It is only when a culture has been superseded that it can be summed up. Early Edo was exactly such an age: its artists, like Totetsu, were able to create works summing up the best of Muromachi. The current time is another such summing up. The very fact that Japan's culture is breathing its last gasp is allowing artists of unprecedented genius to flourish.

Like Tamasaburo. *Onnagata* of Tamasaburo's beauty probably never existed before. When I look at photos of past actors and listen to the recollections of old-timers, it seems that *onnagata* were never as attractive as Tamasaburo; they didn't need to be. Kabuki was alive: audiences were able to project an image of beauty and didn't need to see beauty with their own eyes. But the Kabuki stage is very far away from the daily lives of today's audiences: it is a 'dream world'. As Kawase puts it, 'Only the most perfect dream approaches reality', and so today's *onnagata* must possess dream-like beauty. Hence Tamasaburo's popularity.

Today, there is at least one extraordinary person active in every field. In design, there is Issey Miyake; in architecture, Tadao Ando; in Kabuki, Tamasaburo; in flowers, Kawase. They are all in their forties or early fifties, and have in common the fact that in their youth, Japan's culture and natural environment were more or less intact. They saw a world which can never be known by today's young people. But merely growing up when the culture is intact is not enough: it is also important to be free. In the 1960s and '70s, when these artists were maturing, they had the freedom to experiment with modern forms and break away from suffocating ancient rules and restrictions. All of them are international in outlook, and some, like Miyake or Ando, are resolute modernists. Thanks to this freedom, they surpassed their predecessors in the early twentieth century, and the result today is an explosion of talent. What we are seeing now is an exciting grand finale – these artists are producing some of the best work to ever come out of Japan.

To the degree that these artists are both a part of tradition and free from it, they resemble Totetsu. Born into the Unkoku family, Totetsu had access to paintings, possibly some by Sesshu himself, which outsiders could never have seen; at the same time, he lived outside the moat – removed from the official mainstream. Kawase is in the same position: he was born and raised in a flower shop right next to Ikenobo, the famous flower-arranging school headquarters, and in his youth he studied with an Ikenobo master; but now Kawase is independent, neither affiliated with an established school, nor aiming to start his own.

None of the great 'artists of the summing up' have successors: the next generation, raised in the era of *pachinko*, does not have the cultural background to draw upon. In mountains planted with a monoculture of industrial pines, they will never hear the birds singing *cuckoo, cuckoo*. Nor do they have the same sort of freedom that Tamasaburo, Kawase and Miyake had, since the lives of young people today are so dominated by bureaucracies and systems which had not yet solidified in the 1960s and '70s.

The artists of Totetsu's period thought that they were summing up the past, but actually they were laying the foundation stones for the future. The *kata*, or characteristic 'forms', of tea ceremony, calligraphy, architecture and many other arts were laid in late Muromachi and early Edo. The chance to create new *kata* comes around only once every three or four hundred years, and the present time is such an opportunity. The challenge is how to bring the ancient wisdom encapsulated in the traditional arts into the modern world. This is the work that these artists are now engaged in, and the *kata* they create will possibly stand for another three hundred years.

'The reason why people end up as "blind mules",' says Tamasaburo, 'is that they are trying to succeed a genius. You never can. All you can do is to take a hint from their work, and create something completely new yourself.' That is why it is not so important that Kawase and the others do not have successors; they are leaving *kata* as building blocks for the future. In coming generations, when artists look back at Japan's traditions, they will have no choice but to turn to the work of the present period.

The other day somebody asked me, 'Why have you spent so many years in Japan? Especially nowadays, there must be so many other more interesting places?' The only answer I could give was to describe the story of the Kabuki dance *Kasane*. In it, Kasane and her lover Yoemon are walking along the bank of a river at night. A strange transformation takes place in which she reverts to the ghastly crippled form of the woman Yoemon had murdered in his former life. He pulls out his scythe, and tries to murder her again. There is a struggle, he slashes her with the scythe, and Kasane falls dead. Yoemon rushes off the stage via the *hanamichi* walkway through the audience. Lights out.

But the play is not over. In the pale light of the stage, Kasane's hand can be seen rising. She turns ghostly fingers towards the *hanamichi* as if grabbing and pulling. Soon Yoemon reappears, pulled backwards by a magic power along the *hanamichi*, back onto the stage. There, he and Kasane meet once more.

Japan has been like this for me. Just at the moment when I am poised to move elsewhere, ghostly fingers reach out and pull me back. In college, when I had my doubts as to whether Japan was a country in which I wanted to spend my life, I discovered Iya Valley. When Iya seemed threatened, I stumbled through the secret door to Kabuki. When my studies at Oxford were drawing me towards China instead of Japan, David Kidd yanked me back to the Oomoto arts seminar. Later, when I was considering taking up a position in the art world in New York, I met Trammell Crow, and he diverted me into the business world, paying me to stay in Japan.

Today, just at the moment when Japan has lost much of its appeal in both natural landscape and culture, it is artists such as Tamasaburo and Kawase and the ferment of creativity surrounding them which draws me back. The present time, it turns out, is the best of all times to be in Japan. The changes taking place in the cultural world, the rumblings of revolution in the bureaucracy and in business – all of this is exciting in a way in which Japan has not been exciting for decades.

'If you think it's not there, it is. If you think it's there, it isn't.' At the very moment of its disappearance, Japanese traditional culture is having its greatest flowering.

Afterword: About Alex

By Bando Tamasaburo

I remember that I must have first met Alex in 1978. It was at Shinbashi Enbujo Theatre, the first time that I danced 'Sagi Musume' (*The Heron Girl*). Alex arrived with an introduction from Kabuki *onnagata* Kawarazaki Kunitaro and a bouquet of roses, and right from the beginning he was someone I could talk to with complete ease.

Around this time I had just traveled to Europe and was suffering from culture shock. At university Alex had studied not only Japanese Studies and Chinese Studies, but he had also traveled widely around America and Europe, and so he taught my culture-shocked self much about foreign countries. In particular, we both loved Italy and that was a true meeting of minds. After this I brought Alex as interpreter with me on trips such as my American tour. His wide-ranging knowledge of unique foreign sayings and culture was very educational and useful to me when I came to do work abroad, and I still feel grateful to him for it.

Unusually for an American, Alex is the type of person who judges things more by intuition than by logic. This has allowed him to ably come to terms with the quality that flows at the base of Japanese culture – an embrace of vagueness and uncertainty. We're people who value things that can't be explained just with clever words. No matter how well the reasons for something are explained to us we're not able to pay much attention to what's being talked about. Both of us have a tendency to respect only what feels right to our intuition about things. I think that's the reason we got on so well together.

233

Tamasaburo and Alex, at a performance of The Heron Girl, 1980

Alex once said, 'The two of us, let's not end up as *cognoscenti*.'
The word originally came from Italian and suggests someone
who knows a lot but doesn't accomplish anything. But that very
same Alex, who had such a rich store of knowledge – beginning
with Greek sculpture and expanding via the Silk Road to a fascination with the Far East – was rather an unworldly innocent when
it came to making his own living. He lived in the general belief
that money would just spring up from somewhere. What changed
him completely was working for the American real estate company Trammell Crow for a period of about six years. Through his
experience in business he acquired knowledge of the world and
gained the techniques of a well-managed life.

That said, Alex's basic qualities – love of humour, preferring intuition over logic, and free-spirited living – have never changed up to this day. He once told me: 'Leonardo da Vinci said, "Beauty lies in the mystery of balance".' In this respect, I'd say Alex has achieved a first-class state of 'balance'. While never losing his original qualities, he gained a mature perspective as a member of society, and this was the first book written by that mature Alex.

Looking at Japan with mature eyes as a person knowledgeable of the outside world, what is the landscape that he sees? This is the selfless Alex who sought only beauty, and that's why he's been able to capture Japan as it is now in such a feat of writing. I hope as many people as possible can read this book, which arose from Alex's passion to preserve Japan's beauty and his love for Japan.

Glossary

bonkei – art form involving the creation of a miniature landscape on a tray

danmari – 'pantomime' scene in Kabuki during which the actors move in slow motion as if in darkness, oblivious to each other's presence

fukusa – silk cloth used by tea masters to wipe utensils during tea ceremony

fusuma – sliding paper doors used to divide the open space of a house into rooms and corridors; both sides of the framework are covered with several layers of strong paper, making them heavier than *shoji*

geisha – (lit. 'person of the arts') professional female entertainer or companion

genkan – (lit. 'hidden barrier') entranceway or foyer; shoes are left here on entering a house

geta – traditional wooden clogs

giri-ninjo – conflict between love and duty, the subject of many Kabuki plays

goma – symbolic geometrical arrangement of ritual utensils placed on a table before the altar in Esoteric Buddhist temples

haboku – ink-painting style, known as 'splashed ink', which features the sparse use of ink and highly abstract compositions

haiku – seventeen-syllable poem

hakama – loose trousers worn by men with kimono

hanamichi – (lit. 'flower path') walkway which is separated from the main stage in Kabuki and used as a dramatic device

hibutsu – (lit. 'hidden Buddha') important Buddha figures which are hidden from view and only rarely displayed

hiragana – cursive script used to transcribe syllabic Japanese

hogai – scholar or artist who works outside official systems

hossu – fly whisk, an ancient symbol of *seidan*, used to 'brush away the flies of care'

ikebana – traditional art of flower arrangement

Kabuki – form of traditional Japanese theater characterized by elaborate costumes, stylized acting and the use of male actors for all roles

kai – special gathering for cultural (e.g. an ikebana display) or commercial (e.g. an auction) reasons

kang – large Chinese sofa

kanji – Chinese calligraphic characters used in Japanese script

kaomise – (lit. 'face showing') performance of Kabuki held in Kyoto in December, featuring leading Kabuki actors

karayo – 'Chinese-style' calligraphy; see also *wayo*

kaso – phenomenon of depopulation of rural areas

kata – characteristic 'forms' of movement in Kabuki; distinctive patterns in the traditional arts

katakana – script used primarily to transcribe foreign words into syllabic Japanese

katsu – meaningless shout, used in Zen to shock or surprise and thereby lead to enlightenment

kaya – see *susuki*

keaki – (zelkova) a precious wood

keren – crowd-pleasing acrobatic tricks in Kabuki

kiseru – long, silver tobacco pipe, often used in Kabuki

koan – illogical Zen Buddhist riddle, used as a meditational tool to achieve enlightenment

koto – thirteen-stringed musical instrument

kuge – Kyoto's highly cultured court nobles of old, descended from the Heian-period's Fujiwara family and having semi-Imperial status

kura – storehouse, traditionally used to store furniture and decorations

e#.b#.#b##.# Glossary

kuroko – Kabuki's black-clad stage attendants who are supposedly invisible to the audience

kuruwa – enclosures or walled areas within a city, which were inhabited by courtesans

ma – distinctive, spatial rhythm featured in traditional Japanese music; rests between notes

machiya – town house

matcha – Japanese-style tea ceremony

men – (lit. 'face') front of an object

mu – concept of 'nothingness' which lies at the core of Zen

nageire – style of ikebana known as 'thrown flowers', in which flowers are dropped into a basket or vase

natsume – lacquered tea caddy used in tea ceremony

oku no in – inner sanctuary of a temple complex

onnagata – male actors who play women's roles in Kabuki

pachinko – gambling game played on a vertical pinball machines

pai-lou – multi-tiered decorative gates of China; in Japan, found only in Chinese-influenced temples such as Manpuku-ji Temple in Kyoto

samisen – three-stringed musical instrument

saniwa – cleared area of raked sand, used in ancient times to stage divinations and the judgment of criminals, from which the Zen raked-sand gardens originated

seidan – term originating in fourth-century Taoist gatherings: the art of 'pure conversation'

seiza – the position of sitting on one's knees required on formal occasions and in many traditional arts, such as tea ceremony and sometimes calligraphy

sencha – Chinese-style tea ceremony

shikishi – square calligraphic plaque

shino – type of thatch, cut in spring after the leaves have fallen from the stalk

Shinto – polytheistic indigenous religion of Japan

shoji – sliding paper doors constructed from a wooden frame-work, covered on one side with a sheet of paper; see *fusuma*

sudare – bamboo blinds

suki – playful architectural style which focuses on details, strongly influenced by tea ceremony

susuki – long grass with blade-like leaves which, when cut and bound, is known as *kaya* and is used as roofing thatch; the grass appears in scrolls and poems as 'autumn grass'

tanzaku – rectangular calligraphic plaque

tatami – woven floor matting, used as a unit of room measurement

tatebana – formal style of ikebana known as 'standing flowers'

tokonoma – decorative alcove found in most Japanese homes in which flowers, a scroll or other artworks may be displayed

torii – entrance gate to a shrine

tsubo – traditional unit of land measurement in Japan, defined as one square bay or two tatami mats (3.3 m^2)

tsuka – mound; at Fushimi-inari Grand Shrine in Kyoto, the word is used to denote collections of small altars or mounds bearing symbolic artifacts

tsutsumi – shoulder drum

ubu – (lit. 'infant') objects which appear at auction for the first time after having been stored in the *kura* for decades

wabi – (lit. 'worn' or 'humble') emphasis on simplicity and humble, natural materials; first incorporated into tea ceremony, *wabi* has come to symbolize all that is unostentatious in the traditional arts

waka – thirty-one-syllable poem

wayo – 'Japanese-style' calligraphy originating in the Heian period, which the *kuge* developed into a range of delicate and flowing styles; the term is used in contrast to *karayo* – 'Chinese-style' calligraphy – the more rigorous and individualistic form favored by monks and the literati

yago – actor's 'house name', which is shouted by members of the audience at dramatic moments during a Kabuki play

yobai – (lit. 'night crawling') pattern of courtship in rural areas, now rare, where the male enters his chosen partner's house at night to sleep with her; if all goes well, the process results in a marriage

yukata – summer-weight cotton kimono

Zen – Japanese school of Buddhism, introduced in the twelfth century from China, which teaches the achievement of enlightenment through inner contemplation

Art travels - mention how museums were ran in 'olden' times - transport, package 'agreements' - how non-moving 'stuffy' galleries changed very quickly to major blockbusters. Recall my first day at GoM in '93